T0382957

'*Sustainability Policy, Planning and Gentrification in Cities* demonstrates how assemblages of social actors intending to create more environmentally sustainable cities also reproduce inequitable cities. The uncritical replication of urban intensification and sustainable master planning approaches has led to the spread of environmental gentrification globally. While plans may promise social justice, when they hit the ground, private for-profit interests trump public-minded goals. Even well-meaning gentrifiers with progressive sustainability ideologies contribute to social displacement. Bunce suggests that a shift toward de-growth and de-commodification discourses and actions may be the best way to promote just sustainability.'

—**Kenneth A. Gould** and **Tammy L. Lewis**,
authors of Green Gentrification: Urban Sustainability
and the Struggle for Environmental Justice

'*Sustainability Policy, Planning and Gentrification in Cities* is a pointed and cogent analysis of contemporary trends in urban environmental gentrification. It offers insightful – but rarely discussed – critiques of sustainability master plans and the aesthetics and preferences of today's urban hipsters.'

—**Melissa Checker**, *Associate Professor,*
PhD Programs in Anthropology and Environmental
Psychology, The CUNY Graduate Center, USA

Sustainability Policy, Planning and Gentrification in Cities

Sustainability Policy, Planning and Gentrification in Cities explores the growing convergences between urban sustainability policy, planning practices and gentrification in cities. Via a study of governmental policy and planning initiatives and informal, community-based forms of sustainability planning, the book examines the assemblages of actors and interests that are involved in the production of sustainability policy and planning and their connection with neighbourhood-level and wider processes of environmental gentrification.

Drawing from international urban examples, policy and planning strategies that guide both the implementation of urban intensification and the planning of new sustainable communities are considered. Such strategies include the production of urban green spaces and other environmental amenities through public and private sector and civil society involvement. The resulting production of exclusionary spaces and displacement in cities is problematic and underlines the paradoxical associations between sustainability and gentrified urban development. Contemporary examples of sustainability policy and planning initiatives are identified as ways by which environmental practices increasingly factor into both official and informal rationales and enactments of social exclusion, eviction and displacement. The book further considers the capacity for progressive sustainability policy and planning practices, via community-based efforts, to dismantle exclusion and displacement and encourage social and environmental equity and justice in urban sustainability approaches.

This is a timely book for researchers and students in urban studies, environmental studies and geography with a particular interest in the growing presence of environmental gentrification in cities.

Susannah Bunce is Assistant Professor in the Department of Human Geography at the University of Toronto, Scarborough, Canada.

Routledge Equity, Justice and the Sustainable City series
Series editors: Julian Agyeman, Zarina Patel, AbdouMaliq Simone and Stephen Zavestoski

This series positions equity and justice as central elements of the transition toward sustainable cities. The series introduces critical perspectives and new approaches to the practice and theory of urban planning and policy that ask how the world's cities can become 'greener' while becoming more fair, equitable and just.

Routledge Equity Justice and the Sustainable City series addresses sustainable city trends in the global North and South and investigates them for their potential to ensure a transition to urban sustainability that is equitable and just for all. These trends include municipal climate action plans; resource scarcity as tipping points into a vortex of urban dysfunction; inclusive urbanization; 'complete streets' as a tool for realizing more 'livable cities'; the use of information and analytics toward the creation of 'smart cities'.

The series welcomes submissions for high-level cutting edge research books that push thinking about sustainability, cities, justice and equity in new directions by challenging current conceptualizations and developing new ones. The series offers theoretical, methodological, and empirical advances that can be used by professionals and as supplementary reading in courses in urban geography, urban sociology, urban policy, environment and sustainability, development studies, planning and a wide range of academic disciplines.

Incomplete Streets
Processes, Practices and Possibilities
Edited by Stephen Zavestoski and Julian Agyeman

Planning Sustainable Cities and Regions
Towards More Equitable Development
Karen Chapple

The Urban Struggle for Economic, Environmental and Social Justice
Deepening Their Roots
Malo Hutson

Bicycle Justice and Urban Transformation
Biking for All?
Edited by Aaron Golub, Melody L. Hoffmann, Adonia E. Lugo and Gerardo Sandoval

Green Gentrification
Urban Sustainability and the Struggle for Environmental Justice
Kenneth Gould and Tammy Lewis

Sustainability Policy, Planning and Gentrification in Cities

Susannah Bunce

Routledge
Taylor & Francis Group

LONDON AND NEW YORK

First published 2018 by Routledge

2 Park Square, Milton Park, Abingdon, Oxfordshire OX14 4RN
52 Vanderbilt Avenue, New York, NY 10017

Routledge is an imprint of the Taylor & Francis Group, an informa business

First issued in paperback 2019

British Library Cataloguing-in-Publication Data
A catalogue record for this book is available from the British Library

Library of Congress Cataloging-in-Publication Data
Names: Bunce, Susannah, author.
Title: Sustainability policy, planning and gentrification in cities / Susannah Bunce.
Description: Abingdon, Oxon ; New York, NY : Routledge, 2018. |
Series: Routledge equity, justice and the sustainable city series |
Includes bibliographical references and index.
Identifiers: LCCN 2017029220 | ISBN 9781138905993 (hardback) |
ISBN 9781315695693 (ebook)
Subjects: LCSH: Sustainable urban development. | Gentrification—Social aspects. |
City planning. | Urban policy.
Classification: LCC HT241 .B86 2018 | DDC 307.1/416—dc23
LC record available at https://lccn.loc.gov/2017029220

ISBN: 978-1-138-90599-3 (hbk)
ISBN: 978-0-367-35836-5 (pbk)

Typeset in Times New Roman
by Florence Production Ltd, Stoodleigh, Devon, UK

Contents

Figures

Acknowledgements

This book builds upon the topic of my PhD dissertation – the convergences of sustainability policy, planning and gentrification in Toronto's waterfront redevelopment – that was guided by a very helpful and thoughtful supervisorial committee at the Faculty of Environmental Studies, York University, Toronto. It has combined with a more recent Social Sciences and Humanities and Research Council of Canada funded research project on urban community land trusts (CLTs). As a comparative study of urban CLTs in Canada, the United States and Britain, this research allowed me to become more familiar with cities such as Boston, New York, Freiburg, Paris and, in particular, London over the past several years. My research experiences in these cities connected my broader and on-going interest in the processes and impacts of environmental gentrification with a more specific study of community-based responses to gentrification and ideas for collective land ownership. It was in these cities that I became familiar with the examples discussed in the following chapters. I am grateful for Social Sciences and Humanities Research Council of Canada (SSHRC) Standard Research Grant #486959 for support for research presented in several sections of this book, as well as for a smaller SSHRC Standard Institutional Grant for additional research on urban eco-villages. I am thankful to my colleagues at the University of Toronto and at other universities who provided suggestions or who gave detailed and helpful comments on particular chapter sections. I wish to thank Julie Mah, PhD candidate in the Department of Geography and Planning at the University of Toronto, who provided research and formatting assistance in the production of the manuscript. I am grateful to Khanam Virjee, Rebecca Brennan, Kelly Watkins and Leila Walker at Routledge Earthscan for their supportive guidance in the coordination of my first effort in writing a book, as well as Julian Agyeman and Steve Zavestoski, co-editors of the Equity, Justice and the Sustainable City book series. Finally, I wish to thank my family and friends for their support, patience and many kindnesses during the different phases of research and writing. This is for Jacob, my daily inspiration.

1 Introduction

Sustainability policy, planning and gentrification in cities

It is not difficult to feel engaged with the benefits of sustainability policies and planning initiatives in the central city of Toronto. As a city where the local government promotes walkable neighbourhoods as progressive spaces, creates infrastructure that supports bicycle commuting and currently owns and manages multiple hectares of park spaces and valley systems, residents can easily engage with environmental spaces and initiatives and often without question. The neighbourhoods of central Toronto represent multiple connections of sustainable urban planning – they can be largely navigated without reliance on an automobile, there are routes of mobility between neighbourhood locations by public transit, the presence of government managed 'tree protection zones' to preserve tree canopy along roadways, and publicly owned and funded green spaces. While further public improvements to and additional funding for environmental initiatives have been a consistent need, Toronto – within a global context – is a city that has been at the frontline of local sustainability policy development as one of the first urban governments in the world to create an official local environmental policy agenda in the 1990s in collaboration with environmental non-governmental organizations (Desfor and Keil, 2004; Fowler and Hartmann, 2002; Gordon, 2016). Following the United Nations Conference on Environment and Development (Rio Summit) in 1992, the city was home to the head office of the International Council for Local Environmental Initiatives (ICLEIs), an organization that formed with the direct purpose of implementing Local Agenda 21 policy. In the early 2000s, Toronto's government used the United Nations' notion of sustainability as the balancing of social development, economic development, and environmental protection to frame the city's official 30-year-long planning and development vision (City of Toronto 2002, 2015). At the core of the plan is an emphasis on urban intensification as a merged strategy to attract global and domestic financial investment in residential and commercial development while mitigating climate change and additional environmental problems through the production of more green spaces and denser, walkable districts with the intention of lessening automobile dependency (Boudreau, Keil, and Young, 2009; Bunce, 2004; Kern, 2007).

Intensification planning in Toronto has largely emphasized the re-development of previously industrialized districts such as Toronto's central waterfront area into mixed residential and commercial areas, increased building densities and heights and the creation of public green space networks and sustainable transportation infrastructure such as increased bicycle and pedestrian pathways. Despite the city-wide nature of the plan, much of its implementation has been directed to the central city while planners have struggled to implement intensification planning, reliant upon private develop-ment interest, in Toronto's expansive, unevenly developed, culturally diverse and more impoverished suburban areas. This has produced a multi-faceted divide between the largely car-dependent, residential, and lower-income suburban areas of the city (Cowen and Parlette, 2011; Hulchanski, 2010) and an intensely developing downtown core; with compact residential and commercial buildings largely visible in the form of privately owned residential and office towers and varied environmental initiatives provided for by local government, private sector interests and civil society organizations. In referring to the creation and implementation of sustainability policy and planning in Toronto over the past three decades, I specifically point to the city, a place where I live and work, as a spatial context where sustainability policy and planning agendas increasingly coincide with experiences of gentrification. While slower patterns of what Zukin (1989) calls 'creeping gentrification' have occurred in Toronto over the twentieth century and into today through the transformation of older working class central city neighbourhoods by middle class, higher income residents (Caulfield, 1994; Mazer and Rankin, 2011; Slater, 2004) over the last decade, and particularly in the last few years, various other forms and pressures of gentrification have emerged. What Lees (2003) and Butler and Lees (2006) have characterized as 'super gentrification', in reference to New York City and London, respectively, has appeared in Toronto with intensive multi-scalar financial speculation and investment occurring most noticeably in the residential property market and demonstrated in public discourse about 'residential bidding wars', 'Toronto's red-hot housing market' and 'house flipping' [buying and quickly selling for a profit] (Gee, 2017; King, 2016; McClearn, 2017). Relatedly, homeownership and the security of affordable housing is rapidly becoming more precarious and out of reach for lower income and even average income earners. Urban green spaces and other environmental infrastructure such as green corridors, parks, gardens and bicycle and pedestrian pathways have, interestingly, added to and not detracted from rapid gentrification. Property agents in Toronto now regularly apply a walkability score, a universal rating system for urban "walkability" produced by US company Walk Score (Zamon, 2013), to highlight pedestrian friendly neighbourhoods and close proximity to recreational pathways and park spaces in the marketing of residential properties (Lissner, 2013; Moranis, 2016). An environmental form of gentrification is emerging in Toronto where environ-mental spaces and amenities such as parks, green roofs and gardens, and bicycle and pedestrian pathways, are increasingly entangled with existing gentrification processes. The notion of a sustainable development paradox (Krueger and Gibbs, 2007), the contradictory associations between the progressive and necessary environmental characteristics of sustainability and the structural mechanics of profit interests and accumulation, applies here. Although official sustainability policy and planning initiatives in Toronto produce necessary and forward-looking environmental practices that attempt to mitigate climate change effects, reduce local-level pollution and encourage residents to participate in environmentally responsible activities, many residents cannot secure affordable living spaces, are struggling to retain housing or are made vulnerable to gentrification outcomes such as displacement.

I rely on the aforementioned example of Toronto in order to contextualize a problem of environmental gentrification that is occurring in cities more broadly through a framework of sustainability policy and planning. This problem raises central questions of why and in what ways environmental practices, commonly produced through both formalized and informal policy and planning initiatives, are interwoven with the structural processes and everyday lived experiences of gentrification in cities? As the starting place for this book, these questions are positioned in relation to the production of sustainability policy and plans, how such policy and plans are implemented, the involvement of government, private sector and citizen actors in the enactment of sustainability initiatives, and connections of these with both neighbourhood-level and wider urban gentrification processes. Such associations are not only explored within the context of Toronto but through examples drawn from cities such as London, New York City, and Paris among others, where governmental sustainability policy and planning directives and local environmental initiatives have converged with the experiences of gentrification.

Environmental gentrification

The broader definitions of gentrification that guide the following chapters engage with critical analyses of gentrification as a process that creates uneven spatial and social development outcomes of community-level eviction and displacement in cities. Hackworth's succinct and widely applied definition of gentrification as the 'production of urban space for progressively more affluent users' (Hackworth, 2002, p. 815) underlines the connections between urban spatial transformation, the presence of higher income earners and associated income-based social and spatial selectivity. This useful definition can interpret the gentrification of already existing urban spaces through residential and commercial changes that benefit the needs of higher income urban residents. Yet, the definition can also be applied to the production of new urban spaces that are 'ready-made' for affluent residents and moves beyond understandings of gentrification as a longer term and transitional process that just occurs in older neighbourhood environments. This is particularly relevant for the notion of *new-build gentrification* (Davidson, 2006; Davidson and Lees, 2005, 2010) as a form of 'instant gentrification' where new residential and commercial developments automatically meet the residential and commercial demands and financial abilities of higher income individuals. It also helps to frame the notion of *policy-led gentrification* conceptualized as the link between public policies strategically aimed at the 'regeneration' of specific areas of cities and the instigation of gentrification through more complex arrangements and involvement of private sector actors and investment practices (Hackworth and Smith, 2001; Smith, 2002). Marcuse's articulation of gentrification, first defined in 1985 but still very relevant today, is directed towards the spatial context of older urban neighbourhoods, but demonstrates how eviction and displacement work in relation to associated issues of class, labour and income and racism in the production of uneven spatial development. He defines gentrification as a process that occurs

> when new residents – who disproportionately are young, white, professional, and technical, and managerial workers with higher education and income levels – replace older residents – who disproportionately are low-income, working-class and poor, minority and ethnic groups, and elderly – from older and previously deteriorate inner-city housing in a spatially concentrated manner, that is, to a degree differing substantially from the general level of change in the community or region as a whole . . .
>
> (Marcuse, 1985, p. 199)

The transformation of urban space that is based upon the problematic displacement of lower income and racialized persons is a critical thread that moves through the following chapters in connection to the production of sustainability policy and planning in cities.

While these definitions anchor gentrification as a socio-spatial process, emerging scholarship that has occurred over the last decade on the topic of *environmental gentrification* or *green gentrification* has primarily focused on the associations between changes to the residential and commercial features of urban neighbourhoods for the benefit of higher income earners and the production of cleaner and healthier environmental spaces through brownfield remediation, the localized mitigation of environmental toxins and creation of environmental amenities in urban communities (Abel and White, 2011; Banzhaf and Walsh, 2006; Checker, 2015; Eckerd, 2011; Gamper-Rabindran and Timmins, 2011; Gould and Lewis, 2016; Hamilton and Curran, 2013; Pearsall, 2013). Other literature suggests that environmental features such as parks, community gardens and sustainable design techniques for buildings are now considered to entice, not dissuade, property investment and are highlighted in the advertising and generation of property sales (Bunce, 2009, 2011; Quastel, 2009). Dooling (2009) employs the term *ecological gentrification*, instead, to underline how environmental initiatives can act to 'greenwash' particular areas of cities and, in the context of her research on a local government environmental planning and design for a park in Seattle and its displacement of existing homeless individuals who used that particular space, defines it as the 'implementation of an environmental planning agenda related to public green spaces that leads to the displacement or exclusion of the most economically vulnerable human population – homeless people – while espousing an environmental ethic' (Dooling 2009, p. 621). The exclusionary practices that Dooling mentions can be expanded more broadly to all residents who are made vulnerable to displacement and exclusion because of ecological gentrification. In particular, they can incorporate the displacement of individuals, often based on issues of racialization, class, and/or income disparity, who conflict with gentrification experiences that are propelled by the aesthetic, residential and commercial demands of higher income gentrifiers that support environmental initiatives and engage in environmentally sustainable practices (Anguelovski, 2015; Checker, 2015). The transformation of urban neighbourhoods into spaces with higher residential property values along with commercial and recreational landscapes that reflect an engagement with environmental issues – such as the growing presence of restaurants that promote organic and 'locally-sourced' ingredients, bicycle shops, crafting boutiques and holistic wellness stores, the proliferation of local farmers' markets, and varied green spaces – suggests a new shape of gentrification that coincides with existing socio-spatial gentrification practices in cities.

In the work of this book, environmental forms of gentrification are addressed in a study of the ways by which assemblages of public, private and civil society actors, governmental policies, public and private sector planning initiatives, and more recent forms of gentrifiers interested in environmental issues co-produce gentrification through legislative and non-legislative urban sustainability policies and planning discourses and enactments. I explore this through three central themes– (i) the issues and predicaments regarding the absorption of often progressive sustainability initiatives aimed at mitigating climate change or fostering public interest in environmental practices into neo-liberalized, profit-oriented urban regeneration and development activities that produce gentrification in cities; (ii) the implementation of urban sustainability policy and planning ideas, both formal and regulated governmental plans for sustainability and the less formalized sustainability planning initiatives of community-based organizations (CBOs) and/or individuals, and the spaces and experiences of social exclusion, eviction and displacement produced by gentrification and (iii) the search for local government and community-based policy and planning alternatives that promote more equitable and just forms of sustainability in planning and which resist gentrification as a process that galvanizes social inequity and displacement. In the following chapters, these themes are discussed through the use of different examples of the convergences of sustainability policy, planning and gentrification in cities and alternatives to these practices. While examples are primarily drawn from North

American and European cities where these connections are more commonly identified in relation to the development and implementation of sustainability policy and planning agendas and rapid gentrification contexts, examples of the policy mobility of sustainable planning – particularly in relation to urban intensification as a sustainable planning strategy – are discussed in connection with global contexts of gentrification.

Assembling urban intensification and sustainable master planned communities and producing gentrification

Associations between sustainability policy and planning ideas and implementation practices with gentrification are first examined through the study of urban regeneration initiatives that support intensification – defined by Jenks, Burton, and Williams (1996) as the densification of population and built form in cities. The creation of sustainable cities and the production of more compact urban form through intensification have been frequently associated over the past two decades by policy-makers and planners for reasons of decreasing sprawled urban development, reducing encroachment on agricultural land and reusing and repurposing existing buildings and space for development in order to generate more sustainable forms of urban land and building consumption, more environmentally considerate human activities in cities, and greener and more 'livable' cities (Burton, 2000; Grant, 2009; Leffers and Ballamingie, 2013; Searle and Filion, 2011; Williams, Burton, and Jenks, 2000). The densification of material infrastructures, such as housing and transportation, and increased population activity within the existing boundaries of cities are considered to mitigate environmental problems caused by the extensive use of oil and gasoline-reliant vehicles and the existence of sprawled commuting distances and instead encourage individuals to engage with more sustainable forms of mobility and condense the spatial distance between their home and work environments (Newman and Kenworthy, 1996; Thomas and Cousins, 1996). Critical analyses of urban intensification have questioned its validity as a sustainable planning approach due to research that has demonstrated a correlation between spaces of intensification and greater traffic concentration (Melia, Parkhurst, and Barton, 2011). It is also considered as a planning discourse that disguises the interests of property developers who stand to generate profits from more intensified development forms through the use of environmentally friendly policy language (Kern, 2007; Rosol, 2013). Yet interestingly has been integrated, largely uncritically, into the work of urban policy-makers and practitioners in cities across the globe and championed as the most comprehensive sustainable method for urban planning and development. The popularity of intensification is demonstrative of policy transfer and mobility, discussed in the next section, that greatly informs the application and implementation of similar urban policies in different global locations. As explored in Chapter 2, urban intensification is an ubiquitous component of smart growth policy agendas in North American cities and urban regions and of urban sustainable regeneration and development policies and planning ideas more widely, but has particular associations with gentrification as explored in research on gentrification and the development of the British government's *Sustainable Communities* policy and planning agenda starting in the late 1990s (Davidson and Lees 2005; Lees 2000; Raco, 2005, 2007; Smith, 2002) as well as current examples of intensification in practice in literature pertaining to new-build gentrification.

Intensification is directly linked with approaches to sustainable master planning and the production of new sustainable neighbourhoods in cities, particularly as a post-industrial planning strategy for the remediation and revaluation of brownfield lands through the creation of new communities. Sustainable master plans, as comprehensive plans for the residential and commercial redevelopment specific urban area, are tied to the implementation of high built form densities, sustainable transportation infrastructure and, more frequently, the inclusion and application of sustainable design rating systems – such as Leadership in Energy and Environmental Design (LEED) in the North American context. Sustainable master planned neighbourhoods that rely on intensification, and even intensification practices that occur independently of master planned areas, are guided by arrangements of actors, interests and policy enactments that represent a neo-liberalized form of governance and a shift to what Swyngedouw (2005) calls governance-beyond-the-state; 'arrangements of "governing" which give a much greater role in policy-making, administration, and implementation to private economic actors on the one hand and to parts of civil society on the other.' (2005, p. 1992). The remediation of industrial lands for new development and the production of new densified sustainable communities relies on these arrangements, sometimes produced through formalized contractual partnerships, in the creation of policy frameworks, site plans and for the development process. Partnership arrangements underline a neo-liberal governance and profit-centred approach in the production of sustainable residential neighbourhoods where governments are responsible for crafting a sustainability policy and planning agenda – increasingly in collaboration with non-governmental actors – while government departments, private sector planning firms, investment and development companies and other non-governmental organizational bodies are involved in the implementation of plans and the construction of new infrastructure. These collections of policies, plans, actors and interests are indicative of urban assemblages, a concept described by McFarlane that helps to explain the making of contemporary urbanism by examining '. . . why and how multiple bits-and-pieces accrete and align over time to enable particular forms of urbanism over others . . .', and which integrates political, cultural, ecological and other 'domains' into a unified understanding of urbanism (McFarlane, 2011, p. 652).

In an application of the concept of assemblages to the production of urban policy, McFarlane (2011, p. 652) argues that political economy enmeshes with the myriad micro-level actions of individuals, relational associations between actors and connections between actors and material objects, among other interactions, that take on different forms of 'power and impact' in varied settings. McCann and Ward (2011) discuss urban assemblages in relation to the global mobility of policy, where policies originate in a particular localized urban environment through assemblages of structural processes, actors and localized practices yet inform the creation of similar policies in locations across the globe – what they call the 'local globalness' of urban policy (2011, p. xvi). While urban assemblages may be different according to their location, Peck (2011) underlines that urban policy ideas are frequently transferred between different urban locations in formalized and essentialized ways without much attention to localized contexts, but without fully achieving 'carbon copy outcomes' (2011, p. 781). In relation to sustainable master planning approaches, sustainable policy and planning ideas are infused through urban assemblages across the globe via the expedient transfer of 'best practices' policy and planning models that are localized in each context. Moore (2013) suggests, in relation to New Urbanism as a commonly adopted sustainable residential planning model, that a largely unquestioned application of these models by policy-makers and planners occurs in different urban spaces. In keeping with Swyngedouw's assertion regarding the increasingly technocratic and managerial ways in which governance actors engage with acknowledging and finding solutions for environmental concerns and impacts (Swyngedouw, 2009, 2010), the role of urban policy-makers, planners and other actors in adopting 'best practices' sustainable planning models reflects a managerial and techno-centric approach to policy creation and implementation. In Chapter 3, assemblages of actors and interests in urban sustainability policy and planning, the mobility of sustainable planning policies and models and their connections with the production of gentrification are explored through studies of the master planning of new sustainable neighbourhood districts in the central waterfront area of Toronto, as part of a larger thirty year public–private waterfront re-development process, and the 'One Planet' sustainable neighbourhood planning model that was created by environmental non-governmental organizations Bioregional Planning and the World Wildlife Federation in 2003 and has been adopted for community-level planning in cities across the globe.

Another important component of the production of urban intensification and sustainable master planned neighbourhoods in cities are the ruptures that occur within localized contexts between visions of sustainability articulated in the crafting of policy documents and plans and their implementation. This refers to the 'paradox of sustainability' in the sense that urban intensification and sustainable master planning are ostensibly holistic, progressive and strategic policy and planning responses and solutions to broader urban environmental problems caused climate change, the presence of toxins in urban air and waterways, the dominance of fossil fuel reliant automobiles, among other sustainability challenges. Often, these visions are crafted in a neutral and apolitical way, with an overall emphasis on achieving sustainability through intensification and the creation of new sustainable neighbourhood spaces without assessments of possible tensions and problems arising during policy and planning implementation. Yet, the unfolding of these policies and plans and the construction of sustainable built form often culminates with different results than articulated in the initial visions (Mapes and Wolch, 2011; Moore and Bunce, 2009). This is often noticed in the disjuncture between sustainability policies and plans for intensification and master planned neighbourhoods that promote social sustainability through directives for encouraging social mix (income diversity within a particular spatial area) and tenure mix (a range of different residential options from affordable rental or ownership units to market-geared housing). Ruptures exist between these policy vision and planning strategies and the 'on-the-ground' realities of planning implementation and property development instigated and managed by private and profit-oriented interests, and which are changed and impacted by emphases on profit accumulation, retractions of public funding and support for affordable housing provision, the financial costs and risks of land development in cities and differences in design aesthetics, among myriad other factors. The translation of sustainability policy and planning visions into implementation practice thus becomes vulnerable to specific motivations and interests within the assemblages of government actors, public and private sector urban planners and designers, private development interests, among others, that are engaged in these practices. Further, these assemblages connect with the mechanics of gentrification through the prevalence of intensification plans and sustainable master planned neighbourhoods that demonstrate environmentally sustainable features but are also oriented towards the accumulation of profits for property developers, investors and homeowners. This corresponds with the concept of new-build gentrification through the construction of new market-oriented planned neighbourhoods in cities, as well as the concepts of 'third wave' (Hackworth and Smith, 2002) and 'fourth wave' (Lees, Slater, and Wyly, 2008) gentrification, which both underline the complex arrangements of governmental and non-governmental actors and interests involved in contemporary urban gentrification processes that are further described in Chapter 2.

Sustainability, gentrification and exclusion

Differences between more progressive ideas for fostering environmental sustainability in cities that are articulated at the stage of policy creation and the materialization of these ideas also demonstrate how sustainability policy and planning can become a component in the production of social exclusion and exclusionary practices connected with gentrification, such as spatial displacement. Environmentally sustainable spaces that are produced and maintained as amenities for the benefit of higher income earners in cities, that increase property values and contribute to the production of more surveilled and controlled surroundings, and that limit and displace the engagement of lower-income, racialized and marginalized persons are considered in the following chapters. Through examples drawn from literature on environmental justice and environmental racism in the context of the production and provision of environmental spaces as well as individual case studies, I discuss the problems of exclusion and displacement that arise from the formalized implementation of sustainability policies and plans as well as informal and more individualized enactments of environmental practices that are produced through planning and which occur in different cities.

Existing and new environmental spaces, and the relational practices within these spaces and between individuals with differing levels of social privilege and interests, can galvanize social exclusion, inequities and injustices and has been readily addressed in research on urban environmental justice, largely through analyses of socio-spatial injustice in relation to the existence of environmental problems. These issues have been considered through empirical and geographical studies regarding the connections between the residential environments of low-income, racialized persons and spatial proximity to concentrated locations of polluted soil, air and water, as well as challenges in obtaining legal rights to mitigate polluted areas and social access to cleaner and healthier environmental spaces and resources in cities (cf. Agyeman, Bullard, and Evans, 2003; Bullard, 1990, 1999; Pulido, 2000; Pulido, Sidawi, and Vos, 1996; Taylor, 2014). In relation to the production of urban green spaces, research on environmental justice and critical urban political ecology has explored the impact of policies and planning initiatives in the management of recreational park uses and how these can isolate and exclude particular 'undesirable' individuals and activities (Byrne, 2007, 2012; Byrne and Wolch, 2009; Foster, 2010; Loughran, 2014; Patrick, 2014), as well as issues of socio-spatial inequity in relation to access to tree canopy in cities (Heynen, 2006; Heynen, Perkins, and Roy, 2006; Landry and Chakroborty, 2009). These topics are relevant for the study of the connections between sustainability policy, planning and gentrification as they are point to role of different actors and interests in the production of environmental spaces in specific relation to which actors and interests are privileged and those which are not.

Exclusionary practices can be either explicit or indirect actions and outcomes of initiated sustainability policies and plans and cause displacement in different ways and in differing socio-spatial scales and contexts. Here, the gentrification literature on issues of social displacement and eviction is particularly useful for considering the links between the production of gentrified environmental spaces in cities and exclusion. Marcuse's (1985) definition of displacement incorporates the notions of direct and exclusionary displacement. Direct displacement is based on physical and economic processes of residential change where local housing is upgraded through renovations and land and housing values increase therefore causing forcing low-income residents to relocate. Marcuse defines exclusionary displacement as occurring when residents are not able to afford housing in a particular neighbourhood or after the renovation of a housing unit, thereby excluding their access to housing and eliminating their ability to reside in certain urban areas. While Marcuse largely emphasizes that displacement is based on income, an understanding of displacement must also include issues of racism as well as discrimination based on gender, sexuality, disability and age in struggles to access housing and as factors in displacement processes within residential environments. Both direct and exclusionary forms of displacement have relevance for interpreting the outcomes of formalized and informal sustainability initiatives in cities, particularly in connection to the production of sustainable residential neighbourhoods and the enactments of gentrifiers who participate in environmental practices.

Exclusionary displacement, originally directed towards older and transforming housing and neighbourhoods, can be applied to understanding how displacement occurs within the context of new planned communities and local responses to displacement. This is specifically discussed in relation to considerations of gentrification as a form of neo-colonialist practice that invokes direct and exclusionary forms of displacement from urban land and residential areas (cf. Atkinson and Bridge, 2005; Clark, 2005; Shaw, 2005, 2006; Smith, 1996). In Chapter 3, displacement as a result of new planned sustainable communities is explored through the planning process for and construction of a sustainable residential project that is located adjacent to the Pembury Estates council housing community in the borough of Hackney in London. Although the project corresponds with local government sustainability policy responses to its development have underlined trepidations about rapid gentrification in surrounding neighbourhoods and in Hackney more widely. Concerns about gentrification and displacement are noted by council housing residents and largely British-Caribbean and British-African communities, raising issues regarding problems of racialization in housing access and long-term support for communities threatened by displacement. Chapter 3 also presents a study of the production of a new sustainable master planned community to be developed upon the traditional and sacred lands of Anishinaabe First Nations people, in Ottawa, Canada. The Zibi development is part of the previously mentioned 'One Planet' sustainable planning agenda and has culminated in the production of instantly gentrified, market-geared residential and commercial spaces with sustainable planning and design features that are oriented towards higher income, professionalized occupants interested in sustainability practices. Its planning process and development have evoked contestation over indigenous rights to the lands, notions of exclusion, dispossession and displacement, associated tensions between supporters and opponents of the master planned community and underlined the predicaments of public engagement in sustainability planning initiatives.

Informal practices of gentrifiers who participate in environmental initiatives have bearing on the transformation of urban neighbourhoods and larger city

districts. Enactments by higher income 'bourgeois-bohemian' or 'hipster' gentrifiers who actively seek out progressive and authentic urban spaces and
experiences, particularly older and socially diverse city neighbourhoods,
and who participate in environmental activities as a way to produce authenticity and cultivate pastoral notions of urban life are explored in Chapter 4.
This section discusses the unfolding of the social privileges of higher income,
urban professionals in sustainability projects that are directed by local government, consumer demand for environmental amenities and services and the
participation of gentrifiers in community-based non-governmental environmental initiatives. Attention is directed towards how gentrifiers co-produce
urban policy through social connections with policy actors and urban practitioners and the associations between sustainability policies and 'creative city'
policies that aim to regenerate cities through urban arts and culture initiatives
and attract higher income, professionalized cultural workers to particular
locations. Included in these analyses are the direct and indirect exclusionary
processes that are produced by gentrifiers through participation and engagement with localized policy and planning agendas.

Resisting gentrification: Searching for equitable and just sustainability policy and planning

In untangling how sustainability policy, planning practices and gentrification
converge and unfold in cities and the problematic impacts of these connections
on issues such as residential affordability, equitable spatial access and socio-
spatial transformations that can produce experiences of exclusion and
displacement, the last section of this book focuses on more hopeful responses
and spaces of resistance to these processes. In place of official urban sustainability agendas and informal environmental initiatives that are complicit with
and act to co-constitute gentrification, this takes the form of projects that
emphasize long-term and 'in place' social and environmental equity and
justice. As gentrification produces rising land and housing values in cities,
individual and organizational responses to these situations have involved
attempts to retain land and housing and raise awareness about rights over urban
spaces, housing, and land as a sustainability strategy. Here, a notion of rights
as a form of resistance to gentrification include the right to 'remain in place'
through agency over and an ability to remain in an existing urban area without
being made vulnerable to socio-spatial eviction and displacement. Two types
of land and housing stewardship practices that are discussed in Chapter 5 –
CLTs and eco-villages – both emphasize community ownership of land and
affordable arrangements of housing in order to produce affordable and socially
accessible housing and equitable uses of green space in cities. CLTs are non-
profit, non-governmental organizations that operate at very local scales and
that own legal title to urban land for uses identified by local residents and for
sustainable, long-term land stewardship (cf. Angotti, 2007; Crabtree 2010,

2014; Davis, 2007, 2010; Sungu-Erylimaz and Greenstein, 2005; Meehan, 2014). Eco-villages (or 'eco-communities') are also situated at the local scale and are more informal in arrangement although they may use a CLT approach as a way to retain community control over land. They primarily focus on using land for a mix of small-scale and independent residential and environmental uses such as permaculture initiatives, small livestock raising and recycling and trading without currency (Boyer, 2015; Ergas, 2010; Litfin, 2014; Pickerill, 2016). Both practices emphasize the de-commodification of land and housing as a form of protest and resistance, and participants ascribe to understandings of social and environmental equity and rights.

The Dudley Street CLT in Boston, the East London CLT in the Borough of Tower Hamlets, London, and the Parkdale Neighbourhood Land Trust in Toronto are discussed as examples of CLT organizations that exist in older, historically working class and immigrant areas of these cities and that work to resist neighbourhood-level gentrification through control over neighbour-hood land by lower-income, racialized and marginalized residents. The Vauban eco-village (Freiburg, Germany) and the Los Angeles eco-village are explored due to Vauban being a large planned community with formal connections with the local government of Freiburg (Schropfer and Hee, 2008). By contrast, the Los Angeles eco-village is a small community that promotes independent, 'do-it-yourself' practices and more informal relational associations with institutions and surrounding communities. Both eco-villages emphasize social and environmental equity through collective decision-making processes and co-operative access to affordable housing forms and environmental projects, although, as discussed in Chapter 5, these approaches differ in each location.

While urban CLTs and eco-villages are not comprehensive solutions to the problems of gentrification that are addressed in this book, these initiatives offer possible alternatives to gentrification and displacement processes in cities. Specifically, they suggest a re-framing of how urban sustainability ideas might operate in equitable ways and which incorporates social rights for low income and other marginalized persons such as the right to remain in an urban place without vulnerability to eviction and displacement, the right to affordable urban land and housing and the right to reside within a sustainable community. Julian Agyeman's important conceptual development of 'just sustainability' over the past decade (Agyeman 2005, 2008; Agyeman, Bullard and Evans, 2003; Agyeman and Evans, 2004; Agyeman, Scholsberg, *et al.* 2016) has connected with environmental justice research and activism through a particular call for a reframing of sustainability that challenges its primary interpretation as an environmental pursuit and instead emphasizes the inseparability of environmental quality and human equality (2008, p. 751). As Agyeman and Evans (2004, p. 163) suggest, the notion of a 'just sustainability' that incorporates an understanding of the associations 'between racial, low income, and environmental injustices' allows for the development of common goals with environmental justice actors and organizations. By doing so, it reclaims the idea of sustainability in principle and in its application and, instead, orients it towards the building of rights for socially marginalized persons as a core, inseparable component of any environmental initiative.

As a departure point for the following chapters, the idea of re-orienting the current universalized notion of sustainability towards a more deeply articulated understanding of and support for equity and justice gives a rationale for the necessity of the following critiques of the formalized and informal associations between sustainability policy, planning initiatives, and gentrification in cities. In relying on specific examples of these associations and how they are produced in various cities, I draw from examples in academic literature, research in cities that I visited and reliance on textual materials in these locations – specifically policy and planning documents and development proposals and plans. In place of interviews in multiple locations, I use community-focused blogs, editorials, and additional articles in locally focused media sources in order to gauge local opinions and responses. These methods have garnered a more comprehensive range of information and perspectives about the urban contexts in which the convergences between sustainability ideas and initiatives and gentrification processes occur. As examined in the following chapters, the entanglements between sustainability policy, planning and gentrification demonstrate the paradoxical associations between the progressive intentions of sustainability policy and planning agendas and the accumulative processes of urban development, and underline how environmental gentrification unfolds in cities and its problematic consequences for the production of equitable and just urban environments.

References

Abel, T. D., and White, J. (2011). Skewed riskscapes and gentrified inequities: Environmental exposure disparities in Seattle, Washington. *American Journal of Public Health*, *101*(S1), S246–S254. https://doi.org/10.2105/AJPH.2011.300174

Agyeman, J. (2005). *Sustainable communities and the challenge of environmental justice*. New York City: NYU Press.

Agyeman, J. (2008). Toward a 'Just' sustainability. *Continuum: Journal of Media and Cultural Studies*, *22*(6), 751–756.

Agyeman, J., and Evans, B. (2004). 'Just Sustainability': The emerging discourse of environmental justice in Britain? *The Geographical Journal*, *170*(2), 155–164.

Agyeman, J., Evans, T., and Bullard, R. (2003). Toward a just sustainability in urban communities: Building equity rights with sustainable solutions. *Annals of the American Academy of Political and Social Science*, *590*(1), 35–53.

Agyeman, J., Schlosberg, D., Craven, L., and Matthews, C. (2016). Trends and directions in environmental justice: From inequity to everyday life, community, and just sustainabilities. *Annual Review of Environment and Resources*, *41*, 321–340.

Angotti, T. (2007). *Community land trusts and low-income multifamily rental housing: The case of cooper square, New York City*. Cambridge, MA: Lincoln Institute of Land Policy.

Anguelovski, I. (2015). Alternative food provision conflicts in cities: Contesting food privilege, injustice, and whiteness in Jamaica Plain, Boston. *Geoforum*, *58*, 184–194.

Atkinson, R., and Bridge, G. (eds). (2005). *Gentrification in a global context: The new urban colonialism*. London: Routledge.

Banzhaf, H. S., and Walsh, R. P. (2006). *Do people vote with their feet? An empirical test of environmental gentrification*. Discussion paper. Washington, DC: Resources for the Future. Retrieved from www.rff.org/files/sharepoint/WorkImages/Download/RFF-DP-06–10.pdf

Boudreau, J.A., Keil, R., and Young, D. (2009). *Changing Toronto: Governing urban neoliberalism*. Toronto: University of Toronto Press.

Boyer, R. (2015). Grassroots innovation for urban sustainability: Comparing the diffusion pathways of three ecovillage projects. *Environment and Planning A*, *45*, 320–337.

Bullard, R. (1990). *Dumping in dixie: Race, class, and environmental quality*. New York: Westview Press.

Bullard, R. (ed.). (1999). *Confronting environmental racism: Voices from the grassroots*. New York: South End Press.

Bunce, S. (2004). The emergence of 'Smart Growth' intensification in Toronto: Environment and economy in the new official plan. *Local environment: International Journal of Justice and Sustainability*, *9*(2), 177–119.

Bunce, S. (2009). Developing sustainability: Sustainability policy and gentrification on Toronto's waterfront. *Local Environment: International Journal of Justice and Sustainability*, *14*(7), 651–667.

Bunce, S. (2011). Public–private sector alliances in sustainable waterfront revitalization: Policy, planning, and design in the West Don Lands. In G. Desfor and J. Laidley (eds), *Re-shaping Toronto's waterfront* (pp. 287–304). Toronto: University of Toronto Press.

Burton, E. (2000). The compact city: Just or just compact? A preliminary analysis. *Urban Studies*, *37*(11), 1969–2006.

Butler, T., and Lees, L. (2006). Super-gentrification in Barnsbury, London: Globalization and gentrifying global elites at the neighbourhood level. *Transactions of the Institute of British Geographers*, *31*(4), 467–487.

Byrne, J. (2007). *The role of race in configuring park use: A political ecology perspective*. PhD dissertation. Faculty of the Graduate School, University of Southern California.

Byrne, J. (2012). When green is white: The cultural politics of race, nature and social exclusion in a Los Angeles urban national park. *Geoforum*, *43*(3), 595–611. http://doi.org/10.1016/j.geoforum.2011.10.002

Byrne, J., and Wolch, J. (2009). Nature, race, and parks: Past research and future directions for geographic research. *Progress in Human Geography*, 653–750. http://doi.org/10.1177/0309132509103156

Caulfield, J. (1994). *City form and everyday life: Toronto's gentrification and critical social practice*. Toronto: University of Toronto Press.

City of Toronto. (2002). *Toronto official plan*. Toronto, ON: Author.

City of Toronto. (2015). *Toronto official plan*. Toronto, ON: Author.

Checker, M. (2015). Green is the new brown: "Old School Toxics" and environmental gentrification on a New York City Waterfront. In C. Isenhour, G. McDonogh, and

M. Checker (eds), *Sustainability in the global city: Myth and practice* (pp. 157–179). Cambridge, UK: Cambridge University Press.

Clark, E. (2005). The order and simplicity of gentrification – A political challenge. In R. Atkinson and G. Bridge (eds), *Gentrification in a global context: The new urban colonialism* (pp. 261–269). London: Routledge.

Cowen, D., and Parlette, V. (2011). *Inner suburbs at stake: Investing in social infrastructure in Scarborough*. Research Paper 220. Toronto: Cities Centre, University of Toronto.

Crabtree, L. (2010). Fertile ground for CLT Development in Australia. In J. E. Davis (ed.), *The community land trust reader* (pp. 464–476). Cambridge, MA: Lincoln Institute for Land Policy.

Crabtree, L. (2014). Community land trusts and Indigenous housing in Australia – beyond mainstream home ownership. *Housing Studies*, *29*(6), 743–759.

Davidson, M. (2006). *New-build 'Gentrification' and London's Riverside renaissance* (Unpublished PhD dissertation). University of London, London. Retrieved from http://epn.sagepub.com/lookup/doi/10.1068/a3739

Davidson, M., and Lees, L. (2005). New-build 'Gentrification' and London's Riverside renaissance. *Environment and Planning A*, *37*(7), 1165–1190. http://doi.org/10.1068/a3739

Davidson, M., and Lees, L. (2010). New-build gentrification: Its histories, trajectories, and critical geographies. *Population, Space and Place*, *16*(5), 395–411. doi:10.1002/psp.584

Davis, J.E. (2007). *Starting a community Land Trust: Organizational and operational choices*. Burlington, VT: Burlington Associates.

Davis, J.E. (ed.). (2010). *The community land trust reader*. Cambridge, MA: Lincoln Institute of Land Policy.

Desfor, G., and Keil, R. (2004). *Nature and the city: Making environmental policy in Toronto and Los Angeles*. Tucson, AZ: University of Arizona Press.

Dooling, S. (2009). Ecological gentrification: A research agenda exploring justice in the city. *International Journal of Urban and Regional Research*, *33*(3), 621–639. http://doi.org/10.1111/j.1468-2427.2009.00860.x

Eckerd, A. (2011). Cleaning up without clearing out? A spatial assessment of environmental gentrification. *Urban Affairs Review*, *47*(1), 31–59. https://doi.org/10.1177/1078087410379720

Ergas, C. (2010). A model of sustainable living: Collective identity in an urban ecovillage. *Organization & Environment*, *23*(1), 32–54.

Foster, J. (2010). Off track, in nature: Constructing ecology on old rail lines in Paris and New York. *Nature and Culture*, *5*(3), 316.

Fowler, E. P., and Hartmann, F. (2002). City environmental policy: Connecting the dots. In E. P. Fowler and D. Siegel (eds), *Urban policy issues: Canadian perspectives*. Toronto: Oxford University Press.

Gamper-Rabindran, S., and Timmins, C. (2011). Hazardous waste cleanup, neighborhood gentrification, and environmental justice: Evidence from restricted access census block data. *American Economic Review*, *101*(3), 620–624. https://doi.org/10.1257/aer.101.3.620

Gee, M. (2017). I won the real estate lottery, but I'm not celebrating. *Globe and Mail Friday*, March 24, 2017. Retrieved from https://www.theglobeandmail.com/news/toronto/torontos-real-estate-frenzy-is-going-to-end-very-badly/article34414410/ Accessed on: May 1, 2017.

Gordon, D. J. (2016). Lament for a network? Cities and networked climate governance in Canada. *Environment and Planning C: Government and Policy, 34*(3), 529–545. https://doi.org/10.1177/0263774X15614675.

Gould, K., and Lewis, T. (2016). *Green gentrification: Urban sustainability and the struggle for environmental justice.* Abingdon, UK: Routledge.

Grant, J. (2009). Theory and practice in planning the suburbs: Challenges to implementing new urbanism, smart growth, and sustainability. Principles *Planning Theory & Practice, 10*(1), 11–33.

Hackworth, J. (2002). Postrecession gentrification in New York City. *Urban Affairs Review, 37*(6), 815–843.

Hackworth, J., and Smith, N. (2001). The changing state of gentrification. *Tijdschrift Voor Economische En Sociale Geografie, 92*(4), 464–477. http://doi.org/10.1111/1467-9663.00172

Hamilton, T., and Curran, W. (2013). From 'Five Angry Women' to 'Kick-ass Community': Gentrification and environmental activism in Brooklyn and beyond. *Urban Studies, 50*(8), 1557–1574. http://doi.org/10.1177/0042098012465128

Heynen, N. (2006). Green urban political ecologies: Toward a better understanding of inner-city environmental change. *Environment and Planning A, 38*(3), 499–516. http://doi.org/10.1068/a37365

Heynen, N., Perkins, H. A., and Roy, P. (2006). The political ecology of uneven urban green space. The impact of political economy on race and ethnicity in producing environmental inequality in Milwaukee. *Urban Affairs Review, 42*(1), 3–25. http://doi.org/10.1177/1078087406290729

Hulchanski, D. (2010). *The three cities within Toronto: Income polarization among Toronto's neighbourhoods 1970–2005.* Toronto: Cities Centre, University of Toronto.

Jenks, M., Burton, E., and Williams, K. (eds). (1996). *The compact city: A sustainable urban form?* London: E&FN Spon.

Kern, L. (2007). Reshaping the boundaries of public and private life: Gender, condominium development, and the neoliberalization of urban living. *Urban Geography, 28*(7), 657–681. http://dx.doi.org/10.2747/0272-3638.28.7.657

King, R. (2016). Canadian real estate market outlook 2016. *Money Sense*, January 20, 2016. Accessed from www.moneysense.ca/spend/real-estate/canadian-real-estate-market-outlook-2016/ Accessed on: May 1, 2017.

Krueger, R., and Gibbs, D. (eds). (2007). *The sustainable development paradox: Urban political economy in the United States and Europe.* New York City: The Guilford Press.

Landry, S., and Chakraborty, J. (2009). Street trees and equity: Evaluating the spatial distribution of an urban amenity. *Environment and Planning A, 41*(11), 2651–2670.

Lees, L. (2000). A reappraisal of gentrification: Towards a 'geography of gentrification'. *Progress in Human Geography, 24*(3), 389–408. http://doi.org/10.1191/030913200701540483

Lees, L. (2003). Super-gentrification: The case of Brooklyn heights. *New York City Urban Studies, 40*(12), 2487–2509.

Lees, L., Slater, T., and Wyly, E. (2008). *Gentrification.* Abingdon, UK: Routledge.

Leffers, D., and Ballamingie, P. (2013). Governmentality, environmental subjectivity, and urban intensification. *Local Environment: International Journal of Justice and Sustainability, 18*(2), 134–151.

Lissner, R. (2013). Toronto is the second most walkable city in Canada, says walk score Huffington. *Post Canada.* Retrieved from http://torontoist.com/2013/01/toronto-is-the-second-most-walkable-city-in-canada-says-walk-score/ Accessed on: May 1, 2017.

Litfin, K. (2014). *Ecovillages: Lessons for sustainable community.* Cambridge, UK: Polity Press.

Loughran, K. (2014). Parks for profit: The high line, growth machines, and the uneven development of urban public spaces. *City & Community, 13*(1), 49–68. http://doi.org/10.1111/cico.12050

Mapes, J., and Wolch, J. (2011). 'Living Green': The promise and pitfalls of new sustainable communities. *Journal of Urban Design, 16*(1), 105–126.

Marcuse, P. (1985). Gentrification, abandonment, and displacement: Connections, causes, and policy responses in New York City. *Washington University Journal of Urban and Contemporary Law, 28,* 195–240.

Mazer, K., and Rankin, K. (2011). The social space of gentrification: The politics of neighborhood accessibility in Toronto's Downtown west. *Environment and Planning D, 29*(5), 822–839.

McCann, E., and Ward, K. (2011). *Mobile urbanism: Cities and policymaking in the global age.* Minneapolis: University of Minnesota Press.

McClearn, M. (2017). Flipped. Globe and Mail Friday, May 7, 2017. Retrieved from www.theglobeandmail.com/news/toronto/condo-flipping-toronto-hot-housing market/article34908345/

McFarlane, C. (2011). Assemblage and critical urbanism. *City, 15*(2), 2014–224.

Meehan, J. (2014). Reinventing Real Estate: The community land trust as a social invention in affordable housing. *Journal of Applied Social Science, 8*(2), 113–133.

Melia, S., Parkhurst, G., and Barton, H. (2011). The paradox of intensification. *Transport Policy, 18*(1), 46–52.

Moore, S. (2013). What's wrong with best practice? Questioning the typification of new urbanism. *Urban Studies, 50*(11), 2371–2387.

Moore, S., and Bunce, S. (2009). Delivering sustainable buildings and communities: Eclipsing social concerns through private sector-led urban regeneration and development. *Local Environment: International Journal of Justice and Sustainability, 14*(7), 601–606.

Moranis, S. (2016). 10 Things to consider for real estate investment property. *Toronto Sun,* Tuesday, July 26, 2016. Retrieved from www.torontosun.com/2016/07/26/10-things-to-consider-for-real-estate-investment-property

Newman, P., and Kenworthy, J. (1999). *Sustainability and cities: Overcoming automobile dependence.* Washington, DC: Island Press.

Patrick, D. (2014). The matter of displacement: A queer ecology of New York City's high line. *Social and Cultural Geography, 15*(8), 920–941.

Pearsall, H. (2013). Superfund me: A study of resistance to gentrification in New York City. *Urban Studies, 50*(11), 2293–2310. https://doi.org/10.1177/0042098013478236

Peck, J. (2011). Geographies of policy: From transfer-diffusion to mobility-mutation. *Progress in Human Geography, 25*(6), 773–797.

Pickerill, J. (2016). *Eco-Homes: People, place, and politics.* London: Zed Books.

Pulido, L. (2000). Rethinking environmental racism: White privilege and urban development in southern California. *Annals of the Association of American Geographers, 90* (1), 12–40.

Pulido, L., Sidawi, S., and Vos, B.(1996). An archaeology of environmental racism in Los Angeles. *Urban Geography, 17*(5), 419–439.

Quastel, N. (2009). Political ecologies of gentrification. *Urban Geography, 30*(7), 694–725. http://doi.org/10.2747/0272–3638.30.7.694

Raco, M. (2005). Sustainable development, rolled-out neoliberalism and sustainable communities. *Antipode, 37*(2), 324–347. http://doi.org/10.1111/j.0066–4812.2005.00495.x

Raco, M. (2010). Spatial policy, sustainability, and state restructuring: A reassessment of sustainable community building in England. In R. Krueger and D. Gibbs (eds). *The Sustainable development paradox: Urban political economy in the United States and Europe* (pp. 214–237). New York City: The Guilford Press.

Rosol, M. (2013). Vancouver's "EcoDensity" planning initiative: A struggle over hegemony? *Urban Studies, 50*(11), 2238–2255.

Searle, G., and Filion, P. (2011). Planning context and urban intensification outcomes: Sydney versus Toronto. *Urban Studies, 48*(7), 1419–1438.

Shaw, W. (2005). Heritage and gentrification: Remembering 'the good old days' in postcolonial Sydney. In R. Atkinson and G. Bridge (eds), *Gentrification in a global context: The new urban colonialism* (pp. 58–72). Abingdon, UK: Routledge.

Slater, T. (2004). Municipally managed gentrification in South Parkdale, Toronto. *Canadian Geographer, 48*(3), 303–325.

Smith, N. (1996). *The new urban frontier: Gentrification and the revanchist city.* New York: Psychology Press.

Smith, N. (2002). New globalism, new urbanism: Gentrification as global urban strategy. *Antipode, 34*(3), 427–450. http://doi.org/10.1111/1467–8330.00249

Sorensen, A. (2010). Urban Sustainability and Compact Cities Ideas in Japan: The diffusion, transformation and deployment of planning concepts. In: Healey, P. and Upton, R. (eds) *Crossing Borders: International Exchange and Planning Practices* (pp. 117–140). London and New York: Routledge.

Sungu-Erylimaz, Y., and Greenstein, R. (2007). *A national study of community land trusts.* Cambridge, MA: Lincoln Institute of Land Policy.

Swyngedouw, E. (2005). Governance innovation and the citizen: The Janus face of governance-beyond-the-State. *Urban Studies, 42*(11), 1991–2006.

Swyngedouw, E. (2009). The antinomies of the post-political city: In search of a democratic politics of environmental protection. *International Journal of Urban and Regional Research, 33*(3), 601–620.

Swyngedouw, E. (2010). Apocalypse forever? Post-political populaism and the spectre of climate change. *Theory, Culture & Society, 27*(203), 212–232.

Taylor, D. (2014). Toxic communities: Environmental racism. *Industrial Pollution and residential.* New York City: Mobility NYU Press.

Thomas, L., and Cousins, W. (1996). The compact city: Successful, desirable and achievable? In M. Jenks, E. Burton, and K. Williams (eds), *The Compact City: A Sustainable Urban Form?* (pp. 53–65) London: E&FN Spon.

Williams, K., Jenks, M., and Burton, E. (eds). (2000). *Achieving sustainable urban form.* New York City: Spon Press.

Zamon, R. (2013). Walkable cities Canada: Walk score grades Canada's cities. *Huffington Post Canada, January* 23, 2013. Retrieved from www.huffingtonpost.ca/2013/01/23/walkable-cities-canada_n_2535699.html Accessed on: May 1, 2017.

Zukin, S. (1989). *Loft living: Culture and capital in urban change.* New Brunswick, NJ: Rutgers University Press.

2 Convergences of urban sustainability policy, planning and gentrification

Varied definitions of gentrification have emerged over the past four decades since it was first defined by sociologist Ruth Glass (1964) through her observations of the transformation of multi-unit housing into single family, middle class homes in London neighbourhoods. While debates over definitions of gentrification, from both critical and celebratory perspectives, have unfolded over the last few decades in gentrification scholarship, current and widened approaches to defining urban gentrification in theory and practice are enormously cogent for understanding the formulation and, in particular, the implementation of contemporary urban policy and planning. Two particularly dominant discourses, urban regeneration and sustainability, have emerged from urban policy and planning, urban growth and increasing assemblages of government, private sector and civil society actors in urban agendas and development. Complex similarities between the conceptual agendas of urban regeneration and urban sustainability policy and planning exist despite appearing to have conflicting objectives – sustainability to mitigate urban environmental problems and urban regeneration to stimulate growth through the development and re-use of urban spaces. Yet, the synchronicity between the two policy and planning agendas in relation to how these are defined and implemented by governments and actors beyond the state have profound effects on how urban spaces are planned and developed within a broader context of neo-liberalized, profit-centred urban growth. Certainly, gentrification is not an explicit policy and planning agenda and the term is argued to be viewed by mainstream urban policymakers and planners as an overtly critical 'dirty word' that dampens celebratory perspectives on gentrification (Slater, 2009; Slater, Curran, and Lees, 2004; Smith, 1996; Wyly, 2015). It is employed by critical scholars and other public actors to unveil the problematic outcomes of 'well-intended' urban development plans and projects. Gentrification is a particularly important lens for enquiry into the uneven development of spatial production in cities, social exclusion and displacement, and environmental injustice. In this chapter, the connections between urban regeneration and sustainability policy and planning agendas, and the roles of governmental and non-governmental actors and institutions in the development and implementation of policy and planning initiatives, will be explored through a discussion of how these two policy directives have become more entwined and how they relate to urban gentrification processes. These associations are particularly evident in policy and planning directives of urban intensification, succinctly defined as the densification of built form and population activity in cities (Jenks, Burton, and Williams, 1996), that have been widely adopted and implemented in cities over the past two decades as way to produce more sustainable urban form and encourage regeneration largely through public–private alliances in planning and development.

Over the past several decades, multi-level governmental policy and planning for urban sustainability has primarily emphasized the cultivation of more environmentally responsible built form and land use patterns in cities, and is integral to shifting perspectives towards addressing the environmental problems caused by traditional forms of urban land consumption. Layard (2001) notes that, '(l) and use planning and sustainable development seem to be ever more inextricably intertwined. References to the ideas, principles and policies underpinning sustainability are everywhere – from planning policy guidance to good practice guides to inclusions in development plans' (p. 1). This has been most noticeable in scholarly and public discussions over what defines and constitutes sustainable urban form and land use (Neuman, 2005). The emphasis on the re-casting of land use policy and planning to connect with sustainability has become most visible, over the past two decades, in urban regeneration policy agendas that emphasize 'compact city' and 'smart growth' planning practices as a way to produce more sustainable cities. The compact city planning model was popularized in continental Europe and Britain (Beatley, 2000, 2007), and has been quickly exported through policy mobility to cities such as Singapore and Tokyo (Han, 2005; Lin and Yang, 2006; Sorensen, 2010; Vallance, Perkins, and Moore, 2005), with a focus on re-creating planning interpretations of the more traditional compact form of European cities through attention to the maintenance and increase of residential population and building densities in the urban core, the encouragement of mixed residential and commercial spatial uses, adaptive reuse of existing buildings and brownfield redevelopment, and strengthening pedestrian, bicycle and public transit infrastructure. Compact city policy and planning has been particularly compatible with Local Agenda 21 policy, hence the success of Local Agenda 21 initiatives in European cities due to a combination of political support and the existence of urban forms that are, to some degree, already compatible with the idea of a sustainable city (ICLEI – Local Governments for Sustainability, n.d.). In North America, smart growth has become embedded in public discourse and policies of urban planning with features and objectives in keeping with the compact city model, however, with a more explicit emphasis on the mitigation of urban sprawl and the impacts of urban development encroachment on agricultural land or the promotion of new sustainable communities through more compact 'new urbanist' design in suburban and exurban locations (Bourne, Bunce, Taylor, Luka, and Maurer, 2003; Bruegmann, 2005; Calthorpe and Fulton, 2001; Chapple, 2015; Krueger and Buckingham, 2009, 2012; Wolch, Byrne and Newell, 2014). It is through urban intensification that an alliance between multi-level government policy and planning and built form development by the private sector development has become increasingly evident (Moore and Bunce, 2009). Intensification, identified as a major urban development process in Britain from the most recent Labour government's 'urban renaissance' agenda onwards (Lees, 2002; Raco, 2005), as a federal urban development policy directive for cities in the United States (Steinacker, 2003) and a provincial government-level policy for urban municipalities in Canada (Bourne, 2001; Filion, Bunting, Pavlic, and Langlois, 2010; Leffers and Ballamingie, 2013), has galvanized new forms of socio-spatial production and consumption that are increasingly connected with gentrification practices in central cities. As critical discussions on gentrification indicate, the 'urban regeneration through intensification' thrust of urban policy, planning and development in Europe and North America has also sparked a co-constituted transformation in the production of residential and labour spaces and an emergence of a new middle class, professionalized demographic of urban residents. Sustainability increasingly connects with gentrification as a result of urban intensification policies and practices that foster increases in residential and commercial value as well as initiatives to expand environmental amenities, such as parks and other green spaces, that meet the needs of higher income residents in cities. Critical gentrification literature has examined the impact of governmental policy and planning, the involvement of private sector planning and development firms and the engagement of civil society in the creation of urban regeneration policy agendas more broadly, and practices of intensification as an approach to producing more sustainable urban form. The following sections explore several recent and current areas of gentrification research – policy-led gentrification, social mix and gentrification, new-build gentrification, 'third' and 'fourth wave' gentrification and environmental gentrification – that provide insight into the associations between urban regeneration and sustainability and how these policy concepts coalesce and unfold at different scales. Recent literature on policy-led gentrification explores the associations between multi-scalar urban regeneration policies, their development-oriented focus at the scale of cities set within the broader context of globalized circuits of property investment and the production of urban gentrification. A majority of writing on policy-led gentrification attends to studies of urban regeneration policy and implementation in Britain, given the wide scope of the UK government's sustainable urban regeneration agenda over the past two decades. In relation to policy-led gentrification, studies on 'social mix' policy in the form of governmental directives that encourage urban development projects to include a mixture of income and residential tenure ranges in order to promote an official discourse of diversity and inclusivity while often hiding social exclusion and displacement. Understandings of 'third wave'

(Hackworth and Smith, 2001) and 'fourth wave' (Lees, Slater, and Wyly, 2008) gentrification couch it within broader structural changes of neo-liberal governance and neo-liberal urbanism and explain the increasing complexity of motivations, arrangements and contexts for and of gentrification. Discussions on new-build gentrification explore the roles of property and property developers in the construction of newly built residential and commercial development that frequently occurs as an extension of policy and regulatory support for brownfield remediation and redevelopment as well as in-fill development, also considered as environmentally sustainable practices. I conclude with an exploration of recent writing on environmental gentrification, which has largely grown to examine localized connections between environmental remediation and property values, the creation of environmental amenities that attract gentrifiers to particular neighbourhoods and the role of environmental activities and spaces in producing social exclusion and displacement.

Policy-led gentrification

Discussions on policy-led gentrification have largely focused on the development and implementation of urban regeneration policies by the British 'New Labour' government in the late 1990s and 2000s, however the notion of 'policy' or 'state-led' gentrification has also now been examined in cities such as Berlin (Levine, 2004), Mumbai (Harris, 2008), Istanbul (Islam and Sakizlioglu, 2015), Lagos (Nwanna, 2015) and Auckland (Murphy, 2008). The development of urban regeneration policy in Britain was a central marker in the shifting of gentrification discourse toward the analysis of a policy agenda that brought together intensified urban development, the establishment of public–private alliances in policy implementation, and private sector involvement in the roll-out of policy. A turn toward the study of government formulated, private sector supported urban regeneration policies and gentrification was particularly relevant for understanding the conceptual design and implementation mechanisms of sustainability within urban regeneration policies. Responding to the emergent British urban regeneration policies of the late 1990s, Lees (2000) notes that, 'gentrification practices have permeated recent urban policy and urban politics' (p. 391). The formulation of governmental policy that promoted guidelines for future urban planning and encouraged private sector-led land development is viewed as a defining feature of gentrification in the 2000s and demonstrated how government urban regeneration and revitalization policies shaped gentrification (Hackworth, 2002; Hackworth and Smith, 2001; Lees and Ley, 2008; Lees *et al.*, 2008; Levine, 2004; Murphy, 2008; Smith, 2002; Watt, 2009) As urban planning literature has also shown, the contemporary creation of governmental urban planning policy has increasingly involved private sector actors and interests in the implementation of urban planning directives (Allmendinger, 2009;

Brindley, Rydin, and Stoker, 1989; Fraser, DeFilippis, and Bazuin, 2012; Healey, Davoudi, O'Toole, Tavsanoglu, and Usher, 1992; Moore and Bunce, 2009; Newman and Thornley, 2002; Oatley, 1998; Tweedale, 1998). Closer associations between government urban policy agendas and private sector involvement have been constituted by a broader paradigmatic shift toward flexible and entrepreneurial neo-liberal urban governance at different scales that has forged deeper alliances between the state and private corporate and investment interests in cities (Brenner, 2004; Brenner and Theodore, 2003; Hackworth, 2007; Harvey, 1989; Jessop, 2002; Kipfer and Keil, 2002; Peck, Theodore, and Brenner, 2013; Peck and Tickell, 2002).

Research on policy-led gentrification has pointed to the ways in which the objectives of urban regeneration policies augment existing and create new gentrification processes through their reliance on private sector involvement. This research has also suggested that urban regeneration policies can frequently obfuscate 'on the ground' gentrification processes through the use of ostensibly progressive and friendly sounding concepts such as sustainability and intensification. Since the late 1990s, British governmental policies for urban regeneration and planning have particularly emphasized what Bromley, Tallon, and Thomas (2005, p. 2408) have called the, 'intertwined goals of regeneration and sustainability' through urban intensification. Lees (2003), in an assessment of the 'New Labour' government's urban policy agenda, notes that 'urban policy statements have invoked a discourse of "urban renaissance" that interweaves calls for urban sustainability with a prescription of concepts and ways of living [a "back to the city" lifestyle] that are closely tied to gentrification practices' (p. 61). She also notes that the Labour government's concept of sustainability was primarily defined in terms of an 'environmentally sustainable urban renaissance', where, 'the foundation for urban renaissance and sustainability is the densification of urban form', ostensibly considered to be a 'magic cure all for a variety of environmental and social ills' (Lees, 2003, p. 75). The scope of the Blair government's urban regeneration agenda was evident in the quantity of policy documents that were developed. The government appointed Urban Task Force, formed in 1998 under the guidance of its first chair, Richard Rogers[1], an architect, urban planner and author of several books on urban sustainability and compact cities, formulated multiple reports that guided intensification practices in British cities under the umbrella of sustainable urbanization. The *Towards an Urban Renaissance* (DETR, 1999) document posited a rationale for intensifying existing urban areas with the first 'priority area' of the document making an explicit connection between the regeneration of British cities through compact development and sustainable design and infrastructure such as pedestrian, bicycle and public transit networks (DETR, 1999, p. ix). The report also emphasized brownfield development through 'flexible' arrangements with private sector and civil society partners, a reregulation of planning mechanisms and tax incentives to entice private engagement and investment in urban regeneration projects, and the

establishment of national public–private companies to attract additional investment (DETR, 1999, p. ix). These directives formed the basis for policy
implementation at the local scale documented in the document, *Our Towns
and Cities: The Future – Delivering an Urban Renaissance* (DETR, 2000),
which detailed sustainability initiatives such as a multi-million pound public
investment in transit infrastructure (2000, p. 10), a comprehensive program to
improve the quality of parks, play areas and open spaces, and the introduction
of a 'Green Flag Awards' program to acknowledge best practices in parks
and other green spaces (2000, p. 9). These policies were followed by the
'Sustainable Communities Plan' in 2003 and the 'Sustainable Communities
Act' in 2007 (since rescinded by David Cameron's Conservative government
in January, 2015). The Sustainable Communities Plan defined and legislated
the production of sustainable communities through local economic growth
initiatives, public space redevelopment and 'place making' through connections between increased housing provision and more compact residential
neighbourhoods, the maintenance and creation of parks and public spaces and
local scale human interactions (ODPM, 2003). A thrust of the plan was the
production of new housing, aimed towards middle-class professionals, in
selected urban regions (Raco, 2004, 2005). Street (2014) notes that the British
government's policy trajectory and emphasis on achieving sustainability
through local economic growth was retained through the global economic crisis
of 2008 and post-recession years and expanded to include the encouragement of local strategies for climate change resiliency and green economic
development.

In a discussion of the Blair government's first urban regeneration policies,
Neil Smith (2002) suggested that the sustainability objectives of urban intensification in both documents connected with a broader neo-liberal project and
national and urban government urgency to stimulate private investment in
property development in British cities. Smith predicted that the intensification
targets and strategies for redevelopment that were outlined in *Toward an Urban
Renaissance*, such as a designated 60 per cent of new housing to be built on
brownfield sites over a 25-year period in conjunction with the role of private
sector investment in and construction of residential housing, would exacerbate
gentrification through property inflation. As Harris (2008, p. 2409) suggests,
the re-development context occurred alongside 'a raft of deregulatory and
liberalisation reforms, and the growth of new corporate-governmental alliances'. Raco (2005) argues that the *Sustainable Communities* plan aligned
important tenets of sustainability, such as environmental responsibility and
community-based planning, with contradictory emphases on private sector
provided, market-oriented development of new housing. He states that the
objectives of the policy were to 'tackle the housing shortage in the South and
East of England, rejuvenate land and housing markets in low demand areas
of northern England and protect rural areas from growing development
pressures' as well as to 'replace obsolete housing with modern sustainable

accommodation' (Raco 2005, p. 332). Davidson (2006) and Davidson and Lees (2005), in studies of new residential development along the Thames River to the west of London's centre, demonstrate how urban regeneration through sustainability, as a policy directive of both national and local level government, informed the creation of new residential communities. Davidson and Lees (2005) note that despite these policy directives, new property developments were geared towards middle to high income earners, in keeping with a concurrent government focus on the attraction of professionals to key urban regional areas of Britain, with small to large flats selling between 240,000 and 825,000 pounds in the mid-2000s (p. 950). These studies, conducted during the first years of urban regeneration policy implementation in Britain, were integral for underlining how urban policies increasingly shape the conditions for gentrification before implementation and how the contradictory mechanisms of 'policy-to-practice' transfer, particularly in relation to the focus on private sector involvement in intensified residential development, can produce 'on the ground' gentrification. In these ways, gentrification was understood as a genuine outcome of both the policy objectives and implementation of urban regeneration policies as a result of the increased practices of residential and commercial intensification and reliance upon private sector developers to enact largely market-oriented 'property-led regeneration' in cities (Adair, Berry, and McGreal, 2003).

Discussions on policy-led gentrification have also pointed to how the British 'New Labour' government's discourse of urban regeneration was shaped through the use of friendly, progressive terms and phrases that cultivated a positive public image while hiding its problematic underpinnings (Davidson, 2008; Lees, 2000, 2003; Smith, 2002). Slater *et al.* (2004) suggest that the policy discourse of sustainability and regeneration, or 'sustainable regeneration', implied a pluralistic, beneficial situation for all British residents, regardless of their socio-economic situation, while avoiding mention of possible negative outcomes of policy implementation such as gentrification. Moreover, they note that the use of friendly, progressive discourse reduced space for public critique of the policies. They state that, 'class-neutral [policy] terms such as urban regeneration, urban sustainability, urban renaissance . . . effectively deflect criticism and resistance' (Slater *et al.*, 2004, p. 1144). Furbey (1999) observes that the use of the term 'sustainable urban regeneration' implied a long-term, beneficial, and organic process of policy creation and 'roll-out' that supported associations between the physical, economic, social, and environmental change of urban communities and resident well-being.

While the use of ecological terms to interpret social functions is not new, it has been re-casted through urban sustainability policy to imply a holistic practice that is transformational as well as visionary; an understanding that sustainability will provide comprehensive benefits that will concurrently mitigate socio-ecological damage and produce better urban environments. Interventions in gentrification research that have critiqued the policy discourse of urban regeneration and sustainable communities are particularly enlightening for understanding how government and non-state actors employ certain discourses in the shaping and marketing of urban policy agendas and broader public attitudes that can veil 'on-the-ground' gentrification outcomes. As discussed in Chapter 4, the policy discourse of the creative city is utilized in conjunction with sustainability in a similar way to attract and produce new spaces of gentrification for middle class professionals in cities.

Third and fourth wave gentrification and sustainability

Alongside policy-led gentrification, the concept of 'third wave gentrification' (Hackworth and Smith, 2001) underlines the increased and more fluid associations and formalized alliances between government and private sector interests and the amelioration of governmental conditions for private investment practices in cities, particularly in urban land development. These associations are evident in government support for more flexible planning and development approaches as well as formalized financial assistance programs for private sector developers in order to ease perceived development risks (Adair *et al.*, 2003). Hackworth and Smith (2001, p. 468) characterize three waves of gentrification that have connected state and private sector interests. They define the first phase as one marked by sporadic government-led interventions intended to ease private market disinvestments in inner-city neighbourhoods alongside the concurrent maintenance of public housing and other social service programs, such as publicly funded urban renewal projects. The second wave, occurring in the late 1970s to the end of the 1980s, demarcated the start of concerted government effort to encourage private sector investment in urban development. In the United States, for instance, federal loans and grants programs for private sector developers were provided through the Urban Development Action Grants program, which inspired the national Urban Development Grant program in Britain in the 1980s (Adair *et al.*, 2003). This period also defined the start of intensive neo-liberal deregulation of urban planning legislation and the government targeting of specific urban land areas for redevelopment, such as the Thatcher government's 'simplified planning zones' (SPZs) in Britain. SPZs were implemented during the 1980s for the dual purpose of 'de-bureaucratizing' planning and development control processes and making the approval process more accessible and expedient for private developers, particularly for the redevelopment of brownfield sites such as London's Docklands area, the largest SPZ in Britain (Allmendinger, 2002)[2]. In their articulation of a third wave of gentrification, Hackworth and Smith identify two defining characteristics that also help to better understand convergences of sustainability policy and planning with gentrification. First, they note that the current period of gentrification underlines an increasing globalization of the real estate sector, which has set the context for larger development corporations leading neighbourhood scale gentrification processes rather than individual investors. Second, is their argument that governments are more comprehensively involved in creating urban policies that produce the conditions for gentrification in cities before policy implementation. Smith noted that gentrification has now become a 'crucial urban strategy for city governments in consort with private capital in cities around the world' (Smith, 2002, p. 440). This strategy has localized variations that are dependent upon the particular routes of global investment capital, government structures, state policies and labour configurations (Ibid., p. 443). As such, governments do not serve as mitigating bodies to counter private sector disinvestments as per the first wave of gentrification, but proactively court globalized investment capital for land development practices and set policy and legislation to support this approach. Davidson and Lees (2005, p. 1169) remark, in their discussion of new-build gentrification, that new residential development 'involves the large-scale deployment of capital by developers who have the capacity and capability to do so'. It necessitates access to larger sources and more complex flows of finance capital in order to arrange financing packages for land purchase and development, particularly in urban areas with high land values.

In relation to the development of new communities that include sustainable materials and design, for example, large property development companies are better able to both attract the financing capital and absorb the additional costs that are related to the construction of sustainable buildings (Bunce, 2009; Roper and Beard, 2006). In Toronto, for instance, two of the largest for-profit residential and commercial developers, Minto and Tridel[3], have led a shift of property developer interest toward the provision of sustainable design in residential and commercial buildings. In addition to their increased dexterity in arranging financing for additional sustainable design construction costs, large property development companies, such as Minto and Tridel, also have the financing to sell the benefits of sustainable design to potential residential purchasers through sales centres, environmental education activities and environmentally focused advertisements (Quastel, 2009), which assist in demonstrating the consumer benefits of sustainable design to potential purchasers and are considered to be an important component of marketing the long-term cost savings of sustainable design to residential purchasers (Kibert, 2013; Lutzkendorf and Lorenz, 2005).

The second characteristic of third-wave gentrification noted by Hackworth and Smith is the increasingly complex role of state engagement with private sector land development. This is often witnessed through the dismantling of supply-side constraints to property development and rests on the notion of providing more certainty to development companies through the reduction of potential risks for companies and their financial lenders (Adair *et al.*, 2003). In the alleviation of risks, it involves governmental enhancement of property developer interest in and assurance about certain urban locations (Ibid.). This is now increasingly being done through state involvement in the highlighting and marketing of sustainable 'green' features of cities (Greenberg, 2015).

Urban governments are emphasizing their high achievement in international city rankings such as the Global Cities Index and the Arcadis Sustainable Cities Index to demonstrate the benefits and assurances of investing in their particular city. The Arcadis Sustainable Cities Index, for example, highlights indicators such as the availability of green space, lower levels of air pollution, governmental planning practices that support compact development and public transit infrastructure and government support for energy efficiency infrastructure. These features are viewed as positive externalities that are measured alongside the corporate and employment climate of cities and the 'ease of doing business' in urban locations (Arcadis Sustainable Cities Index, 2015). Another example is the cultivation of private sector engagement with sustainable property development through state-funded and facilitated educational programs intended to provide technical assistance for private developers in sustainable design and construction. For instance in Canada, such incentives include new programs formulated by the national government's Canada Mortgage and Housing Corporation (CMHC), such as the EQuilibrium Housing Demonstration program, which offers 'builders and developers across the country a powerful new approach to establish a reputation for building healthy and sustainable, quality homes that will meet the needs of Canadians now and well into the future' (CMHC, 2016) through the provision of technical resources and sustainable design models. The Canadian federal government's Ministry of Natural Resources has also established sustainability workshops on energy-efficient development for private developers. As part of their program, ecoENERGY for Buildings and Housing, the Office of Energy and Efficiency 'promotes stakeholder networks, provides information for owners and professionals, training and feedback on energy solutions, and tracks baseline data for new commercial, institutional and multi-unit residential buildings' (Natural Resources Canada, 2016). The same office has held consultative forums for private developers on improving energy reduction practices in Canadian cities, with one being held in Toronto to coincide with a large private sector property development conference (Natural Resources Canada, 2007/2016). Such sustainability programs highlight how governments assist the real estate market through the offer of direct financial incentives and educational programs to private development companies.

Lees *et al.* (2008) add a 'fourth wave' of gentrification and define it as an 'intensified financialization of housing combined with a consolidation of pro-gentrification politics' (p. 179). They use the example of the rebuilding of New Orleans, following the destruction of nearly half of the city's residential and commercial infrastructure (Gotham and Greenberg, 2014) after Hurricane Katrina in 2005. Lees *et al.* underline the role of different scales of government investment and policy making as practices in the rebuilding of New Orleans that has created a type of 'policy laboratory and template for broader urban redevelopment priorities' (Lees *et al.*, 2008, p. 186). They note that the U.S. federal government's disaster aid of approximately $10 billion offered homeowners the opportunity to rebuild or sell their properties and move else-where while local government initiatives created an open door for private sector involvement in redevelopment (Ibid., 2008). As Greenberg suggests, an interest in compact development sustainable residential design, new green space production, waste reduction and pedestrian and bicycle infrastructure has since become a central component of the redevelopment process and a way of re-branding New Orleans as a sustainable city (Greenberg, 2015), instigated by policies such as the multi-sector Louisiana Disaster Recovery Foundation's 'GreeNOLA' sustainability plan that states that 'New Orleans is poised to become one of the greenest-built cities in the world' (Louisiana Disaster Recovery Foundation, 2008, p. 16). The 'GreeNOLA' plan advocates for private sector and NGO involvement in the rebuilding process, with an emphasis on streamlining and expediting development permits and incentivising green design for private developers (Louisiana Disaster Recovery Foundation, 2008). Also encouraged is the involvement of non-governmental philanthropic organizations in rebuilding efforts, which has been noticeable in such initia-tives as the 'Make it Right Foundation', founded by Hollywood actor Brad Pitt, that has invested in the design, financing and construction of new sustainable residential buildings (Gotham, 2012; Greenberg, 2015). As Greenberg notes, the sustainability agenda for rebuilding in New Orleans has coalesced with economic growth approaches to attracting new creative industries and 'start up' enterprises to the city, with green technology now being a leading industry. She notes that, '(t)he combination of hip, urban culture and experienced with the nation's greatest environmental challenges gave New Orleans an unexpected cachet and leg-up amongst [green technology] start-up firms' (Greenberg, 2015, p. 123). These practices have also contributed to direct and indirect displace-ment of low-income residents through the production of 'environmentally friendly' communities that have increasingly become gentrified areas for 'bourgeois bohemian' residents who are attracted to alternative and environ-mentally oriented lifestyles (Campanella, 2013).

The concept of third wave gentrification and the analyses of Lees *et al.* regarding the complexity of government and private sector involvement in fourth wave gentrification and the direct relationship of policies and plans to the strategic production of gentrification offers helpful guidance for unpacking these complex arrangements in the convergences of sustainability and gentrification. These connections will be further examined in Chapter 3, in a discussion of particular urban local-level contexts of sustainability policy, planning and development.

Sustainability, social mix and gentrification

The integration of sustainability principles into urban policy incorporates the discursive application of other ecologically related terms such as 'diversity'. It is one of the key characteristics of environmental sustainability, as evidenced through biodiversity (Cowell, 1998; Hostetler, Allen and Meurk, 2011; O'Riordan and Stoll-Kleemann, 2002), and a progressive tenet of social sustainability in relation to the enhancement of social diversity (Dempsey, Bramley, Power, and Brown, 2011; Holland, 2004; Polese and Stren, 2002). In urban regeneration policy and planning, diversity has been frequently captured in the concept of 'social mix', a way to forward a social sustainability angle of urban regeneration through a dismantling of planning approaches that have created income-segregated urban communities, often symbols of the failures of mid-twentieth century modernist, state-managed and delivered planning efforts such as public housing and council estates. In social sustainability discourse, a diversification of urban residents, labour and incomes, ethno-cultural backgrounds and diverse and socially inclusive uses of urban space is connected with the longer-term vitality of a city and a way to counter the formation of homogeneous and socio-spatially marginalized communities based upon race/ethnicity, income and/or residential tenure (Polese and Stren, 2002). Gentrification research has demonstrated, however, how the urban policy discourse of social diversity, through cultivating 'social mix', is frequently altered in implementation practice. A disjuncture between policy language and implementation is evident in policy directives that suggest equitable mixtures of incomes, residential tenures and spatial uses in new urban residential developments yet do not consider structural issues and contexts of power differences and social inequalities in the production of these developments. Although a pluralistic social mix is the desired outcome of urban regeneration policies, the results often demonstrate conflicts between the interests of higher income earners and the needs of low income residents, with the interests, expectations and social access of higher income residents having more influence (August, 2014; Davidson, 2008; DeFilipis and Fraser, 2010; Lees, 2014; Rerat, Soderstrom, and Piguet, 2010). The discourse of social mix is also considered to advance a paternalistic, neo-colonialist assumption that lower income residents will benefit from close proximity to and interactions with more affluent individuals (Davidson, 2008; DeFilippis and Fraser, 2010; Kipfer and Petrunia, 2009; Lipman, 2008).

'Social mixing' and the production of mixed communities with features of intensificiation, provides a softer public image to urban regeneration yet produces gentrification through the insertion of market-oriented housing and associated commercial amenities for higher income earners (August, 2008, 2014; August and Walks, 2012; Blomley, 2004; Cameron, 2003; Davidson, 2006, 2008; Davidson and Lees, 2005; Lees, 2014; Lees and Ley, 2008; Rose, 2004; Rose *et al.*, 2013; Slater, 2006; Uitermark, Duyvendak, and Kleinhans, 2007). As Bridge *et al.* (2012) argue, social mixing is done through 'stealth' policy practices that quietly suggest beneficial arrangements yet limit opportunities for resistance to these practices. Government directives for social mixing have been frequently noticeable in the redevelopment of aging public (social) housing complexes in cities through mixed forms of rental and homeownership housing and the involvement of private sector developers as a way to off-set government expenses and stimulate private property investment and development in the provision of market-oriented residential units, which has contributed to the gentrification of these spaces (August, 2014; Davidson, 2008; Hackworth, 2007; James, 2010; Lees and Ley, 2008; Lees, Slater, and Wyly, 2008; Shaw, 2007). Lees (2014, p. 924) states that the 'rhetoric of mixed communities policy in the UK echoes the rhetoric of Labour's "urban renaissance"' and has become integrated into national and local government urban regeneration policy and planning agendas as part of the mandate to build sustainable communities and combat social exclusion. Her research on the redevelopment of the Aylesbury Estate council housing area in Southwark, London, cited as a 2.4 billion (pound) redevelopment project over a 20-year period, discusses the comprehensiveness of a 'social mix' approach in justifying and normalizing the vision of redevelopment for the area in the public realm. She notes that the redevelopment plan outlined that, 'Aylesbury was going to be more socially inclusive, better designed and contain more social capital' (Lees, 2014, p. 933). Yet, this vision was re-directed by a planning strategy that also supported the demolition of social housing units, a reduction in the availability of renewed social housing units, and the construction of 3200 new market-oriented homes (Ibid., p. 933), which has placed strain on residential arrangements for low-income, existing tenants, and contradicted the objectives of social mixing.

Similarly, the redevelopment of Toronto's Regent Park, Canada's oldest public housing complex located in the central downtown area of the city, was started by the City of Toronto in conjunction with multiple private sector and community-based actors as a way to regenerate aging housing through the encouragement of intensification, the diversification of incomes, tenures and land uses, and the insertion of market-oriented housing (August, 2014; August and Walks, 2012; Dunn, 2012; James, 2010, 2015; Rowe and Dunn, 2015). August (2014) notes that the redevelopment plan has been implemented through a reduction in public housing units and the construction of 5400 market-oriented condominium residences. She observes that '(O)nce complete, there will be a more than three-fold increase in density and a dramatically altered social composition in which rent-geared-to-income (RGI) subsidized homes will have been reduced from 100 per cent to (at most) 26 per cent of on-site units' (2014, p. 1317). The redevelopment has involved the forced relocation of existing public housing tenants during the construction of new public housing rental units and new market-oriented units (August, 2014; James, 2010). Additionally, the local government redevelopment plan was formulated with an explicit emphasis on sustainability through population densification, the production of parks and rooftop garden spaces and sustainable building and design criteria (de Schutter, 2009) and 'crime prevention through environmental design' (James, 2010), while, at the same time, aiming to increase social inclusion through community gardening practices (Toronto

Community Housing, 2007). Adherence to sustainability guidelines has been marketed by property developers in Regent Park, with one development firm noting that

> Regent Park leads the way in sustainable development. From lush green roofs that keep Toronto cool in summer, to gardening plots that allow people to grow their own organic food, to forward-thinking electric car recharging stations, Regent Park is setting the benchmark for the city. And, with the brand new 6-acre Park and its greenhouse, gardens, Farmers' Market, community oven and so much more, this vibrant neighbourhood is making others green with envy.
>
> (Daniels, 2016)

This 'eco-friendly' image of Regent Park, a neighbourhood that has been publicly stigmatized as an area of impoverishment and criminal activity (James, 2010), connects with August's analysis that redevelopment through a social mix approach in Regent Park suggests a broader strategy of 'vilify, then gentrify' (August 2014, p. 1322). The role of sustainability in the Regent Park project joins with the interests of government redevelopment policy and private developers in re-valorizing the site and as a way for the neighbourhood to be regenerated through environmental amenities that are intended to improve the social conditions of the community yet, at the same time, act to veil reduction in affordable housing and increase in market-oriented residences. In this way, environmental amenities factor into the reinforcement of needs-based differences and tensions between existing public housing residents and new condominium owners. These practices raise new issues regarding the role of sustainability practices in forwarding 'social mix' policy and planning objectives, and how this relates to gentrification more broadly.

New-build gentrification and sustainability

Newly constructed residential and commercial buildings on previously developed urban land, particularly in light of intensification strategies, has influenced a widening of the classical definition of gentrification from its more traditional emphasis on the renovation of existing, and largely residential, buildings at the neighbourhood scale. Discussions on new-build gentrification emphasize a changing gentrification process in land development and property construction practices such as 'in-fill' developments between existing buildings and often on small land parcels in cities as well as brownfield redevelopment on previously industrialized land. While the achievement of sustainable urban form through intensification is a directive of policy and planning initiatives in these redevelopment practices, material sustainability components are frequently being added to such new developments as a result of increasing property developer interest in consumer demand and governmental support for sustainable building design. This has particularly emerged through the use of sustainable design rating systems for new developments such as the Building Research Establishment Environmental Assessment Method (BREEAM) system, the first sustainable building design rating system that was developed in Britain in 1999 and has transferred to European countries such as the Netherlands and Germany, and the LEED system that emerged in the United States in 2000 and is now commonly used in North America (Kibert, 2013; Reeder, 2010). The rating systems provide a yardstick by which to measure 'levels' of sustainability in the construction of new buildings primarily focused on the use of sustainable materials and technologies, alongside ratings for planning initiatives surrounding new developments such as sustainable transportation and waste reduction infrastructure. Kibert (2013) notes that sustainable building design ratings are now used in approximately 60 countries across the globe, with localized variations of the BREEAM and LEED approaches.[4] Referring to engagement with LEED in the United States, Kibert observes that sustainable building design is considered to be one of the most successful environmental initiatives in the United States based on the involvement of multiple government and private sector actors in LEED building practices and the particular support for LEED from the property development industry. He states that, '(T)he green building movement provides a model for other sectors of economic endeavour about how to create a consensus-based, market-driven approach that has rapid uptake, not to mention broad impact' (Kibert, 2013, p. 2). As discussed in case examples of new build sustainable development in Chapter 3, developers of new mixed use sustainable communities incorporate a framework and rubric for sustainable design into development plans from the beginning and often in conjunction with broader governmental policies for sustainable urban regeneration. Urban sustainability policies, sustainable planning approaches and sustainable design ratings are particularly impactful in 'new build' contexts in cities and are connected with processes of new-build gentrification.

Research on new-build gentrification demonstrates how new residential and commercial development in cities is associated with gentrification as a result of the involvement of private developers, its market orientation, as well as the role of indirect or exclusionary social displacement that is caused by these developments (Badcock, 2001; Cameron, 2003; Davidson, 2006, Davidson and Lees, 2005, 2010; He, 2010; Kern, 2010; Murphy, 2008; Rerat, Soderstrom, and Piguet, 2010; Rerat, Soderstrom, Piguet, and Besson, 2010; Rose, 2004; Stabrowski, 2014; Visser and Kotze, 2008). New-build gentrification is considered to be a hallmark practice of 'third wave gentrification' (Murphy, 2008; Rerat, Soderstrom, Piguet, and Besson, 2010). Davidson and Lees' (2005) formative work on new build gentrification in London underlines it as a process that occurs through the provision of new market housing by private developers, the socio-economic power of middle to upper income purchasers of newly built housing and the revalorization and reproduction of brownfield sites and other vacant or underused areas into new residential and commercial areas in cities. They state that it is a practice that 'involves middle class resettlement of the central city, the production of a gentrified landscape, and lower income displacement in the adjacent residential communities' (p. 1169). Additionally, 'new build gentrification involves the large-scale employment of economic capital by developers who have the capacity and capability to do so, and then the deployment of economic capital by consumers buying into a different version of urban living' (Ibid., p. 1169). The transition of these spaces is articulated as a sign of revalorization and 'progress' in terms of urban land development towards what urban planners call the 'highest and best' land use; a re-configuration of land use with the intention of achieving the most value from the land. This approach is particularly used in brownfield redevelopment where there is a notably marked transition from contaminated, deindustrializing land into residential and commercial uses of land. He (2010), for example, observes that new build gentrification has occurred in Shanghai, as a result of an implementation of a land price gradient that has increased land value in the central city area and galvanized the construction of new buildings on brownfields and the renovation of low-income central city neighbourhoods for more 'value-added land use' (2010, p. 348). Stabrowski (2014), through research on waterfront redevelopment in Brooklyn, NY, notes that New York City's city council and Department of City Planning rezoned the industrialized waterfront districts of Greenpoint and Williamsburg from industrial to mixed residential and commercial use in 2005 with a focus on new build redevelopment. The rezoning encompassed 184 blocks of industrialized area and is considered to be the largest rezoning exercise ever undertaken by New York City's government (2014, p. 794). Stabrowski argues that the rezoning was a public enterprise with the explicit strategy of repurposing the land areas for new residential and commercial development by private developers and revalorizing the land (2014, p. 813). The re-zoning of urban brownfield locations is also evident in the government funded redevelopment of Toronto's central waterfront, that has significantly emphasized a change in waterfront land use from industrial into residential and commercial under the umbrella of a comprehensive 'sustainability framework' policy that has guided the on-going redevelopment process since 2004 (Bunce, 2009, 2011; Toronto Waterfront Revitalization Corporation, 2004). In a similar way to the redevelopment of Regent Park in Toronto, the regeneration of Toronto's waterfront has focused on the role of sustainability in 'improving' the social and land quality of waterfront areas. This approach has been demonstrated in government and media discourse that described the city's waterfront before redevelopment as, 'derelict and dirty, unloved, unvisited and minimally used – a wasteland' (Stevens, 2002, p. 98) and a blank slate requiring new development despite its industrial and recreational significance (Desfor and Laidley, 2011). Alongside discourse used to rationalize waterfront redevelopment is an ascription of higher use and exchange value to waterfront land primed for new residential and commercial development, through government managed and funded environmental assessments and contaminated soil removal and remediation. As futher noted in Chapter 3, this approach was augmented by a multiplicity of local government and waterfront redevelopment agency policy and legislation for the planning and design of new build neighbourhoods on publicly owned brownfield lands and directions for private sector property developers to build new sustainable and 'smart' (high technology) communities in accordance with LEED specifications after the sale of public land (City of Toronto, 2002; Toronto Waterfront Revitalization Corporation, 2005).

As new-build gentrification widens classical definitions of gentrification to include new buildings and newly built communities it also alters the methods traditionally used to measure and assess gentrification such as the rent gap hypothesis (Smith, 1987; Smith and Williams, 1986). This change has sparked concern among some gentrification scholars as to whether new building construction can be defined as a gentrification practice due to the lack of existing building stock, and, by extension, the absence of a gentrification measurement. Critiques of the concept of new build gentrification have focused on the challenges of using the theory of rent gap as a measurement of gentrification in the existence of newly built development. As Davidson and Lees (2005) point out, one of the discrepancies between new build gentrification processes and rent gap theory is that governments are increasingly playing a role in revalorization processes in contexts where, for example, publicly owned land is sold to private developers. Critics of the concept of new build gentrification suggest that without the application of rent gap theory to empirically assess the existent conditions for gentrification, new build development cannot truly be classified as gentrification. For example, Boddy (2007), in a study of new build residential development in Bristol, UK, suggests that new build development does not constitute gentrification because the gap between the 'site value' of land as a commercial and industrial use and the site value potential of this land, in the form of newly built residences, does not prove the potential occurrence of gentrification as per the definition originally articulated by Smith (1979, 1984, 1987, 1996) and Smith and Williams (1986). Smith (1979, p. 545) defined rent gap as the, 'disparity between the potential ground rent level and the actual ground rent capitalized under the present land use'. The intention of the rent gap formula, instigated by Hoyt's 1933 study of land value changes on individual lots in Chicago, is to assess the transformation of land values over time in order to measure the potential occurrence of gentrification. In order to determine the possibility of gentrification, Smith (1987) noted that, 'gentrification is most likely to occur in areas experiencing a sufficiently large gap between actual and potential land values' (p. 464). Boddy's (2007) rationale for why the rent gap formula does not signify conditions for gentrification in the case of newly built areas is based upon the argument that the strength of the urban housing market in Britain during the 2000s, and the consequent increase in housing prices encourage governments and developers to 're-zone' urban land from non-residential to residential use, thus a traditional 'widening' of the residential rent gap cannot be measured over time in an existing place. Boddy, however, does not offer the demarcation that Smith articulated between housing and land value. Smith (1987, p. 463) made a clear distinction between land value and housing price, stating that,

> (it) [the rent gap] refers to the value of the land separate from any structures or improvements built on it. The value of the land is appropriated in economic transactions as ground rent: hence the notion of 'rent gap'. House value is conceptually separate from land value, even if the actual selling price of a structure usually incorporates the value of a building and the land into a single monetary figure.

As Davidson and Lees (2010) note, Boddy's argument focuses more on dispelling why new build residential development cannot be categorized as gentrification rather than offering an analysis of how gentrification can be re-conceptualized given the increasing occurrence of private sector new-build construction in cities.

An additional critique of new-build gentrification suggests that new-build sites cannot be understood as spaces of gentrification because social displacement of pre-existing residents does not tend to occur. Boddy (2007) argues that income-based displacement, a measure of gentrification, cannot be evaluated because new-build development most frequently occurs on lands that have been changed from a non-residential to residential use without an already existing residential population. Davidson (2008), Davidson and Lees (2005, 2010), Slater (2006, 2009), and Quastel (2009) draw upon Marcuse's (1985) definition of exclusionary displacement, as discussed in the introduction of this book, to demonstrate that new-build developments do enact displacement through the exclusion of individuals who cannot afford market-rate housing in new developments. Davidson and Lees (2005) note that this involves price shadowing, a form of indirect displacement through the prevalence of high property values. Davidson (2008) expands on a notion of indirect displacement by suggesting that the displacement caused by new-build gentrification differs from traditional gentrification forms: 'in the classical process of gentrification, where single properties are vacated by non-gentrifiers because they cannot afford to stay or are forced to leave, the economic displacement is direct' (2008, p. 2390). Indirect displacement does not have the same embodied process of eviction that occurs in displacement caused by traditional gentrification practices, but instead displaces and evicts lower income individuals and families from the outset as a result of the market cost of new build housing. Davidson and Lees (2005) note that indirect displacement expands to areas in close proximity to new build developments through increases in property values and the consumer demands of higher income professionals. Slater (2006) asserts that critiques of new-build gentrification focus too heavily on maintaining a classical definition of gentrification and its measurement at the expense of developing new and widened definitions of gentrification. In discussing the difference between classical definitions of gentrification and new-build gentrification, Davidson and Lees (2005, p. 1169) remark that, 'the contrast between traditional and new build gentrification demonstrates how the capital deployment processes of gentrification have changed, because the new build landscape has significantly different associations with cultural and economic capital'. The economic, socio-cultural, and environmental practices involved in new-build gentrification necessitate a wider recasting of gentrification in order to include the role of public policy and regulation, post-industrial land use, environmental remediation and sustainable design. In the early 2000s, Smith (2002, p. 443) stressed the need to understand gentrification in light of the redevelopment of larger swathes of urban land as a 'vehicle for transforming whole areas into new landscape complexes that pioneer a comprehensive class-infected urban re-make'. The concept of new-build gentrification expands a critical understanding of how urban developments are increasingly taking the form of public policy and planning supported, private sector-supplied, and market-oriented new development, with the growing inclusion of sustainability approaches in the form of policy, planning and design.

Environmental gentrification

Environmental gentrification research emerged in the mid-2000s to address the increasing associations between environmental discourses, environmental strategies and gentrification processes, particularly in relation to the location and remediation of 'locally unwanted', environmentally hazardous sites. Banzhaf and Walsh's (2006) quantitative empirical research on facilities in California that report their use of chemicals on the United States Environmental Protection Agency's Toxic Release Inventory, and their relation to the impacts of environmental quality on community demographics was one of the first studies of environmental gentrification. Their use of the term environmental gentrification added a layer to the environmental justice focus of this work by suggesting that high income earners 'voted with their feet' (Banzhaf and Walsh, 2006, p. 4) by moving out of urban communities with facilities listed on the Toxic Release Inventory and into areas with better environmental quality. Conversely, communities with facilities listed on the inventory became 'poorer and less white' over time (Ibid., p. 4). While not explicitly providing a definition of environmental gentrification, the study provided groundwork to link 'negative externalities' such as poor air quality and other forms of pollution with residential movement – predicated on differences in income, class and race – towards 'better' urban areas; processes that are extensively discussed in environmental justice discourse but which had not yet been explicitly connected with gentrification in cities or fully addressed in gentrification research. More recent definitions and statements regarding environmental gentrification include Eckerd's (2011, p. 32) hypothesis that 'environmental improvements may encourage environmental gentrification – gentrification that is spurred by increased demand for land in areas where environmental conditions have improved'. Checker (2015, p. 159) more broadly defines environmental gentrification as, 'the relationship between the up-scaling of low-income neighborhoods and the amelioration of environmental burdens (i.e. the closing of a power plant, bus depot or waste transfer station) and/or green initiatives that appeal to elite ideas about "livability"'. Literature discussing environmental gentrification also frequently refers to terms such as 'green gentrification' (Lugo, 2015) and 'ecological gentrification' (Dooling, 2009), which are used interchangeably to address similar issues. I identify three important areas that are explored in literature on environmental gentrification: (i) locally unwanted land uses, (ii) community-based activism, and (iii) social exclusion. These research areas help to inform a broader discussion of sustainability policy, planning and gentrification in cities and also a specific analysis of the associations between particular sustainability practices, such as community gardening, and the cultivation of sustainable urban lifestyles and gentrification in Chapter 4.

Research on locally unwanted land uses, and environmental gentrification has largely focused on neighbourhood-based and/or ethnographic studies in American urban contexts and primarily in New York City (Abel and White, 2011; Checker, 2015; Eckard, 2011; Gamper-Rabindran and Timmins, 2011; Pearsall, 2013). Several studies, such as Eckard's research on environmental remediation of hazardous waste sites in Portland, Oregon during the 1990s, concentrate on measuring whether gentrification does or does not take place during or following the clean-up of contaminated sites in urban neighbourhoods. Pearsall's (2013) study, for example, of the Gowanus Canal in Brooklyn, NY, a heavily contaminated location noted on the US Environmental Protection Agency's Superfund National Priorities List, demonstrates that the canal's listing as a toxic site deterred municipal government plans for and private developer interest in residential and commercial development along the waterway. She states that,

> (P)roposals to redevelop the contaminated waterfront properties along the Gowanus Canal into 'environmentally sensitive' mixed-use commercial and residential venues polarised the neighbourhood and local government officials in 2009, leading not to expedited and developer-funded redevelopment as supported by the municipal government, but to the designation of a toxic stigma . . . that would lower property values and stifle economic growth.
>
> (2013, p. 2294)

Pearsall concludes by suggesting that the listing process and connected local resident discussion about the merits of remediation and plans for redevelopment signified a resistance to gentrification by slowing down redevelopment, but she also notes that 'developer-led gentrification could resume following remediation' (Ibid., p. 2308). Research on contaminated land, remediation efforts and gentrification has also examined connections between the location of toxic sites, racialization practices and gentrification in a similar vein to the broader literature on environmental racism. Checker (2015), through an ethnographic study of toxic dumping and the location of communities in the north shore area of Staten Island, NY, near the polluted Kill Van Kull waterway, notes a correlation between the residential communities of lower-income African American, Hispanic, and Asian communities and their proximity to the Kill Van Kull. She associates federal and municipally directed efforts to remediate brownfield sites through the creation of 'Brownfield Opportunity Areas' in the north shore area with local government plans to encourage new mixed use residential and commercial development as an implicit environmental gentrification strategy. Checker concludes by suggesting that strategies to de-industrialize and beautify the north shore as processes of environmental gentrification were contradicted by political and economic motivations for the continuation of industrial uses and development in the area. Such a contradiction ultimately jeopardized the interests of lower income and racialized communities on Staten Island and reflected larger competing economic agendas between industrialization and post-industrial environmental gentrification, both of which would have negative impacts on local communities (Checker, 2015).

This work connects with research on community-based environmental activism and gentrification. Hamilton and Curran (2013) provide a different perspective on the context of environmental gentrification in light of the role of community-based environmental activists in their study of the Greenpoint neighbourhood of Brooklyn. They suggest that government involvement in the soil remediation of oil seepage in the neighbourhood directly coincided with gentrification in the 1980s and that remediation processes were expedited when private development interest in the gentrification of Greenpoint and surrounding neighbourhoods became more rapid. Yet, Hamilton and Curran also note that certain gentrifiers in Greenpoint added their voices to environmental activist concerns about environmental toxins in the area by supporting environmental clean-up and have also, conversely, allowed activists to educate new gentrifier residents about the negative impacts of gentrification (Ibid., 2013). Their study presents a more nuanced approach to understanding environmental activism in suggesting that there can be syncopated interests between gentrifiers and environmental activists which can lead to the sharing of knowledge and lived experiences. Checker's research (2011) on environmental planning and activism in Harlem, examined how the GreenX:Change plan (2010) for sustainable development in the area, formulated by New York

City's Department of Transportation, the Harlem Community Development Corporation, and the local community board of Harlem, as part of the City's larger 'PlaNYC 2030' sustainability plan, was a project that side-lined other resident and activist concerns about environmental needs in order to implement quick, technical environmental amenities. She suggests that the GreenX: Change plan sought to enhance the business interests and private developer opportunities in the neighbourhood through sustainable design and the marketing of new developments as being 'green'. Checker (2011) posits that the efforts of community-based and environmental activists to address environmental injustices in Harlem have improved conditions to a certain extent but, at the same time, 'materially, the efforts of environmental justice activists to improve their neighbourhoods (i.e. the removal of environmental burdens and the installation of environmental benefits) now help those neighbourhoods attract an influx of affluent residents' (2011, p. 212). Importantly, she also notes that the language of environmental activists that focuses on sustainability and environmental improvements has been co-opted and is also now used by government actors and developers to market the benefits of environmental amenities in private, market-orientated development.

The third area of environmental gentrification focuses on social exclusion and examines the tensions and contestations over the role of gentrification in galvanizing income-based exclusion practices in cities. Quastel (2009), in a study of environmental amenities such as community gardens provided for by private sector developers in Vancouver, discusses the larger context of changing urban environmental governance in Vancouver that was initiated by local government in the 1990s and 2000s and which encouraged intensification ('eco-density' in Vancouver) and brownfield redevelopment. He observes that intensification through market-oriented, high-rise condominium development quickly took on sustainability characteristics that catered to environmental concerns of gentrifiers and which merged green initiatives with gentrification practices. Further, he argues that this has cultivated a new category of high income 'eco-gentrifiers' who help to shape urban landscapes through a demand for environmental amenities and environmental consumption practices that have produced social and spatial exclusivity in certain city neighbourhoods. Associated with this, Dooling (2009) explains how environmental planning and design for urban parks can exclude already marginalized urban residents, while simultaneously 'improving' these spaces to meet the needs of middle to high income earners in cities. She uses the term 'ecological gentrification' and defines it as the 'implementation of an environmental planning agenda related to public green spaces that leads to the displacement or exclusion of the most economically vulnerable human population – homeless people – while espousing an environmental ethic' (Dooling, 2009, p. 621). Dooling's study of the City of Seattle government's official public consultation process for green space planning provides a detailed account of how planning and design 'charettes' [participatory design workshops] allowed residents to outline their visions for green spaces in the city but also selectively excluded their use by homeless individuals, in particular. She notes that the workshop participants altered spaces that were being used by homeless persons along with infrastructure that supported homeless residents, such as shelters, through the insertion of green infrastructure as a replacement in their participatory design drawings. The implementation of planning and design ideas from the charette eventually involved the actual eviction of homeless and transient persons that frequently used a specific riverside location in order to create new park space. Dooling suggests that, 'ecological gentrification relocates gentrification within the environmental discourses and in the discourses related to the exclusionary aspects of public spaces' (2009, p. 631). The exclusionary impacts caused by certain urban environmental practices have also raised the notion of how city spaces can be defined as being 'just green enough' to be meaningful to communities without contributing to gentrification (Curran and Hamilton, 2012; Wolch, Byrne and Newell, 2014). The idea of 'just green enough' environmental spaces can be linked with the concept of 'development without displacement' to suggest how sustainability initiatives, through community-based ownership and engagement, can enhance urban communities without stimulating gentrification and displacement. This is further explored in Chapter 5 through a focus on diverse community-based socio-environmental resistances and solutions to gentrification. The literature on environmental gentrification and social exclusion helps to inform an understanding of the role of environmental amenities in relation to income-based desires and visions and how the production of green spaces in cities can be covertly and explicitly intertwined with exclusionary practices; issues that are addressed through case examples of master planned sustainable communities in the next chapter.

Conclusion

An exploration of recent scholarly framings of gentrification through the concepts of policy-led gentrification, third- and fourth-wave gentrification, social mix and gentrification, new-build gentrification, and environmental gentrification demonstrates how sustainability policy, planning and in some cases, design are integrated into perspectives of gentrification. As identified in Chapter 3 through the study of different examples on sustainable urban residential projects and park space production, these different types of gentrification frequently occur simultaneously.

Scholarly perspectives that observe different contemporary forms of gentrification provide a framework for the interpretation of sustainability policy formulation and planning implementation strategies, and how these coalesce in 'on the ground' contexts, particularly at the local scale. The concept of policy-led gentrification has broadened classical definitions of gentrification by emphasizing the role of different scales of governmental policy discourse and implementation approaches and emphasizing how policy increasingly guides gentrification through reliance on private sector interest and involvement in urban property development. As noted through existing gentrification analyses of British urban regeneration policies, the implementation of a sustainability agenda has been entwined with the production of urban intensification, primarily through market-oriented property development in cities and urbanized regions. Policy directives for increasing 'social mix' through income and tenure diversification, which have been particularly evident in public–private alliances in public housing redevelopments in cities such as Toronto and London, underline the contradictory assumptions of urban regeneration policies and the 'roll-out' of intensification as a way to produce more sustainable cities. Policy-led gentrification connects to broader frameworks of third and fourth wave gentrification, both of which demonstrate increasingly closer and more complicated assemblages of government and private sector interests in gentrification. Both periodizations of gentrification provide space for interpreting coalescences between sustainability policies, government and private sector actors and their involvement with policy implementation and planning initiatives, and the intersections between environmental concerns and economic growth agendas. The concept of new-build gentrification is considered as the built form extension of governmental urban regeneration policies that emphasize intensification through mixed residential and commercial development on existing urban land such as 'in-fill' sites and brownfields. This form of new development is increasingly connected with sustainable planning and design approaches such as rezoning and the remediation of contaminated land as a frequent planning and regulatory requirement for development, as well as sustainable building design ratings as a way for property developers to gauge 'sustainability levels' in new projects and draw upon growing consumer interest in and concern for sustainability and the natural environment. Although newly built development offers a different spatial and built form context than traditional gentrification practices, the public–private alliances – particularly in brownfield redevelopment – and the production of new market-oriented housing, geared towards middle to high income urban professionals, directly connects with gentrification as a process that 'produces space for more affluent users' (Hackworth, 2002). Lastly, the emerging literature on environmental gentrification, as a whole, provides an important additional layer to gentrification discourse. It is particularly informative in light of increasing governmental, civil society, and private sector engagement with environmental issues and concerns and the role of environmental initiatives and amenities in transforming urban spaces with particular benefit for the interests of private developers, governmental sustainability agendas, and the needs of middle to high income residents in cities. Local level research on the associations between environmental remediation and 'clean-up' and increasing property values, the engagement of gentrifiers with local-level environmental initiatives and activism, and the production of environmental amenities and its links with social exclusion, indicates the growing intersections between urban environmental practices with both the production and consumerist characteristics of gentrification. Although primarily focused on environmental remediation and green space production, the concept of environmental gentrification helps to inform a study of the convergences between sustainability policy, planning and gentrification.

Notes

1 In 1997, Rogers co-edited *Cities for a Small Planet*, a collection of writing on sustainable urban planning, and wrote *Cities for a Small Country,* on urban intensification as a sustainable urban planning strategy for Britain, with Anne Power in 2000. Rogers was also the Chief Advisor on Architecture and Urbanism to the Mayor of London and Chair of the Greater London Authority's Design for London Advisory Group. He coordinated the Sustainable London Exhibition in early 2007.
2 The Adam Smith Institute, a British right-wing think tank, viewed the concept of SPZs as a practical strategy through which to embed neo-liberal logic within planning and land development and forwarded the policy idea to the Thatcher government in 1983 (Allmendinger, 2002).
3 Minto Ltd. developed the first LEED Gold accredited commercial building in the province of Ontario. Tridel Corporation bills itself as 'the largest builder of sustainable Toronto condominiums and communities'. Tridel also states that our commitment to green building practices is evident in our sustainable building designs, adherence to green construction techniques, and dedication to corporate stewardship that focuses on the elements of conservation, sustainability and healthier living (www.tridel.com/tenyork/tridel-built-green/)

References

Abel, T. D., and White, J. (2011). Skewed riskscapes and gentrified inequities: Environmental exposure disparities in Seattle, Washington. *American Journal of Public Health*, *101*(S1), S246–S254. https://doi.org/10.2105/AJPH.2011.300174

Adair, A., Berry, J., and McGreal, S. (2003). Financing Property's Contribution to Regeneration. *Urban Studies*, *40*(5–6), 1065–1080. http://doi.org/10.1080/0042098032000074326

Allmendinger, P. (2002). *Planning theory* (1st edn). Basingstoke, UK: Palgrave Macmillan.

Allmendinger, P. (2009). *Planning theory* (2nd edn). Basingstoke, UK: Palgrave Macmillan.

Arcadis Sustainable Cities Index. (2015). *Arcadis sustainable cities index*. Retrieved from www.sustainablecitiesindex.com/

August, M. (2008). Social Mix and Canadian Public Housing Redevelopment: Experiences in Toronto. *Canadian Journal of Urban Research*, *17*(1), 82–100.

August, M. (2014). Challenging the rhetoric of stigmatization: The benefits of concentrated poverty in Toronto's Regent Park. *Environment and Planning A*, *46*(6), 1317–1333. https://doi.org/10.1068/a45635

August, M., and Walks, A. (2012). From social mix to political marginalization? The redevelopment of Toronto's public housing and the dilution of tenant organizational power. In G. Bridge, T. Butler, and L. Lees (eds), *Mixed communities: Gentrification by stealth*. Bristol, UK: The Policy Press.

Badcock, B. (2001). Thirty years on: Gentrification and class changeover in Adelaide's inner suburbs, 1966–96. *Urban Studies*, *38*(9), 1559–1572. http://doi.org/10.1080/00420980120080441

Banzhaf, H. S., and Walsh, R. P. (2006). *Do people vote with their feet? An empirical test of environmental gentrification* (Discussion Paper). Washington, DC: Resources for the Future. Retrieved from www.rff.org/files/sharepoint/WorkImages/Download/RFF-DP-06-10.pdf

Beatley, T. (2000). *Green Urbanism: Learning from European cities*. Washington D.C.: Island Press.

Beatley, T. (2007). Planning for Sustainability in European Cities: A Review of Practice in Leading Cities. In R. LeGates and F. Stout (eds), *The City Reader* (4th edn), (pp. 411–421). London/New York: Routledge.

Blomley, N. K. (2004). *Unsettling the city: Urban land and the politics of property*. New York: Routledge. Retrieved from http://link.library.utoronto.ca/eir/EIRdetail.cfm?Resources__ID=761527&T=F

Boddy, M. (2007). Designer neighbourhoods: New-build residential development in nonmetropolitan UK cities – the case of Bristol. *Environment and Planning A*, *39*(1), 86–105. http://doi.org/10.1068/a39144

Bourne, L. S. (2001). The urban sprawl debate: Myths, realities and hidden agendas. *Plan Canada*, *41*(4), 26–28.

Bourne, L. S., Bunce, M., Taylor, L., Luka, N., and Maurer, J. (2003). Contested ground: The dynamics of peri-urban growth in the Toronto region. *Canadian Journal of Regional Science*, *26*(2–3), 251+.

Brenner, N. (2004). *New state spaces: Urban governance and the rescaling of statehood*. New York: Oxford University Press.

Brenner, N. and Theodore, N. (eds). (2003). *Spaces of Neoliberalism: Urban Restructuring in North America and Western Europe*. NJ: Wiley-Blackwell.

Brindley, T., Rydin, Y., and Stoker, G. (1989). *Remaking planning: The politics of urban change in the Thatcher years*. London: Unwin Hyman.

Bromley, R., Tallon, A., and Thomas, C. (2005). City centre regeneration through residential development: Contributing to sustainability. *Urban Studies*, *42*(13), 2407–2429. http://doi.org/10.1080/00420980500379537

Bruegmann, R. (2005). *Sprawl: A compact history*. Chicago, IL: University of Chicago Press.

Bunce, S. (2004). The emergence of 'smart growth' intensification in Toronto: Environment and economy in the new official plan. *Local Environment*, *9*(2), 177–191. http://doi.org/10.1080/1354983042000199525

Bunce, S. (2009). Developing sustainability: Sustainability policy and gentrification on Toronto's waterfront. *Local Environment*, *14*(7), 651–667. http://doi.org/10.1080/13549830903097740

Bunce, S. (2011). Public-private sector alliances in sustainable waterfront revitalization: Policy, planning, and design in the West Don Lands. In G. Desfor and J. Laidley (eds), *Reshaping Toronto's waterfront* (pp. 287–304). Toronto: University of Toronto Press.

Calthorpe, P., and Fulton, W. B. (2001). *The Regional City: Planning for the end of sprawl*. Washington, DC: Island Press.

Cameron, S. (2003). Gentrification, housing redifferentiation and urban regeneration: 'Going for Growth' in Newcastle upon Tyne. *Urban Studies*, *40*(12), 2367–2382. http://doi.org/10.1080/0042098032000136110

Campanella, R. (2013). Gentrification and its discontents: Notes from New Orleans. *NewGeography.com.* Retrieved from www.newgeography.com/content/003526-gentrification-and-its-discontents-notes-new-orleans

Canada Mortgage and Housing Corporation (CMHC). (2016). *Equilibrium TM sustainable housing demonstration initiative.* Retrieved from www.cmhc.ca/en/inpr/su/eqho/eqho_008.cfm

Caulfield, J. (1994). *City form and everyday life: Toronto's gentrification and critical social practice.* University of Toronto Press.

Chapple, K. (2015). *Planning sustainable cities and regions: Towards more equitable development.* Abingdon, UK: Routledge.

Checker, M. (2011). Wiped out by the 'Greenwave': Environmental gentrification and the paradoxical politics of urban sustainability. *City & Society, 23*(2), 210–229. http://doi.org/10.1111/j.1548–744X.2011.01063.x

Checker, M. (2015). Green is the new brown: 'Old School Toxics' and environmental gentrification on a New York City Waterfront. In C. Isenhour, G. McDonogh, and M. Checker (eds), *Sustainability in the global city: Myth and practice* (pp. 157–179). Cambridge, UK: Cambridge University Press.

Cowell, D. (1998). Ecological landscape planning techniques for biodiversity and sustainability. *Environmental Management and Health, 9*(2), 72–78.

Curran, W., and Hamilton, T. (2012). Just green enough: Contesting environmental gentrification in Greenpoint, Brooklyn. *Local Environment, 17*, 1027–1042.

Daniels. (2016). *Daniels goes green.* Retrieved from http://danielshomes.ca/innovative-programs/daniels-goes-green

Davidson, M. (2006). *New-Build 'gentrification' and London's riverside renaissance* (Unpublished Ph.D. Dissertation). University of London, London. Retrieved from http://epn.sagepub.com/lookup/doi/10.1068/a3739

Davidson, M. (2008). Spoiled mixture: Where does state-led 'positive' gentrification end? *Urban Studies, 45*(12), 2385–2405. https://doi.org/10.1177/0042098008097105

Davidson, M., and Lees, L. (2005). New-build 'gentrification' and London's riverside renaissance. *Environment and Planning A, 37*(7), 1165–1190. http://doi.org/10.1068/a3739

Davidson, M., and Lees, L. (2010). New-build gentrification: Its histories, trajectories, and critical geographies. *Population, Space and Place, 16*(5), 395–411. doi:10.1002/psp.584

DeFilippis, J., and Fraser, J. (2010). Why do we want mixed-income housing and neighborhoods. *Critical Urban Studies: New Directions,* 135–147.

Desfor, G., and Laidley, J. (eds). (2011). *Reshaping Toronto's waterfront.* Toronto: University of Toronto Press.

Dempsey, N., Bramley, G., Power, S., and Brown, C. (2011). The social dimension of sustainable development: Defining urban social sustainability. *Sustainable Development, 19*(5), 289–300. https://doi.org/10.1002/sd.417

Department of the Environment, Transport, and the Regions (DETR). (1999). *Towards an urban renaissance.* London: Author. Retrieved from http://dclg.ptfs-europe.com/AWData/Library1/Departmental%20Publications/Department%20of%20the%20Environment,%20Transport%20and%20the%20Regions/1999/Towards%20an%20Urban%20Renaissance.pdf

Department of the Environment, Transport, and the Regions (DETR). (2000). *Our towns and cities: The future – Delivering an urban renaissance.* London: Author.

Dooling, S. (2009). Ecological gentrification: A research agenda exploring justice in the city. *International Journal of Urban and Regional Research*, *33*(3), 621–639. http://doi.org/10.1111/j.1468–2427.2009.00860.x

Dunn, J. R. (2012). 'Socially mixed' public housing redevelopment as a destigmatization strategy in Toronto's regent park. *Du Bois Review: Social Science Research on Race*, *9*(1), 87–105. https://doi.org/10.1017/S1742058X12000070

Eckerd, A. (2011). Cleaning up without clearing out? A spatial assessment of environmental gentrification. *Urban Affairs Review*, *47*(1), 31–59. https://doi.org/10.1177/1078087410379720

Filion, P., Bunting, T., Pavlic, D., and Langlois, P. (2010). Intensification and Sprawl: Residential density trajectories in Canada's largest metropolitan regions. *Urban Geography*, *31*(4), 541–569. https://doi.org/10.2747/0272–3638.31.4.541

Fraser, J., DeFilippis, J., and Bazuin, J. (2012). HOPE VI: Calling for modesty in its claims. In G. Bridge, T. Butler, and L. Lees (eds), *Mixed communities: Gentrification by stealth*. Bristol: The Policy Press.

Furbey, R. (1999). Urban 'regeneration': Reflections on a metaphor. *Critical Social Policy*, *19*(4), 419–445. http://doi.org/10.1177/026101839901900401

Gamper-Rabindran, S., and Timmins, C. (2011). Hazardous waste cleanup, neighborhood gentrification, and environmental justice: Evidence from restricted access census block data. *American Economic Review*, *101*(3), 620–624. https://doi.org/10.1257/aer.101.3.620

Glass, R. (1964). *London: Aspects of change*. London: Macgibbon & Kee.

Gotham, K. (2012). Make it right? Brad Pitt, Post-Katrina rebuilding, and the spectacularization of disaster. In R. Mukherjee and S. Banet-Weiser (eds), *Commodity activism: Cultural resistance in neoliberal times*. New York and London: New York University (NYU) Press.

Gotham K., and Greenberg, M. (2014). *Crisis cities: Disaster and redevelopment in New York and New Orleans*. New York: Oxford University Press.

Greenberg, M. (2015). 'The Sustainability Edge': Competition, crisis, and the rise of green urban branding. In C. Isenhour, G. McDonogh, and M. Checker (eds). *Sustainability in the global city* (pp. 105–130). Cambridge, UK: Cambridge University Press.

Hackworth, J. (2002). Postrecession gentrification in New York City. *Urban Affairs Review*, *37*(6), 815–843. http://doi.org/10.1177/107874037006003

Hackworth, J., and Smith, N. (2001). The changing state of gentrification. *Tijdschrift Voor Economische En Sociale Geografie*, *92*(4), 464–477. http://doi.org/10.1111/1467–9663.00172

Hackworth, J. R. (2007). *The neoliberal city governance, ideology, and development in American urbanism*. Ithaca, NY: Cornell University Press.

Hamilton, T., and Curran, W. (2013). From 'Five Angry Women' to 'Kick-ass Community': Gentrification and environmental activism in Brooklyn and Beyond. *Urban Studies*, *50*(8), 1557–1574. http://doi.org/10.1177/0042098012465128

Han, S. S. (2005). Global city making in Singapore: A real estate perspective. *Progress in Planning*, *64*(2), 69–175. http://doi.org/10.1016/j.progress.2005.01.001

Harris, A. (2008). From London to Mumbai and back again: Gentrification and public policy in comparative perspective. *Urban Studies*, *45*(12), 2407–2428. https://doi.org/10.1177/0042098008097100

Harvey, D. (1989). From Managerialism to Entrepreneurialism: The Transformation in Urban Governance in Late Capitalism. *Geografiska Annaler. Series B, Human Geography*, *71*(1), 3. http://doi.org/10.2307/490503

He, S. (2010). New-build gentrification in central Shanghai: Demographic changes and socioeconomic implications. *Population, Space and Place*, 16(5), 345–361. https://doi.org/10.1002/psp.548

Healey, P., Davoudi, S., O'Toole, M., Tavsanoglu, S., and Usher, D. (eds). (1992). *Rebuilding the city: Property-led urban regeneration*. London: E. & FN Spon.

Holland, L. (2004). Diversity and connections in community gardens: A contribution to local sustainability. *Local Environment*, 9(3), 285–305. https://doi.org/10.1080/13549830420002193888

Hostetler, M., Allen, W., and Meurk, C. (2011). Conserving urban biodiversity? Creating green infrastructure is only the first step. *Landscape and Urban Planning*, 100(4), 369–371. https://doi.org/10.1016/j.landurbplan.2011.01.011

ICLEI – Local Governments for Sustainability. (n.d.). *Home / ICLEI global*. Retrieved from www.iclei.org/

Islam, T., and Sakizlioglu, B. (2015). The making of, and resistance to, state-led gentrification in Istanbul, Turkey. In L. Lees, H.B. Shin, and E. Lopez-Morales (eds), *Global gentrifications: Uneven development and displacement* (pp. 245–264). Bristol: Policy Press.

James, R. K. (2010). From 'slum clearance' to 'revitalisation': Planning, expertise and moral regulation in Toronto's Regent Park. *Planning Perspectives*, 25(1), 69–86. https://doi.org/10.1080/02665430903421742

James, R. K. (2015). Urban redevelopment and displacement from Regent Park to El Cartucho. *Canadian Theatre Review*, 161, 17–21. https://doi.org/10.3138/ctr.161.003

Jenks, M., Burton, E., and Williams, K. (eds). (1996). *The compact city: A sustainable urban form?* New York: E & FN Spon.

Jessop, B. (2002). Liberalism, neoliberalism, and urban governance: A state–theoretical perspective. *Antipode*, 34(3), 452–472.

Kern, L. (2010). Gendering reurbanisation: Women and new-build gentrification in Toronto. *Population, Space and Place*, 16(5), 363–379. https://doi.org/10.1002/psp.581

Kipfer, S., and Keil, R. (2002). Toronto, Inc? Planning the competitive city in the New Toronto. *Antipode*, 34(2), 227–264. https://doi.org/10.1111/1467-8330.00237

Kipfer, S., and Petrunia, J. (2009). 'Recolonization' and public housing: A Toronto case study. *Studies in Political Economy*, 83, 111–139.

Krueger, R., and Buckingham, S. (2009). Creative-city scripts, economic development, and sustainability. *Geographical Review*, 99(1), iii–xii.

Krueger, R., and Buckingham, S. (2012). Towards a 'consensual' urban politics? Creative planning, urban sustainability and regional development. *International Journal of Urban and Regional Research*, 36(3), 486–503. https://doi.org/10.1111/j.1468-2427.2011.01073.x

Layard, A. (2001). Introduction: Sustainable development – Principles and practice. In A. Layard, S. Davoudi, and S. Batty (eds), *Planning for a sustainable future*. New York: Spon Press.

Lees, L. (2000). A reappraisal of gentrification: Towards a 'geography of gentrification'. *Progress in Human Geography*, 24(3), 389–408. http://doi.org/10.1191/030913200701540483

Lees, L. (2003). Visions of 'urban renaissance': The urban task force report and the urban white paper. In R. Imrie and M. Raco (eds), *Urban renaissance? New Labour, community and urban policy*. Bristol: Policy Press.

Lees, L. (2014). The urban injustices of new Labour's 'New Urban Renewal': The case of the Aylesbury Estate in London. *Antipode, 46*(4), 921–947.

Lees, L., and Ley, D. (2008). Introduction to special issue on gentrification and public policy. *Urban Studies, 45*(12), 2379–2384. https://doi.org/10.1177/0042098008097098

Lees, L., Slater, T., and Wyly, E. K. (2008). *Gentrification*. New York: Routledge/ Taylor and Francis Group.

Leffers, D., and Ballamingie, P. (2013). Governmentality, environmental subjectivity, and urban intensification. *Local Environment, 18*(2), 134–151. https://doi.org/ 10.1080/13549839.2012.719016

Levine, M. A. (2004). Government policy, the local state, and gentrification: The case of Prenzlauer Berg (Berlin), Germany. *Journal of Urban Affairs, 26*(1), 89–108. https://doi.org/10.1111/j.0735–2166.2004.007.x

Ley, D. F. (1993). Past elites and present gentry: Neighbourhoods of privilege in the inner city. In L. S. Bourne, and D. F. Ley (eds), *Changing social geography of Canadian cities*. Montréal: McGill-Queen's Press – MQUP.

Lin, J.-J., and Yang, A.-T. (2006). Does the compact-city paradigm foster sustainability? An empirical study in Taiwan. *Environment and Planning B: Planning and Design, 33*(3), 365–380. http://doi.org/10.1068/b31174

Lipman, P. (2008). Mixed-income schools and housing: Advancing the neoliberal urban agenda. *Journal of Education Policy, 23*(2), 119–134. https://doi.org/10.1080/ 02680930701853021

Louisiana Disaster Recovery Foundation. (2008). *GreeNOLA: A strategy for a sustainable new Orleans – A resource for neighborhoods and residents to engage in the master planning process and ensure sustainable redevelopment.* City of New Orleans. Retrieved from www.nola.gov/getattachment/bece551e-5cf8–421c-ac27–48db26194c40/Appendix-Ch-13-GreeNOLA-A-Strategy-for-a-Sustainab/

Lugo, A. (2015). Can human infrastructure combat green gentrification? Ethnographic research on bicycling in Los Angeles and Seattle. In C. Isenhour, G. Mcdonogh, and M. Checker (eds), *Sustainability in the global city: Myth and practice*. New York: Cambridge University Press.

Lutzkendorf, T., and Lorenz, D. (2005). Sustainable property investment: Valuing sustainable buildings through property performance assessment. *Building Research & Information, 33*(3), 212–234.

Marcuse, P. (1985). Gentrification, abandonment, and displacement: Connections, causes, and policy responses in New York City. *Washington University Journal of Urban and Contemporary Law, 28*, 195–240.

Moore, S. and Bunce, S. (2009). Delivering Sustainable Buildings and Communities: Eclipsing Social Concerns Through Private Sector-led Urban Regeneration and Development. *Local Environment: International Journal of Justice and Sustainability, 14*(7), 601–606.

Murphy, L. (2008). Third-wave gentrification in New Zealand: The case of Auckland. *Urban Studies, 45*(12), 2521–2540. https://doi.org/10.1177/0042098008097106

Natural Resources Canada. (2016). *Office of energy efficiency*. Retrieved from www.nrcan.gc.ca/energy/offices-labs/office-energy-efficiency

Neuman, M. (2005). The compact city fallacy. *Journal of Planning Education and Research, 25*(1), 11–26. http://doi.org/10.1177/0739456X04270466

Newman, P., and Thornley, A. (2002). Globalisation, world cities, and urban planning: Developing a conceptual framework. In A. Thornley and Y. Rydin (eds), *Planning in a global era*. Aldershot, UK: Ashgate.

Nwanna, C. (2015). Gentrification in Nigeria: The case of two housing estates in Lagos. In L. Lees, H.B. Shin, and E. Lopez-Morales (eds), *Global gentrifications: Uneven development and displacement* (pp. 311–328). Bristol, UK: Policy Press.

Office of the Deputy Prime Minister (2013). *Sustainable Communities: Building for the Future*, Office of the Deputy Prime Minister (Crown Copyright), London, UK.

O'Riordan, T., and Stoll-Kleemann, S. (2002). *Biodiversity, sustainability and human communities: Protecting beyond the protected*. Cambridge, UK and New York: Cambridge University Press.

Oatley, N. (ed.). (1998). *Cities, economic competition and urban policy*. London: Paul Chapman Publishing.

Pearsall, H. (2013). Superfund me: A study of resistance to gentrification in New York City. *Urban Studies, 50*(11), 2293–2310. https://doi.org/10.1177/0042098013478236

Peck, J. (2005). Struggling with the creative class. *International Journal of Urban and Regional Research, 29*(4), 740–770.

Peck, J., Theodore, N., and Brenner, N. (2013). Neoliberal urbanism redux? Debates and developments. *International Journal of Urban and Regional Research, 37*(3), 1091–1099. https://doi.org/10.1111/1468-2427.12066

Peck, J., and Tickell, A. (2002). Neoliberalizing space. *Antipode, 34*(3), 380–404. https://doi.org/10.1111/1467-8330.00247

Polese, M. and Stren, R. (2002). *The Social Sustainability of Cities, Diversity, and the Management of Change*. Toronto: University of Toronto Press.

Quastel, N. (2009). Political ecologies of gentrification. *Urban Geography, 30*(7), 694–725. http://doi.org/10.2747/0272-3638.30.7.694

Raco, M. (2004). Urban regeneration in a growing region: The renaissance of England's average town. In C. Johnstone and M. Whitehead (eds), *New horizons in British urban policy: Perspectives on new labour's urban renaissance*. Aldershot, UK; Burlington, VT: Ashgate. Retrieved from www.loc.gov/catdir/toc/ecip0415/ 2004 003995.html

Raco, M. (2005). Sustainable development, rolled-out neoliberalism and sustainable communities. *Antipode, 37*(2), 324–347. http://doi.org/10.1111/j.0066-4812.2005. 00495.x

Redclift, M. R., and Woodgate, G. (eds). (1995). *The sociology of the environment*. Brookfield, VT: E. Elgar Pub.

Reeder, L. (2010). *Guide to green building rating systems*. Hoboken, NJ: John Wiley & Sons.

Rérat, P., Söderström, O., and Piguet, E. (2010). d debates: Guest editorial. *Population, Space and Place, 16*(5), 335–343. https://doi.org/10.1002/psp.585

Rérat, P., Söderström, O., Piguet, E., and Besson, R. (2010). From urban wastelands to new-build gentrification: The case of Swiss cities. *Population, Space and Place, 16*(5), 429–442. https://doi.org/10.1002/psp.595

Roper, K., and Beard, J. (2006). Justifying sustainable buildings – championing green operations. *Journal of Corporate Real Estate, 8*(2), 91–103.

Rose, D. (2004). Discourses and experiences of social mix in gentrifying neighbourhoods: A Montreal case study. *Canadian Journal of Urban Research, 13*(2), 278–317.

Rose, D., Germain, A., Bacqué, M.-H., Bridge, G., Fijalkow, Y., and Slater, T. (2013). 'Social mix' and neighbourhood revitalization in a transatlantic perspective: Comparing local policy discourses and expectations in Paris (France), Bristol (UK) and Montréal (Canada)–Local discourses of 'social mix' in Paris, Bristol and Montréal. *International Journal of Urban and Regional Research*, *37*(2), 430–450. https://doi.org/10.1111/j.1468–2427.2012.01127.x

Rowe, D. J., and Dunn, J. R. (2015). Tenure-mix in Toronto: Resident attitudes and experience in the Regent Park community. *Housing Studies*, *30*(8), 1257–1280. https://doi.org/10.1080/02673037.2015.1013091

Satterthwaite, D. (ed.). (1999). *The Earthscan reader in sustainable cities*. London: Earthscan Publications.

de Schutter, J. (2009). *Community consultation and environmental justice in the Regent Park Revitalization* (Theses and Dissertations, Comprehensive). Paper 969. Wilfrid Laurier University, Waterloo.

Scott, J. W. (2007). Smart growth as urban reform: A pragmatic 'recoding' of the new regionalism. *Urban Studies*, *44*(1), 15–35. http://doi.org/10.1080/00420980601074284

Sewell, J. (1993). *The shape of the city: Toronto struggles with modern planning*. Toronto: University of Toronto Press.

Slater, T. (2006). The eviction of critical perspectives from gentrification research. *International Journal of Urban and Regional Research*, *30*(4), 737–757. http://doi.org/10.1111/j.1468–2427.2006.00689.x

Slater, T., Curran, W., and Lees, L. (2004). Guest editorial: Gentrification research– New directions and critical scholarship. *Environment and Planning A*, *36*(7), 1141–1150. http://doi.org/10.1068/a3718

Smith, N. (1979). Toward a theory of gentrification: A back to the city movement by capital, not people. *Journal of the American Planning Association*, *45*(4), 538–548. http://doi.org/10.1080/01944367908977002

Smith, N. (1984). *Uneven development: Nature, capital, and the production of space*. Oxford: Blackwell.

Smith, N. (1987). Gentrification and the rent gap. *Annals of the Association of American Geographers*, *77*(3), 462–465. http://doi.org/10.1111/j.1467–8306.1987.tb00171.x

Smith, N. (1996). *The new urban frontier: Gentrification and the revanchist city*. London and New York: Routledge.

Smith, N. (2002). New globalism, new urbanism: Gentrification as global urban strategy. *Antipode*, *34*(3), 427–450. http://doi.org/10.1111/1467–8330.00249

Smith, N., and Williams, P. (eds). (1986). *Gentrification of the city*. Boston: Allen & Unwin.

Sorensen, A. (2010). Urban Sustainability and Compact Cities Ideas in Japan: The diffusion, transformation and deployment of planning concepts. In P. Healey and R. Upton (eds), *Crossing Borders: International Exchange and Planning Practices* (pp. 117–140). London and New York: Routledge.

Stabrowski, F. (2014). New-build gentrification and the everyday displacement of Polish immigrant tenants in Greenpoint, Brooklyn. *Antipode*, *46*(3), 794–815. https://doi.org/10.1111/anti.12074

Steinacker, A. (2003). Infill development and affordable housing: Patterns from 1996 to 2000. *Urban Affairs Review*, *38*(4), 492–509. http://doi.org/10.1177/1078087402250357

Stevens, R. (2002). Carve out a canal system to funnel the Don's flood water out to the lake. *Toronto Life*. June issue, 98.

Street, E. (2014). Sustainable governance and planning in London. In R. Imrie and L. Lees (eds), *Sustainable London? The Future of a Global City* (pp. 67–89). Bristol, UK: Policy Press.

Toronto Community Housing. (2007). *Regent park social development plan – Executive summary*. Toronto: Author.

Toronto Waterfront Revitalization Corporation. (2005). *Sustainability framework*. Toronto: Author.

Tweedale, I. (1998). Waterfront redevelopment, economic restructuring and social impact. In B. S. Hoyle, D. A. Pinder, and M. S. Husain (eds), *Revitalising the waterfront: International dimensions of dockland redevelopment*. London: Belhaven Press.

Uitermark, J., Duyvendak, J. W., and Kleinhans, R. (2007). Gentrification as a governmental strategy: Social control and social cohesion in Hoogvliet, Rotterdam. *Environment and Planning A*, *39*(1), 125–141. http://doi.org/10.1068/a39142

Vallance, S., Perkins, H. C., and Moore, K. (2005). The results of making a city more compact: Neighbours' interpretation of urban infill. *Environment and Planning B: Planning and Design*, *32*(5), 715–733. http://doi.org/10.1068/b31157

Visser, G., and Kotze, N. (2008). The state and new-build gentrification in central Cape Town, South Africa. *Urban Studies*, *45*(12), 2565–2593. https://doi.org/10.1177/0042098008097104

Watt, P. (2009). Housing stock transfers, regeneration and state-led gentrification in London. *Urban Policy and Research*, *27*(3), 229–242. https://doi.org/10.1080/08111140903154147

Wolch, J. R., Byrne, J., and Newell, J. P. (2014). Urban green space, public health, and environmental justice: The challenge of making cities 'just green enough'. *Landscape and Urban Planning*, *125*, 234–244. https://doi.org/10.1016/j.landurbplan.2014.01.017

Wyly, E. (2015). Gentrification on the planetary urban frontier: The evolution of Turner's noösphere. *Urban Studies*, *52*(14), 2515–2550. https://doi.org/10.1177/0042098015601362

3 Sustainable master planning and gentrification

Master planning, defined as the comprehensive planning and design of a new residential area, has been linked with sustainability goals most significantly in the emergence of New Urbanism over the last two decades as a planning strategy to create new compact, 'pedestrian friendly', sustainable neighbourhoods (cf. Duany and Seaside Institute, 2008; Grant, 2006; Helbrecht and Dirksmeier, 2012). New Urbanism has been quickly adopted by private development firms as a way to provide and market sustainable residential environments, largely in the North American context (Grant, 2006; Moore, 2010). The Congress for New Urbanism, an American organization that promotes New Urbanism as a planning approach,[1] was one of the partners involved in creating the LEED sustainable planning and design rating system for neighbourhood development (LEED ND[2]) (Mapes and Wolch, 2011). Support among urban practitioners for New Urbanist planning has largely been influenced through 'best practice' policy mobility between urban municipalities (Moore, 2013). While New Urbanism is largely applied to the planning of new residential neighbourhoods, its general tenets – such as built form intensification, social and residential tenure mix, blended residential and commercial spatial uses and sustainable forms of mobility – have also influenced the production of small and individual housing developments. An ubiquitous planning and aesthetic approach has emerged through policy and planning attention to New Urbanism that is easily modelled and localized in various urban areas, leading to a similarity in the land use form and design of newly built sustainable urban communities.

What can be considered as a reproduction of rational comprehensive ideas of planning, with private developers acting as the master planners of new mixed use communities, is demonstrated in a history of comprehensively planned, environmentally focused, urban communities and neighbourhoods. This has been demonstrated, for example in the development of planned environmental or 'garden' communities in late nineteenth century Britain through the efforts of philanthropic business owners who were influenced by an emergent public health movement and who made a link between social class standing and societal obligations to improve the health and spatial environments of working class labourers through access to 'clean air' and green space. This sentiment was often manifested in benevolent and moralistic public discourse about the rejuvenation of individuals through the production of new spaces (Furbey, 1999). The development of industrial villages in England, such as Port Sunlight, a factory town constructed by soap and detergent makers Lever Brothers, as well as Bournville, planned by the Cadbury chocolate company, were examples of Victorian ideals of morality, social ordering and public health in planning practice; master planned industrial and residential communities that aimed to benefit the urban working poor through the private sector provision of access to better air quality, park and garden spaces, adequate housing and social class mixing (Harrison, 1999; Rees, 2012; Sarkissian and Heine, 1978). These visions are similarly noticeable in the transnational scope of Garden City planning at the turn of the twentieth century, which emphasized the private sector-led master planning of new residential communities, with ample garden and park space, as a way to improve the health and environment of residents (Geertse, 2016; Lewis, 2015). The Garden City model sparked localized interpretations in its transfer across the globe throughout the twentieth century increasingly merged into governmental planning policies and initiatives, and was adopted in master planning projects such as the Romerstadt garden city initiative in Frankfurt (Henderson, 2010), Ciudad Jardin Lomas del Palomar in Buenos Aires (Gallenter, 2012) and Jhong-Sing New Village and Yonghe City in Taiwan (Wang and Heath, 2010). The model was also used as a colonialist strategy in British and French settlement and city building practices in the early-to-mid twentieth century, in Nigeria, South Africa, British Malaya, Tanzania and Morocco, among other colonized countries (Bigon and Katz, 2014; Home, 1990; Jelidi, 2014; Myers and Muhajir, 2014). Others have noted the role of Garden City planning tenets in the evolution of contemporary master planned eco-cities such as Guangzhou (Biqing, Peng, and Hou, 2013).

These approaches to the production of greener residential communities share similar undercurrents of thought and visioning about 'social betterment' through access to improved environmental quality of urbanized spaces. These underlying moral claims are evident in current master planning approaches to the planning and development of new sustainable communities in cities. While there is a benevolence in efforts of private and public sector planners and developers to address environmental issues in the production of master planned, sustainable residential communities, there are also problematic connections with policy-led and new-build gentrification practices and outcomes, tensions caused by efforts to create social mix in new communities and issues of environmental gentrification through the remediation and land use conversion of brownfield sites and creation of new environmental amenities. In this chapter, associations between the production of new sustainable urban residential communities and processes of new-build and environmental gentrification are analyzed through a narrative-based exploration of three studies of sustainable master planning and development in Toronto and

Ottawa, Canada, and London, UK. The last part of the chapter examines the role of comprehensive public planning for urban parks, the involvement of private sector and civil society actors and connections with environmental gentrification through the production and management of urban parks as environmental amenity spaces. It also discusses the relationship of parks with surrounding gentrifying neighbourhoods and issues of social inclusion, exclusion and displacement within and around urban park spaces. The recent construction of recreational greenways in cities, a transnational planning idea that is frequently created through the combined involvement of local governments, private planners and landscape architects and civil society organizations, highlights many of the underlying tensions caused by environmental gentrification and are explored through the planning and development of the Coulee Verte Rene-Dumont pathway in Paris, the Highline and Lowline parks in New York City and the Green Line in Toronto.

In the context of the recent central city waterfront redevelopment project in Toronto, the production of a comprehensive public sustainability policy agenda to guide new waterfront residential community planning and development is observed alongside the provision of privately developed, market-oriented housing in a New Urbanist style along with high-rise buildings and the use of LEED standards in two master planned communities, River City and the Canary District. With the involvement of private development interests, the provision of market-oriented residential buildings and limited quantities of affordable housing, Toronto's new waterfront communities indicate a move towards the construction of socially exclusive, environmentally focused master planned spaces. On a smaller scale, the identification of similar processes in the production of a new mixed-use residential project in the Dalston neighbourhood in the borough of Hackney, London, where rapid gentrification has occurred over the past decade (Butler and Hamnett, 2011; Butler, Hamnett, and Ramsden, 2013; Dyckhoff, 2013), demonstrates how a new privately built residential project with sustainable planning and design features is promoted as a way to transform and improve the surrounding neighbourhood's social and environmental character. The project, named Pembury Circus, is adjacent to a council housing estate, Pembury Estates, and has raised local concerns about its role in neighbourhood-based gentrification; underlining tensions between social needs and issues of racialization and stigmatization in relation to Pembury Estates, increasing forms of gentrification in the surrounding area and in Hackney more broadly, and local government and private provision of environmental amenities. These associations are also evident in the example of the master planned Zibi community in Ottawa, Canada, which is one of ten sustainable 'One Planet' communities across the globe. 'One Planet' is a sustainable planning model created by Bioregional, a UK-based environmental NGO, and the World Wildlife Federation to cultivate sustainable community planning as a best practice that can be adopted and localized in different global regions. The Zibi project is located on land on the Albert and Chaudiere islands in the Ottawa River that is owned by Windmill Developments, who are the main planners and developers of the community. Significantly, the planning of the Zibi community has conflicted with inherent indigenous rights of Anishinaabe First Nations people to the lands and their attempts to reclaim the lands under indigenous title and stewardship. The production of a new sustainable community and the shaping of environmental spaces for new residents underlines processes of new-build and environmental gentrification. It also exemplifies a notion of gentrification as a neo-colonialist process of land acquisition and development and its role in the reproduction of British, Irish and European settler-colonialist practices (in previously colonized countries) (Atkinson and Bridge, 2005; Blomley, 2004; Clark, 2005; Coulthard, 2014; Shaw, 2005; Smith, 1996). In the context of the Zibi project, gentrification is understood as a neo-colonial process of land acquisition at the expense of indigenous rights to the lands and as a way to produce socially exclusive environmental aesthetics and practices under a master planned framework of sustainable community building. All three examples explored in the following sections underscore the connectivity between different forms of gentrification, most significantly new-build gentrification, social mix and gentrification and environmental gentrification. In relation to concepts of third and fourth wave gentrification, the cases also demonstrate the tight and often complex assemblages of public policy and planning objectives and the interests and involvement of private sector actors such as property developers and planning and design firms, as well as civil society organizations and citizens that can either support or contest these objectives and interests in the production of gentrification. Although a sustainable approach to master planned developments offers a necessary movement towards environmental protection and conservation efforts, while done within a context of privatized, market-oriented property development and the production of new environmental spaces for 'social and environmental betterment' it raises questions about social exclusion and the role of sustainable master planning in producing exclusive environmental spaces in cities.

Sustainable master planning and development: central waterfront development and gentrification in Toronto

The redevelopment of Toronto's largely industrialized central city waterfront, started in 2002 as the largest publicly funded spatial redevelopment project in Canada (Toronto Waterfront Revitalization Corporation [TWRC], 2003), has focused on making the city's waterfront along Lake Ontario a 'national and global model for sustainability' (TWRC, 2006c, p. 35). The redevelopment was guided by the TWRC, now called Waterfront Toronto, which was given a mandate by the municipal, provincial and federal levels of government to coordinate a comprehensive planning and redevelopment process on the central waterfront, negotiate competing waterfront uses with other agencies such as the port authority, and encourage private sector investment in waterfront planning and redevelopment. These goals were shaped by a broadened emergence of a larger neo-liberal competitive city agenda in Toronto in the early 2000s that was cultivated through political support for private–public partnerships in infrastructure development and the development of a global city image intended to attract both real and imagined interests of global capital and investment (Kipfer and Keil, 2002). Public discussions about the need to address the quality of the natural environment in Toronto and particularly in industrialized brownfield areas of the waterfront also coincided with these broader political and economic objectives. The early 2000s in Toronto marked an increase in municipal plans for sustainable urban revitalization, with both the City of Toronto Official Plan and the City of Toronto Central Waterfront Secondary Plan – a supporting by-law of the Official Plan – strongly proposing the intensification of residential and commercial built form on major streets and deindustrializing areas of the central city waterfront as a primary sustainability strategy (City of Toronto, 2002a, 2002b). A connection between environmental concerns and economic growth objectives had also been deepened by local government and civil society initiatives, with emergent public discourse about the perceived connections between the poor environmental quality of certain central city locations and the challenges of attracting new investment in land redevelopment (Desfor and Keil, 2004). Environmental practices by government agencies, such as the remediation of contaminated soil and water, ecological restoration projects and environmental flood prevention methods along Toronto's Don River, were examples of initiatives that sought to galvanize economic interest and investment while also alleviating environmental concerns (Keil and Graham, 1998; Desfor and Keil, 2004; Laidley, 2007, 2011).

Over the past decade, Waterfront Toronto has furthered an approach to building amicable connections with private sector interests and property developers. This has been present since the beginning of the redevelopment process, as underlined in the *Development Plan and Business Strategy* (2002). The plan prescribed private sector investment strategies to augment the public financing of waterfront redevelopment over the course of 30 years, with an expectation of an annual return of approximately 14 per cent on government investment in redevelopment through the sale of large areas of publicly owned waterfront land to private developers (TWRC, 2002). The agency's *Sustainability Framework* policy, finalized in 2005, has provided an overarching strategy for the redevelopment process with a broad mandate to balance social, economic and environmental objectives in all future waterfront developments (TWRC, 2005a). This broad approach is encapsulated in Waterfront Toronto's statement that,

> a precise definition [of sustainability] is not critical . . . it is important to the revitalization of Toronto's waterfront that there is general agreement about the key aspects of a sustainable community, including social

progress that meets the needs of everyone; effective protection of the environment; prudent use of natural resources; maintenance of high and stable levels of economic growth and employment.

(TWRC, 2005a, p. 4)

The agency's vision for sustainability has been tied to a marketing of Toronto and the waterfront as places for capital investment, with an emphasis on a vision of sustainable urban regeneration for the waterfront as a way to 'build Toronto'. This strategy was represented in a discussion about global city growth and the claim that '(S)ustainability is the new imperative for cities in the 21st century and the Toronto waterfront will be distinguished by its leadership on sustainability. The question is not when we will do it but how we will do it' (TWRC, 2005a, p. 1).

As the guiding policy for waterfront redevelopment, the agency's Sustainability Framework has also directed a multiplicity of area-specific policies and plans for the construction of new communities with the requirement of LEED targets for all new residential and commercial build-ings. The policy document prescribes five 'sustainability visions' that guide the implementation of sustainability in planning and development practice: (i) 'Sharing the Benefits: Net Plus™' is Waterfront Toronto's corporatized sustainability concept of 'Net Plus', broadly intended to express, 'the idea that revitalization will provide sustainability benefits in a way that has an overall positive net impact on-site and to the city as a whole'; (ii) 'Global Hub of Creativity and Innovation', which refers to the establishment of new commercial spaces and 'smart' high technology communities with sustainable design techniques; (iii) 'The Urban Cottage', a sustainability vision that is meant to recreate the summer vacation atmosphere of northern Canadian 'cottage country' (a largely white, middle-to-high income lifestyle practice) and cultivate a sense of 'tranquility . . . and natural wildness of a northern lakeside cottage' in newly built waterfront communities; (iv) 'Feels Like Home' underlines Waterfront Toronto's objective of enhancing 'social networks, community health and safety' as a nod towards Toronto's reputation as a 'safe' city and; (v) 'Strength Through Diversity' denotes an 'ecological systems approach' to enhance both bio-physical diversity, through new ecological restoration projects, and social diversity, through social mixing in new water-front communities (TWRC, 2005a, pp. 8–12). These five sustainability visions are directly connected with technical implementation methods – a few examples of these being the minimization of noise pollution in new communities through the reduction of ambient noise levels in residential areas, a mandatory siting of new commercial spaces within a 350 m radius of new residential units to discourage automobile use (TWRC, 2005a, p. 30), and 'durability targets' for new residential and commercial infrastructure such as 150 years for new plumbing systems and 50 years for new electrical systems (TWRC, 2005a, pp. 3–26).

Waterfront Toronto's economic growth and sustainability agenda have merged most noticeably in the development of new-build sustainable neighbourhoods. The agency's master plan for the West Don Lands, an 80-acre area of deindustrialized and emptied government-owned land in close proximity to the Don River mouth and Lake Ontario, has been a showcase sustainable neighbourhood for Waterfront Toronto and is the first waterfront area to undergo redevelopment. Neighbourhood planning has been directed by Waterfront Toronto, despite the eventual sale of land to private developers. The agency's planning process has consisted of three separate plans that were devised by private urban planning and urban design firms contracted to manage the planning process, including public consultation. The West Don Lands comprehensive plan (TWRC, 2005b), divided the land area, that would eventually be parcelled and sold to private developers, into four proposed high density sections with an emphasis on creating new neighbourhoods that are, as the plan suggests,

> inherently sustainable in terms of land utilization and achieving smart growth principles, reducing the risk of natural hazards through flood proofing controls, remediating brownfields within the city core, increasing the supply of affordable housing, reducing air pollution associated with commuting, making public transit, cycling, and walking the primary modes of transportation, efficiently using existing infrastructure, increasing the amount of park land and community services, increasing economic development opportunities, and demonstrating the feasibility of green buildings.
>
> (TWRC, 2005b, p. 35)

The master plan policy was augmented by the *West Don Lands Block Plan and Design Guidelines,* a detailed policy document that prescribed the density, height and building quantity for each section of the new neighbourhood, and the *Performance Specifications for Green Building Initiative for West Don Lands* ('green design guidelines') that specified 'LEED Gold' certification,[3] the second highest rating level of LEED, for all new buildings. This has expanded to include a designation of LEED Gold ND (LEED for Neighbourhood Development) as a comprehensive rating for the entire West Don Lands area, based upon the neighbourhood master plan and individual LEED certified buildings (Waterfront Toronto, 2015a). Together, the plans have forecasted the construction of 6000 new residential units with additional commercial spaces covering nearly half of the total redevelopment, with the remaining space incorporating new streets, parks and easements, including the production of a flood protection landform, with surrounding park space and marshland, in order to mitigate flooding from the Don River into the new neighbourhood. The plans have served as a type of 'redevelopment guidebook' for private developers, who submitted bids to purchase and develop land parcels. Additionally, selected private developers were expected to legally adhere to the agency's plans and sustainability specifications, which was ascertained through land sale contracts (Bunce, 2011). The development and bidding selection process followed a government regulated environmental assessment that required soil remediation on the land before development could commence that was funded by the waterfront agency before the commencement of land sales.

The planning and redevelopment of the West Don Lands has largely been underlined by the complex assemblage of public-private associations with the redevelopment agency as the 'master planner' of a new sustainable neighbourhood, the outsourcing of plan formulation to private sector planning and design firms, government funding and management of new public infrastructure – such as new roadways, water and sewage pipes, schools and parks – and the private sector construction of new residential and commercial buildings. Connections between the waterfront agency and private sector interests and involvement in waterfront redevelopment have continued since the formulation of planning documents, despite a hesitation in developer interest caused by the global financial crisis of 2008. A plan to off-set recessionary effects was created through the (since successful) municipal government bid to host the 2015 Pan Am/Parapan Am Games in Toronto and a strategy to locate the athlete residences in the West Don Lands as a 'stop-gap' development project in land sections that had not yet been sold. Along with soil remediation, the construction of the flood barrier landform to mitigate flooding from the adjacent Don River was completed in 2013 alongside the development of the first mixed residential and commercial buildings in the northern section of the West Don Lands area to follow the planning and green design guidelines. The project, named 'River City',[1] has consisted of four different townhouse complexes and mid-size and high-rise condominium towers built to the LEED Gold building specifications. In addition to Waterfront Toronto's sustainability requirements, the developer of River City, Urban Capital, comprehensively markets the sustainability features of the new buildings in their promotional material as a way to attract purchasers:

> (s)urrounded by beautiful new parks and public spaces, and just minutes from the downtown core, River City is unlike any other development in Toronto today. Designed for excellent livability and maximum sustainability, it is the community for the 21st century. Winner of BILD's [Toronto's private sector Building Industry and Land Development Association] Best Design Award, River City is a LEED Gold community.
> (River City, 2015a)

As an example of new-build gentrification, the production of residential units in River City are immediately costly, with new units in the most recent building complex priced between $200,000 to $900,000 CAD for units that range in size from 372 to 1663 square feet (CondoNow, 2015). The size and cost of the units are instantly geared towards more affluent individual residents rather than larger families and individuals with lower incomes. This is supported by a vision for River City that outlines it as a type of 'environmentally friendly oasis' for high income earning urban professionals. The developers cultivate an image of an environmentally gentrified new community and produce spaces in the development that connect with perceived consumer interests in healthy and environmental lifestyles and are additional to LEED specifications, such as on-site yoga studios and a 'crafting' studio. The advertising material for River City also highlights environmental externalities of the development, '(I)magine being able to walk out your front door and into the city's most spectacular urban park. The Don River Park [produced by Waterfront Toronto] is a lush urban retreat of rolling hills, native woodlands and open lawns – and River City is situated right beside it. Perfect for running, walking, cycling and just hanging out, it's a beautiful setting for city living' (River City, 2015b). In this way, the cultivation of 'sustainable lifestyle' practices and appreciation for sustainable buildings, as well as proximity to manufactured natural spaces such as the aforementioned Don River Park, are components of the sale of the development to purchasers and a central part of the overall marketing practices and image construction for the neighbourhood.

This approach is replicated in the second redevelopment area located in the southern part of the West Don Lands. The 'Canary District', a project by Canadian property development firm Dundee Kilmer, so far consists of one market geared condominium building, a students' residence for a local community college, a YMCA (fitness centre), the athletes' residences for the Pan Am/Parapan Am Games that were held in July 2015, as well as three additional market-oriented condominium residential complexes that were constructed after 2015. The Canary District developers, in following Waterfront Toronto's *West Don Lands Block Plan and Design Guidelines* and green design guidelines, emphasizes a comprehensive vision for sustainability that blends a notion of urban lifestyle with healthy living and environmental amenities. Their marketing material suggests that the development will

> maximize qualities that contribute to urban livability such as access to fresh air, the outdoors, sunlight, views, amenity, and public transit as well as a balance of public and private space. The overall design meets LEED Gold criteria and honours [the municipal government of] Toronto's Mandatory Green Building requirements to create a self-sufficient and diversified neighbourhood in which residents can live, work, and play.
>
> (Canary District, 2015)

As is the case of River City, the development is informed by a complex layer of policies from Waterfront Toronto, the developer's adherence to these policies along with their own partnership with private sector architects and construction engineers, and the 'green design guidelines' of the waterfront agency and the Toronto municipal government's mandatory requirements for green building for all new development, a program that provides financial incentives for developers.

The market-oriented focus of the River City and Canary District areas of the West Don Lands has been supported by policy encouragement of 'social mix' by the way of tenure and income diversity, produced through the provision of affordable housing units. This directive connects with Toronto municipal government's local by-law for affordable housing on the waterfront that was specified in the government's plan for waterfront redevelopment, *Making Waves: Central Waterfront Part II Plan* (2002), in conjunction with Waterfront Toronto. The by-law specifies that 25 per cent of all new waterfront residential units must be classified as affordable, in keeping with municipal government affordable housing criteria. The municipal government's public housing corporation, Toronto Community Housing, owns and manages 243 units of affordable rental housing for families and seniors who meet income criteria within three buildings that were constructed by private developers. There are also 253 affordable rental housing that were made available through the conversion of Athletes' Village housing and plans for 100 new units in market-oriented buildings for affordable homeownership (Waterfront Toronto, 2015b). Given that market-oriented residential units in the waterfront redevelopment will total over 6000, the current availability of 600 units is quite a small contribution to acknowledging affordability and equitable accessibility in the new developments. It is also an insertion of affordable housing into an area that is primarily designed and built for market-oriented residential and commercial development, which raises concerns about power differences in regard to the future growth of the new neighbourhoods and whose voices and interests will dominate. The nod towards affordable housing underlines the larger tensions and contradictions inherent in the production of Toronto's master planned waterfront communities. While espousing the benefits of social, economic and biophysical sustainability in municipal government and waterfront agency policies, the waterfront agency extensively relies upon on private development interests to fulfil the implementation of planning and redevelopment.

The redevelopment is reflective of policy-led gentrification including a nod towards social mix in addition to new-build gentrification in the shape of immediate market-oriented residential and commercial development (with a negligible quantity of affordable housing) and environmental gentrification through soil remediation requirements for new development, the production of green spaces as environmental amenities to complement new residential and commercial neighbourhoods, and the cultivation of a middle class, professionalized and environmentally friendly urban lifestyle orientation.

Gentrification and sustainability in Hackney, London, UK: Pembury circus

In contrast to the expansive plans for Toronto's waterfront redevelopment, the newly built Pembury Circus residential project encapsulates the connections between sustainability and gentrification in a small project located on Dalston Lane and near to the Lower Clapton and Dalston areas of the Borough of Hackney, London; an eastern borough that has experienced significant gentrification over the past decade in neighbourhoods such as Shoreditch, Hoxton, Dalston and Victoria Park (Butler and Hamnett, 2011; Butler *et al.*, 2013; Dyckhoff, 2013; Perry, 2015). The developers of Pembury Circus, Peabody Trust – a London-based housing association – and Bellway Homes – a market-geared residential development firm – were granted planning and development permission from the Borough of Hackney in 2011 and construction was completed in 2015. The project is considered as a sustainable urban regeneration initiative for the immediate area that includes the Pembury Estates, a large council housing complex that was built in the 1930s (Figure 2.1). Pembury Estates has been stigmatized over time as a result of racism against African/Caribbean-British residents of the housing estate in combination with perceptions of the area as being impoverished and 'crime-ridden' (Addo, 2011a). This public sentiment was reiterated during the British urban riots of August 2011, when Pembury Estates became a central area for rioting and arson fires in Hackney and the community was represented by media as a place of youth crime and violence (Addo 2011a; Lewis, 2011). The Pembury Circus development contributes to the regeneration of the Pembury Estate through the provision of a small number of new council units to be rented through Peabody Trust, the housing association manager for Pembury

Figure 2.1 Photo of Pembury Circus beside Pembury Estates, Hackney, London

Estates, alongside 149 market-rate units and 40 shared ownership units to be sold by Bellway, for a total of 268 new residences (Bellway, 2014). The affordable units were achieved by Hackney Council through affordable housing gain, in keeping with the Council's *Local Development Framework – Core Strategy* that outlines an affordable housing target of 50 per cent (60 per cent social rent and 40 per cent 'intermediate' rent) in new residential buildings (London Borough of Hackney, 2010, p. 110).

Sustainable planning and design components have been emphasized by Bellway and Peabody Trust since the inception of the project and Fraser Brown MacKenna, an east London-based architecture firm, was contracted to design the buildings and units in accordance with the technical guidelines for Level 4 of the UK Department for Communities and Local Government's *Code for Sustainable Homes* policy (Bellway, 2014). These guidelines were revoked by the UK government in March 2015 but can be applied to developments in process prior to their cancellation (UK Department for Communities and Local Government, 2015). The ground level commercial spaces and community centre that are included in the development have been constructed to the sustainable design specifications of the 'BREEAM Excellent' rating (Fraser Brown MacKenna Architects, 2016). Sustainable planning and design features include brownfield redevelopment, energy efficient lighting, techniques for reduced water usage, photovoltaic rooftop panelling, green roofs, interior courtyard green space and large areas for bicycle storage. The site is also considered to be the largest car-free development in Hackney (Bellway, 2014; Fraser Brown MacKenna Architects, 2016; MLM, 2016).

Embedded in discourse about the development is a correlation between the sustainable regeneration of the site and a reduction in the perceived social problems on Pembury Estates. The project architects state that they have created 'a vibrant new mixed-use development that [has] replaced an under-utilised and unsafe part of the neighbourhood, which had become associated with crime and anti-social behaviour' (Fraser Brown MacKenna Architects, 2016). The aesthetic character of Pembury Circus is intended to have 'ripple effects' for a type of cleansing of broader existing neighbourhood challenges. This discourse is connected with plans for the move of some Pembury Estate residents to the new development, within a larger plan for the regeneration of the Pembury Estate by Peabody Trust. As part of their partnership with Bellway, Peabody Trust will provide approximately 80 affordable rental units in the Pembury Circus development to residents of the council estate who currently reside in units with surplus bedrooms. This is intended to alleviate residential overcrowding on the estate by opening up the availability of larger units while at the same time moving a group of existing residents to the new development. Of the approximately 80 new affordable housing units provided by Peabody Trust in the Pembury Circus development however, 58 units will be made available at between 55 and 75 per cent of the average market rent for the neighbourhood and 21 units will be available for social housing rent, thus pointing to a reduction in the number of social housing rental units.

Additionally, the market housing sold by Bellway was listed in 2014 at a price range between 250,000 and 850,000 pounds for one to three bedroom units (Bellway, 2014; Vyas, 2014). This context has raised concern among area residents about the role of Pembury Circus within the community, its impact on gentrification and struggles over access to affordable housing in the area and negative effects on existing resident populations. The local newspaper, *Hackney Gazette*, has noted that construction noise from the development has negatively affected low-income tenants living in Pembury Estates and the surrounding area. In a news article about the development, a local resident notes that, 'I have lived here for six years. When I moved here there were trees and wildlife. Now I feel like I am being forced out' (in Vyas, 2014). Other local citizens underline the role of Pembury Estate in contributing to gentrification in Hackney. One neighbourhood blogger states that, '(T)he establishment of this new housing development [Pembury Circus] is a small case study in how redevelopment can redefine a neighbourhood. . . however, the Circus – whose name appears loosely inspired by the adjacent roundabout – is not isolated from the wider phenomenon of soaring Hackney property prices or the increasing slipperiness of the term "affordable"'. The writer also questions whether, 'Pembury Estate is the latest example of developers and the council surrendering precious territory to private interests and (primarily) affluent incomers to no great benefit for the existing community' (Hill, 2014).

Concerns from members of the local area connect with broader problems of gentrification in Hackney, most notably an increasing presence of environmental gentrification. The association of Pembury Circus with the gentrification of the area, including regeneration plans for Pembury Estates, occurs within a broader context of rising property values and housing prices in Hackney, where the average market rate for a house was 700,000 pounds in 2014, double the average cost of a residential property from 2013 and where the average monthly cost for a two bedroom private rental flat was 1500 pounds in 2014 (Borough of Hackney, 2014, p. 4). The quickly rising housing prices in Hackney are also occurring at the same time as the borough is considered to be the 'greenest' area of London. Rankings by estate agencies, for example, cite the borough's quantity of open parks, lower than average carbon emissions, and recycling practices as markers of its top ranking in relation to environmental spaces and practices. A reference by *Homes & Property* magazine to a report written by Chestertons estate agents states that, 'homes in the greenest locations in the capital regularly outperform grubbier neighbours when it comes to housing price growth' and that Hackney's quickly rising property values were 'thanks to low levels of carbon emissions and the fact that 90 per cent of its residents live within a short walk of open space' (Bloomfield, 2015). Hackney's 'greenest borough' status is echoed by the Borough of Hackney government which lists Hackney has having the most parks and green spaces of any inner borough of London (London Borough of Hackney, 2016a) and has increasingly prioritized attention towards sustainability practices and the maintenance and production of environmental spaces. The local government strategic master plan (*Local Development Framework*) for Hackney's development between 2010 and 2025, for example, stresses the importance of social and biophysical sustainability planning through proposed comprehensive supports for educational and health infrastructure, renewable technologies, emission reduction practices (London Borough of Hackney, 2010) and the creation of 'Green Action Zones' throughout Hackney with specific efforts in these spaces to improve air quality. This is set within the context of local government statements that note Hackney as already having one of the lowest C02 emissions output rate, per capita, in the U.K.; thought to be derived from an absence of heavy industry in the borough (London Borough of Hackney 2016b, p. 26). The council's *Sustainable Communities Strategy*, which guides sustainable community planning between 2008 and 2018, supports initiatives that reduce C02 emissions and waste diversion strategies such as composting and recycling (London Borough of Hackney, 2008).

Alongside environmental initiatives, the local council has addressed affordable housing challenges in Hackney by setting affordable housing targets in the master plan (London Borough of Hackney, 2010). It acknowledges a crisis of affordability for lower income residents of Hackney and notes that housing affordability and the provision of affordable housing infrastructure is a key concern for residents (London Borough of Hackney, 2010, p. 110). A 2015 report on poverty in London by the New Policy Institute indicates that a higher unemployment rate than the London average for Hackney and rates the borough as one of the four (out of 32 inner and outer boroughs studied) most impoverished London boroughs in the areas of homelessness and the number of residents receiving unemployment benefits and family tax credits. It also states that Hackney is one of the eight most unaffordable boroughs in London in relation to housing (New Policy Institute, 2015a). The report notes that the borough has experienced increased signs of wealth, which is cited as being a result of generated economic benefits from legacy infrastructure projects developed in Hackney for the 2012 Olympic Games, however, it also considers that 'this has been as much gentrification as regeneration, with many natives being priced out of the housing market' (New Policy Institute, 2015b). A recent local government review of affordable housing in Hackney notes that the recent delivery of new subsidized, affordable housing has been largely produced through affordable housing gains that have been yielded in new private developments and through the work of housing associations. The review also suggests, however, that Hackney council is not meeting its own policy targets set for achieving affordable housing for 50 per cent of all new private residential developments as a result of the higher land purchase and connected financing costs faced by developers who plan to build in Hackney (London Borough of Hackney, 2014). This is occurring alongside challenges now faced by housing associations in Hackney as a result of a 60 per cent reduction in governmental subsidies, expected to occur between 2015 and 2018. The review notes that the reduction in subsidies will negatively impact registered housing associations and cause challenges for their future operation due to the increased cost of property in the borough (London Borough of Hackney, 2014). Together, these issues demonstrate that gentrification pressures in Hackney are creating difficulties for existing local government affordable housing policies and the provision of affordable housing. Significantly, these challenges are contrasted against celebrations of Hackney as the greenest and most 'environmentally friendly' borough in London. Further, these plaudits are supported by property agents and developers who highlight the relationship between the benefits of green space and rising property values in Hackney; promoting the connections between the location and proximity of environmental spaces and gentrification.

The challenges of securing affordable housing within an area that is experiencing intensive gentrification is noticeable in the Pembury Circus project, which falls short of the affordable housing target set by Hackney government. The project sets a precedent for new residential development in Hackney in the sense that it both celebrates and normalizes profit oriented private development with sustainability features, with a negligable number of affordable housing units as an example of progressive planning and development. It is also viewed by supporters of the projcet as a way to successfully revitalize the lower-income Pembury Estate through the production of a new gentrified space, an idea which is underlined in the statement by the site architects who use a discourse of 'redundancy and regeneration' to emphasize that they have 'delivered a vibrant new mixed-use development that replaced an under-utilised and unsafe part of the neighbourhood, which had become associated with crime and anti-social behavior' (Fraser Brown MacKenna Architects, 2016). Their statement bypasses the histories and everyday realities of individuals and families who live on the Pembury Estate out of economic necessity and promotes a 'liberating' role for gentrification in transforming the social and aesthetic characteristics of the area. Community-based resistance against the Pembury Circus development has come from individuals who reside in Pembury Estate and view the project as a problematic symbol of gentrification. Franklin Addo, an African-British youth resident of Pembury Estate, has recently written in national newspaper, *The Guardian* about the housing complex from a resident's perspective. He notes that Pembury Estate was particularly stigmatized after the London riots in August 2011, with public commentators finding blame for arson fires and vandalism among residents of the housing complex (Addo, 2011b). Addo makes an important distinction between community regeneration in the form of needed community-based services and programs that help to mitigate problems caused by poverty and racialization and the discourse of regeneration that promotes gentrification. He contrasts the socio-economic realities of everyday life for Pembury Estate residents with the symbolism of Pembury Circus for this area of Hackney: 'Many people have the odds stacked against them from the outset, their class of origin holding them back in too many ways to list here, choking the vast potential everyone possesses. They continue to live, as I do, in marginalised, confined areas such as Pembury estate in Hackney – while luxurious complexes like Pembury Circus are built tauntingly next door' (Addo, 2014). The under-lining of socio-spatial differences and tensions in relation to the development of Pembury Circus suggest that while the site is promoted as a hallmark of new, sustainable, mixed use residential and commercial development it also ignores existing social inequities in Hackney, particularly in relation to affordable housing challenges, as well as the project's role in reproducing gentrification.

Through the example of Pembury Circus, connections between new-build gentrification and environmental gentrification are notable in the redevelop-ment of a brownfield site into a new-build, market-oriented, mixed residential and commercial community with sustainable design certification. This sits alongside the purported role of the development in regenerating the local area by making it 'safer' and more aesthetically pleasing. What is apparent in this context is the notion that improving environmental features of the site will, in turn, encourage social norms and behaviours that are in accordance with desires and practices of gentrification. It points to the cultivation of a form of environmental determinism through planning and design and the role of this type of a form of environmental determinism within site-specific environmental gentrification and current processes of gentrification more broadly.

Exclusionary displacement through sustainable community master planning: Zibi, Ottawa, Canada

As previously noted in Chapter 2, gentrification can produce displacement through indirect and direct practices of exclusion that have negative impacts for residents with lower income levels and/or who experience racialization. The example of Zibi, a master planned sustainable development in Ottawa, Canada, offers a study of how master planned sustainable communities can act to instantly exclude certain populations. Yet, displacement can also appear to have a 'soft' edge through the provision of, often tokenistic, overtures towards social inclusion while at the same time excluding more meaningful and just ideas of rights over urban space. In the context of the Zibi development, this is demonstrated through the exclusion of concerns from aboriginal groups over the inherent ownership of the development lands while at the same time indigenous culture is celebrated by the site's developers and indigenous arts and cultural events are incorporated into the development plans for the community. The Zibi project is one of several 'One Planet Living' (One Planet) 'concept communities' that derive from a formalized planning and design vision for sustainable communities produced by a British 'entrepreneurial charity' organization, Bioregional, in conjunction with the World Wildlife Federation (WWF). Bioregional and WWF created the One Planet model in 2003, while Bioregional was creating sustainability plans for Beddington Zero, Britain's first master planned carbon neutral community located in Hackbridge in south London and a 'testing site' for the implementation of the One Planet planning concept and model. Through policy mobility and the promotion and marketing of the One Planet concept by Bioregional and the WWF across the globe, One Planet has evolved into a global initiative with master planned sustainable communities now developed in Australia, France, Tanzania, Luxembourg and the United States, in addition to Britain and Canada. The model emphasizes ten sustainable planning and design features, defined as 'zero carbon, zero waste, sustainable transport, local and sustainable materials, local and sustainable food, sustainable water, land use and bio-diversity, culture and community, equity and local economy, and health and happiness' (Bioregional, 2015). The developers of each planned community are expected to integrate these features into a localized 'One Planet Action Plan' that identifies technical planning and design approaches for the particular spatial context and environmental needs. This approach, similar to the mobility and transfer of other sustainable planning and design systems such as LEED and BREEAM, points to an emerging universalization and standardization of sustainability planning and design with the incorporation of localized characteristics and aesthetics. In the context of the Zibi development, the project has focused on the production of a new market-oriented residential community and directed through a partnership between Windmill Development Group (Windmill Development), an Ottawa-based property development firm specializing in sustainable design, its financing arm Windmill Green Fund, and Dream Unlimited Corporation, a large pan-Canadian real estate management company.

The Zibi development site is located on the Chaudière and Albert Islands in the Ottawa River near the downtown core of Ottawa (approximately 18 acres of land) and also incorporates part of the central waterfront area of Gatineau, an urban municipality on the north side of the river and situated in the province of Quebec (Ontario Municipal Board [OMB], 2015). A large part of the land on Chaudière and Albert islands is de-industrialized space that requires extensive environmental remediation as a result of its ownership by Domtar Corporation (pulp and paper) and the use of land for saw and pulp factories and resultant soil contamination. A hydro-electricity plant with multiple generating stations, owned by Hydro Ottawa, is the remaining structure in use on the island lands and connects with Chaudière Falls, where a hydro dam was constructed in 1908 (Ibid., 2015). The Albert and Chaudière Islands, including the Chaudière Falls, are unceded indigenous territory of the Algonquin-Amikwa-Nippissing-Anishinaabeg (Anishinaabe) first nation of Canada (Ontario Superior Court of Justice, 2014); unceded territory defined as land that was not formally relinquished by indigenous groups through treaties with Canadian governments (McCreary and Milligan, 2014; Payne, 2015). As such, the island lands have been 'unofficially' taken through multiple colonialist strategies and practices over centuries. These practices, within the broader context of Canada, have privileged the use of land for white settlers and produced devastating impacts on indigenous groups through the eradication of their inherent title to and relationships with land (Coulthard, 2014; Dickason

1992; Gehl, 2014; Razack, 2002). The closure of the Domtar factory in 2005, and the subsequent re-sale of the island lands to Windmill Developments, marked a point at which Anishinaabe communities could actively pursue the reclamation of traditional territory. Yet, instead, the sale of the lands has reproduced white settler land practices but with a type of consultation whereby Anishinaabe communities have been asked for formal input into the planning process for land redevelopment.

The development plans for Zibi community, the name taken from the Anishinaabemowin language and word for 'river', proposes the construction of thirteen development blocks consisting of 1200 market-oriented residential units in low and high rise buildings, with a limited 7 per cent of this housing to be categorized as affordable, alongside varied retail and café spaces that emphasize sustainability and an 'active, outdoorsy' lifestyle. With the creation of a 'One Planet Action Plan' for Zibi that was finalized by Windmill Development in April 2015, particular dimensions of sustainable planning and design methods for the site are connected to the sustainability agenda articulated in the One Planet guidelines. The Zibi plan proposes the construction of a district energy system for heating and cooling (heat derived from waste and water provided for cooling) with the aim of providing carbon neutral energy to the site by 2020, a waste diversion strategy to limit land fill residential waste to 2 per cent of all generated site waste, a reduction in average per capita water use by half through the installation of building efficiency mechanisms, and an increase in biodiversity through the production of new green spaces with native vegetation and encouragement of wildlife in these spaces (Windmill Development Group, 2015a). The plan also emphasizes the creation of sustainable transportation infrastructure and street design that mitigates car use (OMB, 2015). Both the plan and development marketing brochures promote images of an environmentally friendly, seemingly bucolic, urban community created from scratch in largely vacant, de-industrialized space where middle-class urban professionals ride bicycles to and from work, eat organic and locally sourced food, collaborate in garden and park creation for leisure and share a common interest in environmental activities. Embedded in this vision is the role of sustainable planning and design in cultivating a general ethos of sustainable urban living and determining the ways by which residents will become more environmentally sustainable in their everyday behaviours. This intention is underlined by the additional inclusion of an 'eco-concierge' for the community, defined in the Zibi plan as a 'lifestyle management service to help inform people about green living. The service covers all aspects of living, such as travel, food, cleaning, etc' (Windmill Development Group, 2015a, p. 5). Despite the cultivated pastoral character-istics found in the plan for Zibi, Windmill Development suggest, both implicitly and explicitly, that their vision is urban focused, situated on the production of more environmentally responsible urban areas and that the company is tasked with 'greening our urban environments' (Windmill Development Group, 2015c). The development marketing material states,

(W)elcome to Zibi, a world-class sustainable community and redevelopment project by Windmill Development Group and Dream Unlimited
Corp. Here you can live an exceptionally unique and balanced lifestyle
combining the best of urbanity and healthy-living principles with a vibrant
waterfront.

(Windmill Development Group, 2015b)

A sense of paternalism lies in the development vision for Zibi, which
prescribes a new form of urban living through the use of ostensibly positive
discourse that encourages the building a healthy urban community and creating
environmentally sustainable urban infrastructure. The development is intended
to be universally acceptable and bring positive effects to the islands and the
larger city of Ottawa. Alongside this paternalistic approach, the planning
process for Zibi has been opposed by particular Anishinaabe and other
indigenous communities through direct action protests and legal actions,
which have produced differences of opinion between Anishinaabe communities
that oppose the project and communities that are supportive of the development
vision. A legal claim was first submitted in 2014 by a representative of the
Amikwabi family of Anishinaabe, in partnership with the West Nippissing
Woodland Metis Association, the League of Indian Nations of North America
and the Algonquin Hunting Party, as an action against the Attorney Generals
of Ontario and Canada, the City of Ottawa government, Windmill Development and the Algonquins of Ontario (AOO), an organization representing ten
Algonquin communities that support the Zibi project. One section of the legal
action states that certain Anishinaabe communities were omitted from
consultation in the planning process for Zibi, that Windmill Development and
the City of Ottawa should be prohibited from developing on sacred indigenous
land, and that indigenous title to the land must be formally granted by
government (Ontario Superior Court of Justice, 2014). The statement of claim
asserts that,

indigenous title to these described lands, as a sacred site, entitles them
[the plaintiffs] to a declaration of indigenous title which confers ownership rights similar to these associated with fee simple, including: the
right to decide how the land will be used; the right of enjoyment and
occupancy of the land; the right to possess the land; the right to economic
benefits of the land; and the right to pro-actively use and manage the land.

(Ibid., 2014, p. 23)

In conjunction with the civil court action, an appeal was submitted to the
OMB, a provincial government level planning review board, in December 2014
with a request to overturn the City of Ottawa's planning approval for the Zibi
development. The appeal was led by Douglas Cardinal, a well-known Canadian
architect with Metis, Blackfoot and Anishinaabe ancestry, and broadly focused
on the inherent tensions between a governmental understanding of 'planning

in the public interest' and a circumvention of indigenous rights to the island lands. It suggested that the planning process for Zibi, including the formal public consultation process, was not in accordance with the Ontario government's provincial policy statement on planning that encourages 'good planning' because it neglected to include comprehensive consultation and engagement with all Anishinaabe groups that have ancestral connections with the island lands. The appeal also noted that Windmill Developments had informed representative and decision-making Anishinaabe councils about their ideas for Zibi but had, instead, chosen to engage in a long-term planning process for the site plan with the Algonquins of Ontario (OMB, 2015). By doing this, the planning process bypassed the concerns of Anishinaabe communities that were critical of the project. In addition to unease about the planning and consultation process, the appeal suggested that there was a lack of recognition regarding unceded territory that contradicted indigenous rights to self-determination within Canada and individual and collective indigenous rights as outlined in the United Nations *Declaration on the Rights of Indigenous Peoples,* more broadly. Both the legal action in Ontario Superior Court and appeal to the OMB were rejected in 2015 on the basis that decision makers believed that there was sufficient evidence of adequate public consultation with Algonquin communities in the planning process. In the case of the appeal to the OMB, the decision stated that developers had fully complied with provincial planning legislation regarding effective public consultation and that the proposed plans for Zibi incorporated aspects of Anishinaabe history and culture (Butler, 2015; Province of Ontario, 2015). As an immediate response to the OMB decision, the Assembly of the First Nations of Quebec and Labrador, including nine Anishinaabe chiefs, passed a resolution to call for the Zibi development to be stopped, to not proceed without the consent of the whole Algonquin First Nation and to request that the federal government purchase all privately owned land on the site (Macdougall, 2015). Given the resistance to the project by particular Anishinaabe communities, the outcome of the legal actions points to how a narrow interpretation of public consultation has been defined in the planning process for Zibi and underscores how the process has not been free from conflict but, instead, has been contentious; issues that are hidden in the promotion and marketing of the Zibi development.

The legal action and appeal have delayed the start of the construction of Zibi, raised public awareness about indigenous rights to the land and sparked direct action protests by indigenous activists against Windmill Development (Figure 2.2). One particular protest occurred at the entrance of the Zibi site and coincided with the opening day of sales for residential units in the development. A report of the demonstration states that, 'protesters angry with a massive residential, commercial, and retail development planned for two Ottawa River islands considered sacred to First Nations people waved placards and approached would-be condo [market rate, homeownership units] buyers . . .' (CBC News, 2015). The protest articulated the exclusion felt by indigenous communities in the planning process for Zibi and underlined a sense of displacement from the island lands (Cardinal in Ibid., November 7, 2015). While the dismissal of the legal actions has allowed the development to proceed, it has galvanized concern and public awareness about indigenous claims to the Chaudière and Albert islands and demonstrated that the production of a new sustainable community on the islands is a contested process, which is juxtaposed against the celebratory and community-oriented overtones of the 'One Planet' sustainability vision. This is contrasted against a plan by Windmill Development for the inclusion of indigenous cultural events in the Zibi community, which, given the ensuing conflict over the site, provokes questions over the extent of full indigenous representation and the use of indigenous culture to promote the development. The finalized Zibi plan highlights the creation of an Advisory Council on Integrity, that is stated in the plan as being 'set up by the Alqonquin-Anishnaabe to ensure the integrity and appropriateness of the Zibi development on issues of First Nation culture, heritage, and socio-economics'. In relation to the Advisory Council on Integrity, the developers suggest that they have created a model for how private development firms can positively engage with First Nation groups in development processes more broadly (Windmill Development Group, 2015a, p. 18). The plan also includes reference to the installation of indigenous artwork

Figure 2.2 Photo of protest outside of the entrance to the Zibi development, Ottawa, Canada (Photo credit: Julie Comber/Permission granted by Julie Comber)

throughout the Zibi site following its construction, a formal acknowledgement by Windmill Development regarding the Albert and Chaudière islands being sacred lands for Anishinaabe people, and the future development of an indigenous cultural centre located on Victoria Island in the Ottawa River, adjacent to the Albert and Chaudière islands (Ibid., 2015a). In addition to information about the sustainability features of mixed land uses and mixed residential tenure arrangements, a concern for the higher than average unemployment rate for aboriginal Canadians (13 per cent as opposed to the national average of roughly 7 per cent), along with a suggestion regarding the importance of socio-economic equity, is noted in the plan. This is, however, contrasted against a mention of affordable housing as representing only 7 per cent of available residential units once the Zibi community is developed. The contradictions of these plan directives suggests that despite overtures towards recruiting the advice of Anishinaabe persons through an indigenous advisory board for the development and the inclusion of components of indigenous culture into the Zibi project indigenous persons will be displaced from full engagement with the residential community as a result of the market orientation of housing. The reality of the development and what it is promoting and creating – a master planned, sustainable and gentrified community with market-rate housing aimed at urban professionals, with acknowledgements regarding indigenous concerns for the land and its uses – reproduces settler assumptions regarding land possession and dispossession. In this way, the Zibi project reperforms settler-colonialist practices of spatial privatization and market-oriented land and property development.

Connections between gentrification and the imperatives that underlie imperialism and colonialism have been raised in relation to the production of gentrification through land possession as well as the role of the gentrifier as a type of neo-colonialist who claims new territory to gentrify while evicting and displacing others in the process (Atkinson and Bridge, 2005; Blomley, 2004; Smith, 1996). The notion of the 'urban frontier' was put forward by Neil Smith (1996) to describe the colonialist imperative of finding new land and pushing past spatial boundaries which is interwoven with gentrification in practice. Gentrifiers are thought to see themselves as 'risky and brave' white settlers in pursuit of what they consider to be new and previously 'undiscovered' investment territory in cities, frequently at the expense of existing residents of these spaces. Smith (1996, p. xiv) remarked, 'in the language of gentrification, the appeal to frontier imagery has been exact: urban pioneers, urban home-steaders and urban cowboys became the new folk heroes of the urban frontier'. Similarly, Clark (2005) notes that, 'gentrification is colonialism at the neigh-bourhood scale, though the structures and mechanisms involved are by no means limited to neighbourhood boundaries, as ties to foreign direct investment and global city politics makes abundantly clear' (p. 266), making a link between the imperialist tendencies of global finance and investment and the localized complexities of gentrification within a (neo)colonialist framework. Address-ing the similarities between colonialism and gentrification with a focus on indigeneity in Australia, Shaw (2005) examines the role of urban heritage preservation in extending white settler-colonialist practices. She suggests that sanitized historical narratives, produced through heritage installations and other spaces, can complement gentrification and are often intended to coddle the emotions of gentrifiers. Through a study of a gentrified area of Sydney, she notes that the production of a particular colonialist narrative in a local historical site has a purpose of making settler descendants 'feel better' about their past through the presentation of a whitewashed colonialist narrative that selectively diminishes or ignores a history of racist and oppressive acts towards indigenous people in Australia.

Indigenous scholar Glen Coulthard (2014), in discussing urban indigeneity in Canada, writes that the current socio-spatial marginalization of indigenous people in Canadian cities extends the settler-colonialist production of dispossession and displacement. Directly referring to gentrification in Canadian cities, Coulthard suggests that it is becoming an additional 'frontier of dispossession central to the accumulation of capital'. He adds that, '(T)hrough gentrification, Native spaces in the city are now being treated as *urbs nullius* – urban space void of Indigenous sovereign presence' (2014, p. 176), thereby further marginalizing urban indigenous persons and reducing their access to housing and community life as well as their traditional land. Coulthard's (2014) assertion regarding a politics of recognition – that indigenous persons in Canada have been forced into a situation of having to be 'recognized' by settler-colonialists, either through attempting to mediate or advocate for settler colonialist practices to recognize indigenous concerns or having their inherent rights 'bestowed' by paternalistic, benevolent governments – provides an important analysis of contemporary indigenous struggles. It can be connected to the development of the Zibi community and helpful for interpreting how Anishinaabe culture and traditional relationships with the Albert and Chaudière Islands are being recognized in the plan for Zibi but only to the extent that it benefits the interests of proponents of the development and future residential property owners. The consultation process with an Anishinaabe organization in the planning of the Zibi site is an example of the developer recognizing and gathering the 'input' of a representative indigenous community but selecting to proceed, instead, against the full consent of the wider Anishinaabe First Nation. Alongside these limited practices of recognition is a process of exclusionary displacement, noticeable through the production of market-rate housing in the Zibi community with a negligible amount of affordable housing. The Zibi development indicates a type of new build, gentrified, master planned sustain-able community that, while having the hallmarks of an environmentally sustainable community, selectively marginalizes and displaces other commu-nities that do not fit within its vision. In this case, the notion of exclusionary displacement includes indigenous displacement from rights over traditional and sacred lands in addition to a lack of affordable housing. The Zibi plan points to the development of an exclusive sustainable community with environmental amenities, aimed at urban professionals who engage with environmental practices and appreciate indigenous culture, that veils underlying contradictory and contested relationships between this vision for the development and issues of limited inclusion and recognition, processes of exclusionary displacement and indigenous land rights.

Gentrification and the Planning of Urban Parks

A study of urban parks in relation to processes of gentrification underlines their role as a major environmental amenity in cities that is frequently tied to the changing socio-economic character of neighbourhoods and increased property values. The historical trajectory of park development in cities demonstrates that parks have also been a means by which to exclude urban residents who are considered to be 'undesirable' and as a strategy to regenerate more marginalized areas with lower land values in cities. For example, the development of Central Park in New York City, first approved by the New York State legislature in 1853, was a large scale public project designed to provide recreational, public health and ecological space to the rapidly growing Manhattan area while at the same time operating as a way to re-regulate the use of urban space through the eradication of working class activities in this section of Manhattan (Sevilla-Buitrago, 2014). This included the decimation of Seneca Village, a community of approximately 250 landowners with the majority being African-American free slaves who had settled in the area in the 1820s and whose land was taken in 1853 through government expropriation for the creation of Central Park – a contested process that resulted in the physical eviction of residents by police (Seneca Village Project, n.d.). A connection between the development of Central Park and the historical gentrification of neighbourhoods surrounding Central Park is made by Crompton (2001), who notes that Frederick Law Olmstead, the park's planner and architect, lobbied for the creation of the park through an increase in property values and taxes in nearby residential areas. The impact of this was evidenced in empirical data compiled by the New York Parks Commission following the construction of Central Park. Drawing on archival data from the Metropolitan Conference of City and State Park Authorities, Crompton (2001) demonstrates that the New York Parks Commission took note of the fact that, before the development of Central Park,, the three wards closest to the park paid 'one dollar in every thirteen the city received in [property] taxes, but after its development they paid one-third of the entire expenses of the city, even though acquiring land for Central Park removed 10,000 lots from the city's tax roll' (p. 4).

Through the application of the proximate principle, which Crompton defines as the 'capitalization of park land into the value of nearby properties' (Crompton, 2001, p. 1), Crompton has gathered data from 30 urban residential neighbourhoods across the United States that are located in close proximity to parks. His findings indicate that in nearly all of the neighbourhood studies there was a 20 per cent increase, at minimum, in property values for properties that abutted parks, with larger and busier parks increasing property values for residential areas several blocks away by an average of 10 per cent (2001, p. 1). The study asserts, more broadly, that urban residential neighbourhoods with parks tend to have higher property values than those without parks, pointing to the role of parks in gentrification processes but also to the spatial inequality of park locations in cities. The connection of urban parks with increased property values (Harvey, 2012) for landowners and associated increased property tax revenues for local governments also suggests that parks are more likely to be found in more affluent urban residential areas and considered as a 'positive externality' for landowners.

The notion that parks act as positive external factors for property values demonstrates how they can contribute to gentrification. Yet, there is also an association between this process and contemporary practices in cities that aim to maintain and create park space for environmental purposes, which poses interesting contradictions for the role of urban parks as ecological spaces and areas that can also contribute to gentrification and displacement. Urban governments, often in collaboration with ENGOs (environmental non-governmental organizations), promote the conservation and production of new park space as a way to mitigate environmental problems that concentrate in cities, such as rising CO_2 emissions and the urban heat island effect that intensifies surface heat storage and decreases evapotranspiration (Grimmond, 2007). Along with the environmental gains produced by the number of park spaces in cities, the conservation and production of parks also aims to address public health concerns regarding air pollution and heat waves that exacerbate medical issues and mortality rates (Coutts, Horner, and Chapin, 2010); currently an urgent concern in cities with high levels of air pollutants such as Shanghai (Tan *et al.*, 2010).

The creation of parks also responds to the social needs of urban residents for recreational and natural space in cities. However, these needs are often constrained by socio-spatial inequities in urban park locations and access to park programs. The location of urban parks and other environmental features of urban spaces, such as tree canopy, are argued to be part of a larger inequitable production and distribution of green spaces in cities. This uneven spatial distribution in studies of American cities, is often related to how income, class and race is spatialized in cities, with poorer and racialized areas experiencing deficiencies in parks, tree canopy and other environmental amenities (Byrne, 2012; Byrne and Wolch, 2009; Heynen, 2006; Heynen, Perkins, and Roy, 2006; Wolch, Byrne, and Newell, 2014; Wolch, Wilson, and Fehrenbach, 2005; Zérah and Landy, 2013). As Wolch, Byrne and Newell (2014) note in relation to park access, 'racial/ethnic minorities and low-income people have less access to green space, parks, or recreational programs than those who are white or more affluent' (p. 3). They point to the common siting of parks in affluent and predominantly white neighbourhoods in American cities, the challenges of accessing fee-based park programming for low-income families, as well as the dominance of what Byrne (2007) has called 'anglo-normative' park programming that implicitly excludes non-Anglo-American residents, as examples of how parks contribute to social exclusion and feelings of displacement. The production of park spaces in cities contributes to more blurred and simultaneous practices of social inclusion and exclusion, where certain residents are included based on more normative socio-environmental practices and others are excluded from these spaces. In certain contexts there are explicit overtures towards social exclusion through official regulatory practices intended to greatly alter or prohibit the use of park space by marginalized urban residents, such as homeless individuals (see Dooling, 2009 in Chapter 2). Urban parks can also appear to be socially inclusive ecological spaces, yet can be socially exclusive based upon more covert micro-level decisions that relate to different approaches to park governance, maintenance and advocacy and how these approaches are enacted.

Urban parks are increasingly being managed and maintained through public-private partnerships (Loughran, 2014) which, as will be discussed in relation to the growing production of high line parks, complements processes of gentrification. Such partnerships are often augmented through practices of community stewardship conducted by non-profit, non-governmental park advocacy organizations in cities. In Canadian cities, for example, there has been a recent surge in community-based NGOs dedicated to the care of parks and the augmentation of recreational program delivery. These organizations are frequently titled as 'friends of' a favourite neighbourhood park, In Toronto, the 'Friends of Christie Pits [Park]' and 'Friends of Dufferin Grove [Park]' community organizations, both based in rapidly gentrifying neighbourhoods of the city's downtown core, are particularly active park NGOs that host regular community events and collaborate in the spatial planning of the parks in conjunction with local politicians and staff from the Parks, Forestry and Recreation department of Toronto's municipal government. These organizations have ostensibly formed to fill in the gaps created by government disinvestments in park maintenance, services and program delivery. In Toronto, this has taken the form of annual cuts to the Parks, Forestry and Recreation department budget over the last decade (City of Toronto, 2015). The organizations support the volunteer-based provision of park care and advocacy by hosting environmentally focused events such as garbage clean-up and community 'environment days', alongside programming such as seasonal organic food markets, community gardening and outdoor cooking events for neighbourhood residents. In addition to event and program planning, the organizations act as informal regulatory entities for the shaping and surveillance of park use by taking representative ownership over community-based visions and decision-making for the parks. Within the context of gentrifying urban neighbourhoods this raises an issue of what types of community interests and visions gentrifiers bring to discussions about parks and how they enact these ideas. Low, Taplin, and Scheld (2005) observe this in relation to the Prospect Park Alliance, a non-profit ENGO formed in 1987 as a community-based stewardship organization in Prospect Park, Brooklyn, New York. Through an ethnographic study of the park they note that the organization, unknowingly, enacted stewardship practices that generated a sense of exclusion from the park among African-American and Hispanic residents of the area and favoured the interests and tastes of middle-to-upper class white gentrifiers (Low *et al.*, 2005, p. 60). In Toronto, for example, the 'Friends of Christie Pits' organization has a local estate agent who promotes the park in advertisements, sponsors a baseball team that plays in the park and uses the organization's social media platform to market the sale of neighbourhood properties. These actions are normalized as being positive and active engagement initiatives with the community and neighbourhood park, rather than being critically interpreted as methods that promote gentrification through the embedding of an estate agency and property sales into the social life of the park and local community.

In relation to urban intensification policy and planning strategies, recent ideas for urban parks have emphasized the use of larger de-industrialized spaces as well as small lots between existing buildings as a way to re-purpose urban land in a sustainable way and as a method of park production in light of geographical constraints on the availability of urban space. Two more recent planning and design strategies for the use of smaller urban spaces and de-industrialized areas are the creation of high line and low line parks, defined as linear greenways frequently planned along unused railway lines and other previously industrial corridors. A recent burst of high line and low-line park planning in cities across the globe such as the Chapultepec Project in Mexico City, the Baana Bike Corridor in Helsinki, the Green Corridor in Singapore, the Belt Line in Atlanta and the 606 Trail in Chicago, all with differing assemblages of public, private and/or NGO sector investment and involvement and a similar motivation to create new green space in formerly industrial urban areas (Untapped Cities, 2013). Yet, although urban high line and low-line parks suggest the creative provision of park and green space for ecological and recreational purposes, recent analyses of their production indicate their association with the activities of gentrifiers and the gentrification of adjacent neighbourhoods.

The utilization of linear greenway corridors as urban park space has gained momentum in parks planning since the creation of the Coulée Verte René-Dumont (Coulée Verte), also known as the 'Promenade Plantée', which opened in Paris in 1993. It was planned and developed by the City of Paris, designed by architect Philippe Mathieux and landscape architect Jacques Vergely in 1998, and has become a prototype for green pathways in other cities, particularly the Highline in New York City. The promenade is located in one section of a decommissioned railway line that was in operation until 1969 between train stations in the Bastille and Varenne-Saint-Maur areas of eastern Paris. The Coulée Verte spans 4.5 kilometres through the 12th arrondissement and includes both street level and elevated walkway alongside public park spaces and residential and commercial uses (Mairie de Paris, n.d.). A municipal plan for a major railway viaduct, created in 1989, focused on the creation of a 'Viaduct des Arts' through the use of arcades under the viaduct for arts and cultural events. The plan emphasized the viaduct redevelopment as a regeneration project for the Bastille, a working class Parisian neighbourhood (Heathcott, 2013) traditionally known to have a thriving alternative counter-culture (Vivant, 2010). In a study of the Coulée Verte, Heathcott (2013) notes that the regeneration of the Bastille coincided with wider state-led regeneration efforts for Paris through the construction of flagship buildings and infrastructure guided by a neo-liberal agenda of property control liberalization and a desire to increase property values in Parisian neighbourhoods. He notes that a change in the socio-economic character of 12th arrondissement areas, including the Bastille, from the 1980s onwards was demonstrated through a marked increase in knowledge economy workers as new residents alongside a decline in manufacturing labourers, tradespeople and low wage service sector workers as well as a decrease in housing vacancy rates (Ibid., 2013). Heathcott observes that the creation of the Coulée Verte contributed to this change by increasing property values through a transformation of the aesthetic character of the area and the provision of high end, artisanal shops in the Viaduct des Arts that replaced squatters and lower-income artists who previously used the arcade spaces. He suggests that the Coulée Verte is a spectacular place that 'has provided Parisians with an exceptionally well-designed addition to the public realm . . . [and has] added substantially to the city's fund of green infrastructure' (Heathcott, 2013, p. 289). Yet, the greenway has become a draw for tourists and both the greenway and Viaduct des Arts have 'exerted a catalytic effect on the neighborhood, increasing property values and recon-figuring the residential landscape' (2013, p. 289). Indeed, a personal visit to the Coulée Verte found it to be a lush, leafy respite from the heat of Paris during summer, with creative uses of landscape design and architectural restoration (Figure 2.3). It also appears, however, as a social and ecological space inhabited by more affluent, 'bourgeois-boheme' families and tourists having picnics, walking and cycling. A description of the greenway by its architect further cultivates its aesthetic character, its role as a middle class leisure area and as a post-industrial space intended to revitalize an 'underdeveloped' neighbourhood:

> (I)t was abandoned for years, becoming an eyesore in an already struggling neighborhood. In the early 1990s, the City of Paris transformed the railroad track into a green walkway. . . . The original 70 red brick arches of the 1.5 kilometre viaduct have been restored, renovated and enclosed with glass. It now houses arts and crafts workshops, galleries, furniture showrooms, a restaurant and a café. The mass of plant-life that borders and sometimes encroaches the already narrow trail can give the impression of being momentarily lost on a forest trail.
>
> (Mathieux, 2015)

Figure 2.3 Photo of Coulee Verte Rene Dumont, Bastille, Paris

The pastoral character of the Coulée Verte links with an additional greenway project in Paris, the Petite Ceinture, also located on a decommissioned railway line. Foster's (2010) study of the Petite Ceinture notes that the City of Paris' landscape planning department formulated the 'Sentier Nature' plan during the mid-1990s for one part of the Petite Ceinture, located in the 16th arrondissement. The plan was implemented by the ENGO, Association Espaces, between 1997 and 2004. Foster suggests a correlation between the selection of the 16th arrondissement for the development of a low-line green corridor and the affluence of the area, as well as the role of the greenway as a leisure space in a highly gentrified area of Paris. She writes that 'property values in this residential arrondissement are some of the highest in France, where there is no industry, little office space and weak demand for public transport' (Foster, 2010, p. 322). Both the Coulée Verte and the Petite Ceinture point to connections between the establishment of high line and low-line parks as new ecological and social spaces in Paris, while at the same time contributing to and maintaining gentrification in the areas where they are situated.

The High Line greenway, located in the downtown west side of New York City and influenced by the Coulee Verte, opened in 2009 and was similarly developed on a decommissioned rail line. The High Line has become a symbol of revitalization for Manhattan and New York City more broadly and is publically celebrated as an innovative recreational green space by local residents, New Yorkers and tourists (Loughran, 2014; Patrick, 2014). This celebration, however, has overlooked the rising property values surrounding the High Line, its privatized nature (Harvey, 2012), and networked associations between the City of New York government, public and private sector planners and designers, organizations such as the 'Friends of the High Line' constituted by members of the Rockefeller family and various Hollywood movie actors, and billionaire funders such as the Dillon and Von Furstenberg families that have donated to the infrastructure of the High Line (Loughran, 2014). These connections have caused the High Line to become, as Loughran (2014) writes, an 'archetypal urban park of the neo-liberal era that constitutes the uneven development of parks in contemporary cities where elite, privatized green spaces are located in affluent urban neighbourhoods and less attention is given to parks in low-income areas' (p. 50). Both Loughran and Patrick, in their separate analyses of the High Line, underline the gentrified characteristics of the greenway. Patrick (2014) suggests that the curated and manicured vegetation that exists on the High Line, that was planted in place of the weed-like Tree of Heaven (A. Altissima) plants that originally inhabited the rail line, is a sign of ecological gentrification that aims to 'cleanse' the original ecology of the site and produce a new socio-ecological space that better connects with the social and economic character of the surrounding affluent neighbourhoods. Here, Patrick posits a unique observation that natural vegetation also suffers from the eviction and displacement processes of gentrification. Loughran (2014) evokes a notion of spatial privilege to describe the greenway, which he defines as the 'hegemonic ability to make claims on public space based on high standing within socially constructed hierarchies of gender, race, class, sexuality and national origin, [which] reproduces social advantages in a process that both affirms individuals' existing cultural capital and enables practices of consumption' (2014, p. 61). He suggests that the High Line is a highly controlled space of social order that is carefully regulated and watched through formal surveillance by security guards and park personnel, alongside greenway uses by artisanal food stalls, cafes and a 'farm-to-table' locavore restaurant (Loughran, 2014). The assemblage of environmentally friendly consumer merchants and goods, private security guards, public park officials, wealthy supporters and everyday users of the High Line presents a new amalgam of gentrified and inter-related environmental, social and economic characteristics in urban parks. In addition to the High Line, an underground greenway, called The Lowline, recently received planning approval from the City of New York in 2016 (Chino, 2016). Proposed by a group of architects and engineers, the plan centres on the implementation of 'the world's first underground park' (The Lowline, 2016) to be located in a former trolley terminal in the Lower East Side area of Manhattan, historically a neighbourhood for working class immigrants that has experienced significant gentrification over the past several decades (Mele, 2000). The Lowline plan emphasizes sustainable design innovations in solar technology to provide underground light for tree and plant vegetation as well as humans, and is expected to be an acre in size and will serve as an 'underground forest' for the area (Chino, 2016; The Lowline, 2016).

A final example of greenway planning and its connections with gentrification lies in plans for a new green corridor in Toronto. The Green Line project proposes to connect nine existing parks, that are currently owned and maintained by the City of Toronto government, along a 5 kilometre long hydroelectricity corridor in the western downtown core of the city. The corridor is adjacent to formerly working class, largely immigrant areas and currently gentrifying neighbourhoods such as Dovercourt Village, which has been identified in popular media as being the next trendy neighbourhood of Toronto and the city's 'Williamsburg' in reference to the gentrified Brooklyn, NY neighborhood (Korducki, 2015). The Green Line initiative is proposed by an ENGO called Park People in conjunction with the 'Friends of the Green Line' organization and a local architecture firm. Park People advocates for local community involvement in public park management, and negotiates partnerships with the private sector (Park People, 2016). One of the organization's roles in the Green Line project is to lobby local government to invest in infrastructure improvements in existing parks along the proposed greenway and to create four new parks (Park People, 2016). Park People is self-tasked as a 'broker' of partnerships between local government, private firms and banks and local community groups concerned with producing new green spaces along the hydroelectricity corridor. The organization celebrates its role as a partnership builder in park development using discourses of creativity and innovation, '(A)s our city grows, we must look for creative opportunities to expand parks and connect communities. Park People is working on a special project to transform disconnected land in the Dupont hydro corridor into a beautiful, continuous park and trail. ... Park People, in partnership with Friends of the Green Line and Workshop Architecture, is building support with the City of Toronto, community, and other partners to realize the Green Line' (Park People, n.d.). Although this mandate envisions a new green pathway and park spaces in downtown Toronto, there is significant potential for the greenway to become an environmental amenity for more affluent residents and new gentrifiers who inhabit adjacent neighbourhoods and to reproduce socio-spatial inequalities in urban park creation and use.

Conclusion

Current approaches to sustainability master planning in cities, as comprehensive strategies for the production of large and small scale residential communities as well as urban parks, constitute and shape gentrification processes in multiple ways. In the production of new sustainable communities, practices of new-build gentrification are evident through the role of private developers in the provision of market-rate housing and commercial spaces that are intended to attract middle-class and more affluent residents, with an additional emphasis on environmental planning, aesthetics and amenities. These characteristics are not limited to the production of individual master planned sustainable communities but also have effects on the gentrification of surrounding areas. Through the example of the Pembury Circus development in Hackney, London, it is observed how proponents of the project expect that the sustainable features of the project will influence and radiate out to the larger neighbourhood as a way to 'improve' (gentrify) the social and environmental characteristics of the area, including the racialized and low-income council housing community of Pembury Estates. Such projects also cultivate social exclusion through indirect or exclusionary displacement; where low-income residents are instantly excluded from accessing new-build sustainable communities because of inabilities to afford and access housing. In addition to instant displacement from housing in new master planned sustainable communities, the Zibi 'One Planet' community demonstrates how displacement from land and the dispossession of inherent rights to land for indigenous persons is intricately woven into the production of a new gentrified sustainable community. This form of displacement underscores existing conceptual associations between neo-colonialism and gentrification and shows how urban land, struggles over rights to urban land ownership and contestations over the environmental stewardship of urban land are connected with gentrification processes; issues that are further explored through the emergent role of CLTs as a community-based solution to gentrification in Chapter 5.

Environmental gentrification is apparent in the remediation of urban brownfield sites for the planning and development of master planned sustainable communities, an increased valuation of land through soil remediation and proximity to 'better and cleaner' environmental spaces and the provision and location of urban parks and concomitant increases in property values around parks and other green spaces. The River City and Canary District neighbourhoods in Toronto's central waterfront redevelopment, the Pembury Circus project and the Zibi development required soil remediation before construction and the application of sustainable design standards to buildings following their construction. This points to an emergence of a linear trajectory in the integration of environmental components in the planning and development of new master planned sustainable communities – from the planning vision for a project to land preparation and to construction and residential settlement. The role of these steps in increasing the exchange value of land parcels and new residential and commercial properties is an important aspect of both new build and environmental gentrification and concomitant exclusionary processes. In conjunction with increased land and property values, absences of social accessibility and affordable homes and other spaces exacerbate the problems of environmental gentrification. The question of who is able to reside within or access new sustainable master planned communities is largely related to one's social privilege, professional status and income – issues that will be further explored in Chapter 4. In the context of urban parks, in particular, exclusionary practices of environmental gentrification take hold in both covert and explicit ways, such as the dominance of public parks programming that implicitly excludes other socio-spatial uses and more explicit forms of planning and design that are intended to exclude impoverished and marginalized urban residents. Woven into the definition of environmental gentrification, direct and indirect or exclusionary displacement suggests environmental practices that materially and discursively marginalize, isolate and decontextualize the everyday realities of residents that do not fit within a gentrifying urban landscape.

Notes

1 Principles of New Urbanist community planning are(i) walkability; (ii) connectivity of streets and pathways; (iii) mixed-use spaces and social mix; (iv) mixed housing; (v) quality architecture and urban design; (vi) traditional neighbourhood structure – compact development and town centres; (vii) increased density; (viii) green transportation; (ix) sustainability [energy efficiency, minimal impact, eco-friendly technologies]; (x) quality of life [the combined principles will produce an improved quality of life] [New Urbanism: Creating Livable Sustainable Communities www.newurbanism.org].
2 LEED for Neighbourhood Development (LEED ND) was created in 2010 by the United States Green Building Council (USGBC), as a partnership between the USGBC, the Natural Resources Defense Council, and the Congress for New Urbanism (Canada Green Building Council, n.d.). LEED ND awards accreditation for the development of comprehensive sustainable planning and design techniques for new communities. The accreditation is largely based on adherence to principles

of new urbanism (higher density, compact, pedestrian and public transit oriented neighbourhoods) along with the construction of LEED accredited buildings.

3   In Canada, LEED Gold certification is obtained through third-party evaluation and accreditation by the Canada Green Building Council the after the building is completed. Developers build according to a points system in areas of indoor environmental quality/innovation and design (innovative architecture), materials and resources (use of recycled and local construction materials), energy and atmosphere (maximized energy performance through district energy and solar panel use) and sustainable site development (brownfield redevelopment, reduction of heat island effect through green roofs and ground level vegetation). Sixty to seventy-nine points are required to obtain LEED Gold certification (Canada Green Building Council, n.d.). Some specific design features of LEED are development density, in order to promote intensification, the re-development of contaminated sites, alternative modes of transportation such as planning and design provisions for bicycles, storm water management through a reduction in impervious road surfaces, green roofing (to cover 50 per cent or more of building roofs), light pollution reduction and water efficiency (TWRC, 2006b).

References

Addo, F. (2011a, August 9). Hackney riots have crushed the Pembury estate community. *Guardian*. Retrieved from www.theguardian.com/commentisfree/2011/aug/09/riots-pembury-estate-community-hackney

Addo, F. (2011b, September 6). How not to understand the riots. *Guardian*. Retrieved from www.theguardian.com/commentisfree/2011/sep/06/understand-riots-communites-unrest

Addo, F. (2014, November 7). Has your class changed over the course of your lifetime? *Guardian*. Retrieved from www.theguardian.com/commentisfree/2014/nov/07/has-class-changed-posh-or-poor

Atkinson, R., and Bridge, G. (eds). (2005). *Gentrification in a global context: The new urban colonialism*. London: Routledge.

Bellway. (2014). *Pembury Circus, Hackney: Sales Information Sheet*. Bellway, London.

Biqing, H., Peng, F., and Zhongyuan, H. (2013). Planning overall landscapes, building a garden city: On the revision of Guangzhou urban green space system planning. *Journal of Landscape Research*, 5(11–12), 22–25

Blomley, N. (2004). *Unsettling the city: Urban land and the politics of property*. New York: Routledge.

Bloomfield, R. (2015, November 24). *Hackney and Haringey: London's greenest boroughs lead the way for house price growth*. Retrieved from www.homesandproperty.co.uk/property-news/hackney-and-haringey-londons-greenest-boroughs-lead-the-way-for-house-price-growth-51166.html

Bunce, S. (2011). Public-private sector alliances in sustainable waterfront revitalization: Policy, planning, and design in the West Don Lands. In G. Desfor, and J. Laidley (eds), *Reshaping Toronto's waterfront* (pp. 287–304). Toronto: University of Toronto Press.

Butler, D. (2015, July 15). Court dismisses First Nation member suit seeking control of 'sacred' Chaudière site. *Ottawa Citizen*. Retrieved from http://ottawacitizen.com/news/local-news/court-dismisses-lawsuit-seeking-control-of-sacred-chaudiere-site

Butler, T., and Hamnett, C. (2011). *Ethnicity, class and aspiration: Understanding London's new East End.* Bristol, UK: Policy.

Butler, T., Hamnett, C., and Ramsden, M. J. (2013). Gentrification, education and exclusionary displacement in east London. *International Journal of Urban and Regional Research, 37*(2), 556–575. http://doi.org/10.1111/1468–2427.12001

Byrne, J. (2007). *The role of race in configuring park use: A political ecology perspective.* University of Southern California.

Byrne, J. (2012). When green is White: The cultural politics of race, nature and social exclusion in a Los Angeles urban national park. *Geoforum, 43*(3), 595–611. http://doi.org/10.1016/j.geoforum.2011.10.002

Byrne, J., and Wolch, J. (2009). Nature, race, and parks: Past research and future directions for geographic research. *Progress in Human Geography.* http://doi.org/10.1177/0309132509103156

Canary District. (2015). The Canary District. Retrieved 17 November 2015, from http://canarydistrict.com/canary-district-community/

CBC News. (2015, November 7). Protesters greet would-be Zibi buyers as first condos go on sale. *CBC News.* Retrieved from www.cbc.ca/news/canada/ottawa/zibi-condo-protest-1.3309074

City of Toronto. (2002a). *Making waves: Central waterfront plan part II.* Toronto: Author.

City of Toronto. (2002b). *Toronto official plan.* Toronto: Author.

City of Toronto (2015). *Toronto Official Plan.* Toronto: City of Toronto.

Clark, E. (2005). The order and simplicity of gentrification – A political challenge. In R. Atkinson, and G. Bridge (eds), *Gentrification in a global context: The new urban colonialism* (pp. 261–269). London: Routledge.

Chino, M. (2016, July 16). New York just approved plans to build the world's first underground park. Inhabit. Retrieved from http://inhabitat.com/new-york-city-just-approved-plans-to-build-the-lowline-the-worlds-first-underground-park/

CondoNow. (2015). New condos & townhomes for sale | Plans, Prices, Reviews. Retrieved from https://condonow.com/

Coulthard, G. S. (2014). *Red skin, white masks: Rejecting the colonial politics of recognition.* Minneapolis: University of Minnesota Press.

Coutts, C., Horner, M., and Chapin, T. (2010). Using geographical information system to model the effects of green space accessibility on mortality in Florida. *Geocarto International, 25*(6), 471–484. http://doi.org/10.1080/10106049.2010.505302

Crompton, J. L. (2001). The impact of parks on property values: A review of the empirical evidence. *Journal of Leisure Research, 33*(1), 1–31.

Desfor, G., and Keil, R. (2004). *Nature and the city: Making environmental policy in Toronto and Los Angeles.* Tucson: University of Arizona Press.

Dickason, O. P. (1992). *Canada's first nations: A history of founding peoples from earliest times.* Toronto: Oxford University Press.

Dyckhoff, T. (2013, July 19). Let's move to Clapton, north-east London. *Guardian.* Retrieved from www.theguardian.com/money/2013/jul/19/lets-move-to-clapton-north-east-london

Foster, J. (2010). Off track, in nature: Constructing ecology on old rail lines in Paris and New York. *Nature and Culture, 5*(3), 124–132.

Fraser Brown MacKenna Architects. (2016). FraserBrownMacKennaArchitects. Retrieved from www.fbmarchitects.com/

Geertse, M. (2016). The international garden city campaign: Transnational negotiations on town planning methods 1913–1926. *Journal of Urban History*, *42*(4), 733–752.

Gehl, L. (2014). *The Truth that Wampum Tells: My debwewin on the Algonquin land claims process*. Halifax: Fernwood Publishing.

Grant, J. (2006). *Planning the good community: New urbanism in theory and practice*. London: Routledge.

Grimmond, S. (2007). Urbanization and global environmental change: Local effects of urban warming. *Geographical Journal*, *173*(1), 83–88. http://doi.org/10.1111/j.1475-4959.2007.232_3.x

Harrison, M. (1999). *Bournville: Model village to garden suburb*. Chichester, UK: Phillimore.

Harvey, D. (2012). *Rebel cities: From the right to the city to the urban revolution*. London: Verso.

Heathcott, J. (2013). The promenade plantée: Politics, planning, and urban design in postindustrial Paris. *Journal of Planning Education and Research*, *33*(3), 280–291. http://doi.org/10.1177/0739456X13487927

Henderson, S. (2010). Romerstadt: The modern garden city. *Planning Perspectives*, *25*(3), 323–346.

Heynen, N. (2006). Green Urban political ecologies: Toward a better understanding of inner-city environmental change. *Environment and Planning A*, *38*(3), 499–516. http://doi.org/10.1068/a37365

Heynen, N., Perkins, H. A., and Roy, P. (2006). The political ecology of uneven urban green space: The impact of political economy on race and ethnicity in producing environmental inequality in Milwaukee. *Urban Affairs Review*, *42*(1), 3–25. http://doi.org/10.1177/1078087406290729

Home, R.K. (1990). Town planning and garden cities in the British Colonial Empire 1910–1940. *Planning Perspectives*, *5*(1), 23–37

Hill, D. (2014, February 24). Even the buses are saying 'Pembury Circus'. Retrieved from http://davehill.typepad.com/claptonian/2014/02/even-the-buses-are-saying-pembury-circus.html

Jelidi, C. (2014). Symbolic usage in the garden city concept during the French protectorate in Morocco: From the Howardian model to garden housing-estates. In L. Bigan and Y. Katz (eds), *Garden cities and colonial planning: Transnationality and urban ideas in Africa and Palestine*. Manchester, UK: Manchester University Press

Keil, R., and Graham, J. (1998). Reasserting nature: Constructing urban environments after fordism. *Remaking Reality: Nature at the Millennium*, 100–125.

Kipfer, S., and Keil, R. (2002). Toronto, Inc.? Planning the competitive city in the New Toronto. *Antipode*, *34*(2), 227–264. http://doi.org/10.1111/1467-8330.00237

Korducki, K. (2015, February 11). *Is Dovercourt village Toronto's next big thing? Torontoist*. Retrieved from http://torontoist.com/2015/02/is-dovercourt-village-torontos-williamsburg/

Laidley, J. (2007). The ecosystem approach and the global imperative on Toronto's central waterfront. *Cities*, *24*(4), 259–272. http://doi.org/10.1016/j.cities.2006.11.005

Laidley, J. (2011). Creating an Environment for Change: The 'Ecosystem Approach' and the Olympics on Toronto's Waterfront. In G. Desfor, and J. Laidley (eds), *Reshaping Toronto's waterfront* (pp. 203–223). Toronto: University of Toronto Press.

Lewis, J. (2015). Preserving and maintaining the concept of Letchworth Garden City *Planning Perspectives*, *30*(1), 153–163 http://dx.doi.org/10.1080/02665433.2014.971127

Lewis, P. (2011, August 8). *Hackney rioters and police in hand-to-hand combat. Guardian*. Retrieved from www.theguardian.com/uk/2011/aug/08/hackney-riot-police-london

London Borough of Hackney. (2008). *Hackney's sustainable community strategy* 2008–2018. London: Author.

London Borough of Hackney. (2010). *Local development framework – Core Strategy: Hackney's strategic planning for* 2010–2025. London: Author. Retrieved from www.hackney.gov.uk/Assets/Documents/Adopted-LDF-Core-Strategy-final-incchaptimagescov-Dec2010-low-res.pdf

London Borough of Hackney. (2014). *Report of the living in Hackney Scrutiny Commission: New residential development and affordable housing gain – final report*. London: Author.

London Borough of Hackney. (2016a). *Parks and green spaces*. Retrieved from www.hackney.gov.uk/parks

London Borough of Hackney. (2016b). *A profile of Hackney, its people and place*. London: Author.

Loughran, K. (2014). Parks for profit: The high line, growth machines, and the uneven development of urban public spaces. *City & Community*, *13*(1), 49–68. http://doi.org/10.1111/cico.12050

Low, S., Taplin, D., and Scheld, S. (2005). *Rethinking urban parks: Public space & cultural diversity*. Austin, TX: The University of Texas Press.

Macdougall, G. (2015). Nine Algonquin chiefs, AFNQL, oppose 'Zibi' condos and resolve to protect sacred area in Ottawa/Gatineau. *Equitable Education: Learning a better world*, November 25, 2015. Retrieved https://equitableeducation.ca/2015/algonquin-chiefs-afnql-oppose-zibi

Mairie de Paris. (n.d.). Promenade Plantée (Coulée verte René-Dumont) – Paris.fr. Retrieved from http://next.paris.fr/english/parks-woods-gardens-and-cemeteries/gardens/promenade-plantee/rub_8212_stand_34230_port_18987

Marcuse, P. (1985). Gentrification, abandonment, and displacement: Connections, causes, and policy responses in New York City. *Journal of Urban and Contemporary Law*, *28*(4), 195–240.

Mathieux, P. (2015). Promenade plantée. *Architects, architecture, architectural*. Retrieved from http://architectuul.com/architecture/promenade-plantee

McCreary, T. A., and Milligan, R. A. (2014). Pipelines, permits, and protests: Carrier Sekani encounters with the Enbridge Northern Gateway Project. *Cultural Geographies*, *21*(1), 115–129. http://doi.org/10.1177/1474474013482807

MLM. (2016). MLM – Pembury Circus Redevelopment. Retrieved from www.mlm.uk.com/projects_pemburycircusredevelopment.php

Myers, G.A., and Muhajir, M.A. (2014). The afterlife of the Lanchester plan: Zanzibar as the garden city of tomorrow. In L. Bigan and Y. Katz (eds), *Garden cities and colonial planning: Transnationality and urban ideas in Africa and Palestine*. Manchester: Manchester University Press.

New Policy Institute. (2015a). *Boroughs / poverty indicators / London's poverty report*. Retrieved from www.londonpovertyprofile.org.uk/indicators/boroughs/

New Policy Institute. (2015b). *Hackney / poverty indicators / London's poverty report*. Retrieved from www.londonpovertyprofile.org.uk/indicators/boroughs/hackney/

Ontario Municipal Board (OMB). (2015). Case No. PL141340. Issue Date: November 17, 2015. Province of Ontario.

Park People. (n.d.). *The green line*. Retrieved from http://parkpeople.ca/project/the-green-line

Park People. (2016, March 24). It's time for the green line. Retrieved from http://park people.ca/archives/1974

Patrick, D. (2014). The matter of displacement: A queer ecology of New York City's high line. *Social and Cultural Geography*, *15*(8), 920–941.

Payne, E. (2015, February 25). Welcome to 'Zibi': Windmill launches Albert, Chaudière islands development. *Ottawa Citizen*. Retrieved from http://ottawacitizen. com/news/local-news/live-windmill-officially-launches-renewal-project

Perry, F. (2015, March 24). 'It has slowly eroded the place away': Your stories of gentrification – From London to LA. *Guardian*. Retrieved from www.theguardian. com/cities/2015/mar/24/it-has-slowly-eroded-the-place-away-your-stories-of-gentrification-from-london-to-la

Razack, S. (2002). Introduction: When place becomes race. In S. Razack (Ed.), *Race, space, and the law: Unmapping a white settler society* (pp. 1–20). Toronto: Between the Lines Press.

Rees, A. (2012). Nineteenth-century planned industrial communities and the role of aesthetics in spatial practices: The visual ideologies of Pullman and Port Sunlight. *Journal of Cultural Geography*, *29*(2), 185–214.

River City. (2015a). Official site of River City phase 3 by urban capital. Retrieved from http://rivercitytoronto.com/

River City. (2015b). Official site of River City – Winner of BILD's best design award. Retrieved from http://rivercitytoronto.com/river-city/

Sarkissian, W., and Heine, W. (1978). *Social mix, the Bournville experience.* Bournville: Bournville Village Trust.

Seneca Village Project. (n.d.). *The history and archaeology of a community of African-American & Irish immigrants in nineteenth century New York City*. Retrieved from www.mcah.columbia.edu/seneca_village/index.html

Sevilla-Buitrago, A. (2014). Central Park against the streets: The enclosure of public space cultures in mid-nineteenth century New York. *Social and Cultural Geography*, *15*(2), 151–171.

Shaw, W. (2005). Heritage and gentrification: Remembering 'the good old days' in postcolonial Sydney. In R. Atkinson and G. Bridge (eds). *Gentrification in a global context: The new urban colonialism* (pp. 58–72). Abingdon, UK: Routledge.

Smith, N. (1996). *The new urban frontier: Gentrification and the Revanchist City*. New York: Psychology Press.

Tan, J., Zheng, Y., Tang, X., Guo, C., Li, L., Song, G., and Chen, H. (2010). The urban heat island and its impact on heat waves and human health in Shanghai. *International Journal of Biometeorology*, *54*(1), 75–84. http://doi.org/10.1007/s00484 –009–0256-x

The Lowline. (2016). Project – The lowline. Retrieved from http://thelowline.org/about/ project/

Toronto Waterfront Revitalization Corporation (TWRC). (2002*). Our waterfront: Gateway to a New Canada – The development plan and business strategy for the revitalization of the Toronto waterfront*. Toronto: Author. Retrieved from www.torontopubliclibrary.ca/detail.jsp?Entt=RDM1433058&R=1433058

Toronto Waterfront Revitalization Corporation (TWRC). (2003). *Building the foundation: Annual report 2002/03.* Toronto: Author. Retrieved from www.water frontoronto.ca/dbdocs/477e7ed7c05a5.pdf

Toronto Waterfront Revitalization Corporation (TWRC). (2005a). *Sustainability framework.* Toronto: Author.

Toronto Waterfront Revitalization Corporation (TWRC). (2005b). *West Don Lands precinct plan.* Toronto: Author.

UK Department for Communities and Local Government. (2015). Planning update March 2015 – Written statements to Parliament – GOV.UK. Retrieved from www.gov.uk/government/speeches/planning-update-march-2015

Untapped Cities. (2013, December 4). 10 Plans for elevated 'high line' parks around the world. Retrieved from http://untappedcities.com/2013/12/04/10-plans-for-elevated-high-line-parks-around-the-world-petite-ceinture-bloomingdale-trail-reading-viaduct/

Vivant, E. (2010). The (re)making of Paris as a Bohemian place? *Progress in Planning, 74,* 107–152.

Vyas, S. (2014, August 8). Hackney building works a 'nightmare' for residents. *Hackney Gazette.* Retrieved from www.hackneygazette.co.uk/news/hackney_building_works_a_nightmare_for_residents_1_3719156

Wang, Y.W., and Heath, T. (2010). Toward Garden City Wonderlands: New town planning in 1950s. Taiwan *Planning Perspectives, 25*(2), 141–169.

Waterfront Toronto. (2015a). West Don Lands. Retrieved from www.waterfrontoronto.ca/explore_projects2/west_don_lands

Waterfront Toronto. (2015b). *Affordable housing.* Retrieved from http://sr.esolutions group.ca/en/social/AffordableHousing.asp

Windmill Development Group. (2015a). *Zibi one planet action plan.* Ottawa: Author. Retrieved from www.bioregional.com/wp-content/uploads/2015/06/Zibi-One-Planet-Action-Plan_2015.pdf

Windmill Development Group. (2015b). Zibi. Retrieved from www.zibi.ca/

Windmill Development Group. (2015c). *Windmill | greening our urban environments.* Retrieved from www.windmilldevelopments.com/

Wolch, J. R., Byrne, J., and Newell, J. P. (2014). Urban green space, public health, and environmental justice: The challenge of making cities 'just green enough'. *Landscape and Urban Planning, 125,* 234–244. http://doi.org/10.1016/j.landurb plan.2014.01.017

Wolch, J., Wilson, J. P., and Fehrenbach, J. (2005). Parks and park funding in Los Angeles: An equity-mapping analysis. *Urban Geography, 26*(1), 4–35. http://doi.org/10.2747/0272-3638.26.1.4

Zérah, M.-H., and Landy, F. (2013). Nature and urban citizenship redefined: The case of the National Park in Mumbai. *Geoforum, 46,* 25–33. http://doi.org/10.1016/j.geoforum.2012.11.027

4 Sustainability, urban lifestyles and gentrification

The role of consumption and the notion of lifestyle production in the connections between sustainability policy, planning practices and gentrification are increasingly important to consider within cities, in particular how these connections blend together at the everyday and localized level of the urban community and neighbourhood. Consumerist practices are a central part of gentrification and are particularly relevant for understanding who gentrifiers are in terms of their embodied experiences and what forms of commercial services, housing and leisure activities are expected by gentrifiers. This chapter turns towards the production of environmentally oriented lifestyles that have become part of current gentrification practices. While not wholly directed by policy or institutionalized within official planning processes, there are notable exchanges between formal policy themes, such as the growing connection between sustainability and creative city policies and adopted by multiple urban governments, and the everyday practices of gentrifiers who engage in environmentally sustainable activities.

The idea of a more fluid exchange between formal policy, lifestyle practices and further, more informal everyday planning processes that occur outside of direct government involvement becomes noteworthy as more diverse assemblages of public sector, private sector and community-based engagement with sustainability-focused activities increasingly occur in cities. The creation of local government sustainability policy in cities is often urged through the advocacy efforts of environmentalists whose lifestyle practices – such as bicycle commuting, community gardening and recycling, among others – help to shape the types of local environmental policies and planning that are produced. For example, the City of Toronto government, considered as one of the first local governments in the world to adopt an official climate change policy and create offices dedicated to climate change reduction strategies (Gordon, 2016), has developed connections with local environmental activists through the formation of working associations with progressive members of local government. Such activists fluently understand government and policy directives and are actively engaged in helping to develop policy and planning initiatives (Desfor and Keil, 2004; Fowler and Hartmann, 2002) In this respect, the mobilization of environmental activism and the shaping of environmental and sustainability policies in Toronto are linked to advocates who are well educated, who have the ability to articulate environmental objectives, and who are able to develop social networks with politicians and policy-makers. Many local community-based and NGO-led sustainability projects in Toronto are well supported by local politicians, publicly celebrated by neighbourhood residents and frequently located in the downtown core of the city and within more affluent residential neighbourhoods. Examples of these initiatives include street-level campaigns to raise awareness about the environmental and spatial impacts of automobile use in the city by the local committee of the 'Reclaim the Streets!' organization, and 'home-grown' initiatives such as 'Pedestrian Sundays Kensington', a City of Toronto endorsed, car-free festival held in the downtown Kensington Market neighbourhood on Sundays during the summer months. Pedestrian Sundays Kensington has been identified as a sustainability initiative that has particularly lent itself to gentrification through a proliferation of artists, cafes, boutiques and tourists, which has cultivated a gentrified and 'festival-like' atmosphere in the neighbourhood (McLean and Rahder, 2013).

Connections between urban government-led policies and planning initiatives and resident and community engagement with these initiatives can be associated with middle-class aspirations regarding cities and urban living and policies that support and are constituted by these visions, such as 'creative city' policies. Creative city policies that emphasize the attraction of more affluent professional workers to cities and the spatial production of amenities for this demographic of urban resident, now implemented in cities across the world, have increasingly coalesced with the objectives of urban sustainability policies and initiatives (Cretella and Buenger, 2016; Krueger and Buckingham, 2009, 2012; Lederman, 2015; McLean, 2016; McLean and Rahder, 2013). Accordingly, this connection has enabled the reproduction of middle-class ideas about environmentalism and participation in environmentally sustainable practices in cities; from urban farms and crafting projects to the production of sustainability-focused consumer spaces such as organic food stores like Whole Foods Markets, 'locavore' restaurants and farmer markets. The associations between sustainability initiatives, creative city policies and gentrification are important to uncover in order to understand how ostensibly progressive and non-harmful sustainability practices can also intersect with the reproduction of middle-class narratives and material enactments of sustainability in cities. The following sections examine the embodiment of environmentally sustainable lifestyles and the production of environmentally oriented consumer spaces in cities as components of gentrification, the associations between the directives of formalized creative city policies and sustainability policies and initiatives, as well as micro-level 'do-it-yourself' (DIY) sustainability activities such as sewing and crafting, bicycle repair and community gardening and how these practices increasingly intersect with the discourses and spaces of urban gentrification, particularly at the neighbourhood level. These practices have been particularly adopted by new types of urban gentrifiers that are comfortable with socially and environmentally progressive initiatives and as methods for cultivating senses of authenticity and nostalgia for more simplistic urban lifestyles within a broader context of gentrification. The desire for environmentally friendly leisure and commercial spaces among gentrifiers raises challenges for how these spaces are then inserted and used in urban locations and, in relation to environmental injustice, the differences in and tensions over visions for these spaces between gentrifiers and communities that are threatened by exclusionary and direct forms of displacement.

Sustainability and the production of gentrified lifestyles in cities: who are the gentrifiers?

The sustainable urban form characteristics of higher density urban living that are encouraged through intensification policies connect well with professionalized, middle-class tastes and activities and the shaping of consumerist lifestyles in cities. Increasingly, urban planning discourse is being presented through cultivated narratives that emphasize local level and place-based visions of urban residents commuting from home to work by bicycle, stopping for organic coffee at a neighbourhood cafe and shopping for vegetables at the community farmers market or health food store. These narratives are now commonly integrated into public policy and planning documents as well as into the marketing materials of property developers (Quastel, 2009). Emerging public interest in environmentally sustainable practices in cities along with public narratives espousing the benefits of more environmentally friendly ways of being and advertising that promotes 'urbane' environmental lifestyles points to the co-production of environmentally oriented, everyday living in cities. These narrative assemblages help to cultivate embodied practices of sustainability; often in relation to consumer interest in environmentally friendly commercial spaces, individualized concern and strategies for mitigating environmental problems, and pursuits of personal health and well-being. Embodied practices of sustainability in cities intersect with gentrification in multiple ways, particularly in regard to how they are enacted by middle-class, professionalized urban residents. Kern (2012), for example observes how yoga, as a spiritual, physical, and environmentally aware practice, is an increasingly popular activity in cities witnessed through the proliferation of yoga studios and clothing in gentrifying neighbourhoods and aimed at middle-class consumers. She notes that yoga has become one of many 'body-centred' signifiers of gentrification. Such embodied symbols of gentrification connect with larger policies and development strategies that aim to increase the presence of middle-class and more affluent professionalized residents in cities.

The forwarding of 'creative class' policy agendas since the early 2000s have been particularly impactful for shaping embodied practices of both sustainability and gentrification and how they intersect. The 'creative class' agenda, based on the premise that vibrant cities are ones with high concentrations of social and cultural diversity, arts and cultural institutions and events and innovative design and aesthetics (Florida 2002, 2005; Landry, 2002), has been informative for the aspirations of middle class and more affluent urban professionals and has augmented a noted increase in professionalized workers in cities (Hutton, 2009; May *et al.*, 2007; Peck and Tickell, 2002). The impact of middle-class professionals has been most noticeable in their residential and occupational location in the central city and involvement in gentrification processes (Ley, 1996; Rose, 1999), as well as in the forms of economic and cultural capital that they wield. The increase in urban professionalized labour is tied to occupations that require formal education and career specialization, such as lawyers, financiers, architects, urban planners, professors and now, more commonly, website and application designers, product designers, start-up entrepreneurs, and so forth. The specialization and level of education required for these occupations and resultant income connects with lifestyle choices and decisions such as housing choices and location, how cities are planned and designed, local political changes, as well as their levels of engagement in philanthropic, social and environmental initiatives. As gentrification research has demon-strated (Bridge, 2001, 2006; Butler and Robson, 2001; Ley, 2003; Podmore, 1998), Bourdieu's concept of habitus – socialized norms and characteristics that shape and reproduce behaviours and attitudes in the world (Bourdieu, 1977) – is particularly helpful for interpreting the role of professionals in gentrification and the methods by which professionals move around cities in ways that extend past their immediate occupations. Building on Bourdieu's notion of habitus, Isin (2002) notes that the re-structuring of labour towards specialized employment has given specific power to urban professionals in cities. He suggests that professionals act as a new class of urban bourgeoisie that permeates urban life by (i) commanding spatial transformation through economic power; (ii) objectifying the city as a place of 'professional expertise, design, planning and engineering'; and (iii) enforcing social norms and the re-production of professionalized behaviours as habitus, where the city becomes the 'natural habitat for members of the professions' (Isin, 2002, p. 250). These points underline the associations between financial capital and social norms of professionals in the production of urban space and lifestyles and their role as gentrifiers not only in terms of financial ability to purchase property, but also in relation to the form and spatiality of their consumer tastes and demands. This also extends to the role of professionals in emergent social trends in cities and the production of new amenity spaces that reflect these trends.

The daily enactments of higher income professionals in cities are expanding past traditional forms of engagement with consumption-oriented activities, such as visiting trendy restaurants, galleries and shops, into practices usually assumed by individuals concerned with mitigating social and environmental problems. This has grown through the presence of new 'bourgeois bohemians' (bo-bos) in gentrification; liberal younger adults who are more 'environmentally aware' (Timm, 2014) and who can easily reconcile their participation in consumerist practices with bohemian/hippie values and activities (Brooks, 2000) Whether called 'bo-bos', 'hipsters', or the 'gauche-caviar' (Choi, 2009; Cowen, 2006), the growing stylization of urban, largely white, liberal, middle-class professionals into supporters of 'cool cultural consumption' (Zukin *et al.*, 2009) with a 'crunchy [granola] chic' character (Kern, 2015) widens an understanding of who participates in gentrification in cities to include individuals who can easily support and participate in social and environmental causes while at the same time being able to afford residential and other consumer luxuries provided by their professional income. This new demographic of 'urban gentry' supports a simultaneous assimilation with and commodification of existing neighbourhood contexts. It differs from traditional forms of 'artist-led' gentrification because of the existence of higher income levels and an ability to instantly participate in expensive property and urban lifestyle consumption practices. While 'bo-bos' or 'hipsters' are not a homogenous group and have varying personal complexities and levels of complicity with gentrification, their characterization provides insight into the transforming role of gentrifiers in cities and, in particular, with their interest in engaging with environmental issues and activities.

Professionalized individuals now appear to seek out more independent, alternative, 'grungier' urban spaces and traditionally low-income and culturally diverse neighbourhoods despite having substantial incomes. This process is noticeable in the commercial gentrification of streetscapes in low-income neighbourhoods, with incremental transformations of local shops – often with an environmentally friendly orientation and viewed as alternative and progressive spaces. A description of 'hipster' gentrification in the Lower Clapton neighbourhood of Hackney, London, for example underlines this trend:

> (O)n Clapton Road, once known as 'Murder Mile' in the 2000s for its gang-related violence, African-Caribbean owned shops, off-licenses, thrift shops, and basic necessity stores, are being increasingly overtaken by 'sustainable lifestyle' enterprises such as organic cafes, 'locavore' restaurants, bicycle repair places, and craft beer stores; indicating a demographic transformation in consumer demand or as what has been called a transition from Murder Mile to Hipster Village.
>
> (Wetherall, 2013)

The diversification of urban professionals now includes high income earners who eschew traditional 'yuppie' pursuits and favour more bohemian lifestyles that attempt to co-opt and replicate counter-cultures and notions of urban authenticity. As Zukin (2008) suggests, this presents as a simultaneous attraction to and commodification of what is defined as authentic in a certain time and place. These interactions also influence urban policy and planning, in keeping with Isin's (2002) observation of how urban professionals employ education and knowledge as a way to infuse their power through formal and informal activities.

This situation is underlined by the participation of 'bo-bo' professionals in urban affairs and local government policy and planning initiatives. In Toronto, for example, this is apparent in the recent proliferation of urban issues and lifestyle magazines such as *Spacing,* an organization that involves a well-connected and vocal network of trend-conscious city residents interested in current urban policy and planning issues, architects, designers and urban planners from local firms, and city government staff. The organization's magazine focuses largely on urban policy and planning issues; particularly on increasing sustainability initiatives in the city in the form of public transit routes, green roofs on public buildings, bicycle lanes, garden and park spaces. *Spacing* members engage in public policy discussions in the periodical and attend public meetings not as a form of resistance towards local government but instead in an amicable, collaborative way in order to encourage more progressive policy and planning initiatives. The organization also has a shop that sells local crafts that celebrate and promote Toronto, such as hats and other clothing items that declare the names of trendy, gentrifying central city neighbourhoods. The practice of professionalized individuals interacting with policy and planning agendas in these celebratory ways can downplay active resistance against complex social and environmental problems and injustices and instead encourage a more 'milquetoast' approach to urban activism. In a discussion of hipster gentrifers in Toronto, Cowen (2006, p. 22) notes that a proliferating 'gentrification of activism' by 'hipsters' who are interested in urban planning and other city issues, including environmental practices, is conducted through what she calls a form of 'violent peace'. This is described as advocacy for urban policy and planning that is conveyed as being inclusive and collaborative but which, at the same time, is not attentive to the issues and needs occurring in areas of the city that are not perceived as gentrifying or trendy, such as the poorer and less easily accessible areas of Toronto's suburbs. She suggests that a 'violent peace' promotes the institutionalization of hipster sensibilities about spatialization, planning processes and aesthetics in Toronto through the cultivation of 'allies in government and business' (Cowen, 2006, p. 22). This point raises important implications for how gentrifiers co-produce urban narratives and material practices that reinforce their taste and attitudes about city living, with the addition of environmentally sustainability lifestyles and spaces, in ways that – on the surface – appear to be authentic, progressive and inclusive of and well-meaning for all urban residents but can ignore differing lived experiences and inequities.

Creative city policy, sustainability and gentrification

The ideas of creativity and innovation as qualitative hallmarks of trans-formation of professionalized labour in cities towards more specialized occupations is a central component of the now well documented creative class argument, developed in the early 2000s (Florida, 2002, 2005; Landry, 2002), and which rests on the premise that 'successful' cities now have two dominant social classes, the creative class – middle-class professionals employed in specialized arts, cultural and technological production – and the service class, defined as individuals employed in retail, restaurant and similar service economy labour (Florida, 2002). Florida suggests that, 'regional economic growth is driven by the location choices of creative people – the holders of creative capital – who prefer places that are diverse, tolerant and open to new ideas' (2002, p. 223). Central to this assertion is the notion that cities must be culturally lively and diverse in order to attract members of the creative class and provide infrastructure that gives creative individuals access to what Florida calls a 'high quality of place' (2002, p. 223).

The creative class/creative city argument has inspired a rise in 'hipster' creative urban professionals largely through the adoption of the core aspects of Florida's argument in urban media and public policy discourses. As a strategy for civic boosterism, it has been quickly picked up by city governments and integrated into policy directives, planning approaches and public forums in a range of small and large cities across the globe, such as Bandung (Indonesia), Amsterdam, Buenos Aires, Toronto, Singapore, Birmingham (United Kingdom) and Austin (United States) (Brown, 2015; Budd, Lovrich, Pierce, and Chamberlain, 2008; Catungal, Leslie, and Hii, 2009; Cohen, 2015; Lederman, 2015; Long, 2016; McLean, 2014; McLean, Rankin, and Kamizaki, 2015; Peck, 2005, 2012; Rankin and McLean, 2015). Perceived causal relation-ships between high levels of cultural diversity, strong cultural industries, economic growth and development and 'successful' cities that are embedded in the creative class/creative city hypothesis have been critiqued as being complicit with neo-liberal urban revitalization/regeneration policies and gentrification (Peck, 2005, 2012; McLean, 2014, 2016; Rankin and McLean, 2015). As Peck (2005, p. 740) suggests, creative class/creative city policies support neo-liberal urban development strategies of 'inter-urban competi-tion, gentrification, middle-class consumption and place-marketing'. Spatial planning and development, guided by creative class/creative city policies, augments the characteristics and form of urban intensification through the creation of ' "authentic" historical buildings, converted lofts, walkable streets, plenty of coffee shops, art and live music spaces, organic and indigenous street culture, and a range of other typical features of gentrifying, mixed-use, inner-urban neighbourhoods' (Peck, 2015, p. 745). The connections between spatial regeneration and creative city policies aimed at producing urban places that are attractive to the individual tastes and activities of 'creative class' workers are echoed in Brown's study of the residential choices of 'creatives' in

Birmingham, UK, a city with several 'creative city' policies formulated by local government. Brown notes the attraction of creative workers toward residing in gentrifying areas of the city that are 'attractive for their mix of local (independent) and "niche" shops, restaurants and cafes' (Brown, 2015, p. 2346).

The connection of creative class/creative city ideas with urban policy and planning emphases on the spatial production of culturally lively, compact and walkable cities raises broader associations between the creation of 'creative class friendly' spaces, gentrification and sustainability policy and planning directives. As Krueger and Buckingham (2009, 2012) note, a conceptual complementarity exists between the discourses of 'creativity' and 'sustainability' that is underlined in public and private sector support for sustainable urban form through brownfield regeneration, public space development, transit-oriented development and the construction of new mixed-use residential and commercial areas. They suggest that these dominant and interconnected visions and practices of sustainable urban planning are similar to 'creative class/creative city' emphases on innovation, design and 'thinking outside the box' (Krueger and Buckingham, 2012). Lederman (2015), in a discussion of how local government sustainability and creative city policies coalesce in Buenos Aires, observes that both creative city and sustainability policy agendas, while derived from an increased global mobility of policy ideas, are largely 'homegrown' and aimed towards local urban communities and projects. He notes that, '(M)uch like creativity, sustainability can easily mean any number of things' and both concepts can also often give an appearance of being locally oriented and community-centred (2015, p. 50) while at the same time frequently informing and constituting an urban economic development agenda.

Creative class/creative city policies and sustainable urban planning agendas tend to emphasize the urban neighbourhood as a suitable place for policy and planning intervention. Cretella and Buenger's (2016) study of Rotterdam's recent local government policies on food sustainability and urban agriculture, '*Food and the City*' and '*Sustainability Program*', demonstrates how these documents were formulated with a focus on the engagement of 'creative' urban professionals in eventual policy implementation. Interestingly, they note that the language of both policies highlights strategies to retain 'creative' professional residents in Rotterdam through the production of new housing for higher income earners and the engagement of 'creative' professionals in permaculture practices in selected urban neighbourhoods (Cretella and Buenger, 2016). Similar emphases are noted in studies of the implementation of creative class/creative city policies in Toronto and their interface with sustainability policy and planning practices at the neighbourhood level. McLean and Rankin's (2015) and McLean *et al.*'s (2015) research on the local government's 'Weston 2021 Strategy', an area plan for Weston-Mount Dennis – a low-income and culturally diverse suburban neighbourhood close to the central city – examines the official vision to transform the neighbourhood into a 'creative/cultural hub' with new arts and cultural spaces alongside new environmental infrastructure such as bicycle pathways, a community garden and a neighbourhood farmers market. McLean and Rankin (2015) note that these planning efforts involve the participation of municipal government staff, representatives from non-profit NGOs, local residents and what they call 'green-creative' professionals (planners, landscape designers and other interested urban professionals). McLean *et al.* (2015) suggest that the official policy and planning vision for the neighbourhood aims to 'replicate the "downtown feel" of gentrified spaces' through the encouragement of the 'creative' adaptive reuse of older commercial and former industrial spaces into cafes, 'pop-up' stores, bicycle repair shops and environmental amenities (such as the community garden) in order to attract middle-class professionals with higher incomes to the neighbourhood (pp. 1294–1295). Importantly, such neighbourhood-based studies underline the increasingly nuanced intersections between local government formulated creative city/creative class policies, urban sustainability ideas and the implementation of these agendas by government and private actors. More broadly, they point to 'on the ground' ways in which creative class/creative city policy agendas in cities play a role in co-producing the social and environmental practices and spaces of gentrifiers.

'Whole Foods is Coming': sustainability, urban lifestyles and the 'Whole Foods Effect'

Connections between new types of gentrifiers and the cultivation of sustainable urban lifestyles through both informal and official engagements with urban policy and planning are noticeable in the development of commercial spaces that cater to their consumer demands. Along with the presence of afore-mentioned bicycle sales and repair shops and local food and organic cafes, a particularly ubiquitous commercial symbol of the emerging interest of gentrifiers in sustainability issues is found in the proliferation of Whole Foods Markets stores in cities in North America and the United Kingdom. Whole Foods Markets (Whole Foods), an American-owned health food and sustainable lifestyle corporation that has locations in cities in the United States, Canada and Britain, is known for selling organic produce and other 'environmentally friendly' merchandise, frequently at high prices, as well as supporting local community and international environmental causes (L. Smith, 2012). It is also recognized as a company that intentionally locates in gentrifying urban neighbourhoods in order to profit from an increase in demand, largely from white, middle-class professionals, for environmentally sustainable, organic food items (Anguelovski, 2015). Coined in popular media as the 'Whole Foods Effect' (Bendix, 2016; Doig, 2012; Miller, 2014), the term is used to describe a connection between the location, planning and development of a Whole Foods store and subsequent increased property values in gentrifying areas of cities (Anguelovski, 2015). This connection is considered to have been first observed in a study commissioned by the regional government of Portland, Oregon (Portland Metro) that examined the impact of particular commercial amenities on property value increases in the Portland urban area. The report cited a residential 'price premium' median of an increased 17.5 per cent for housing that was already located or newly built near a specialty grocery market such as Whole Foods (Johnson Gardner, 2007, p. 32) Bendix (2016) suggests, based on a review of real estate profiles of gentrifying neighbourhoods in cities in the United States where a Whole Foods is located – such as East Liberty in Pittsburgh, Jamaica Plain in Boston, Midtown Detroit, Logan Circle in Washington, DC, and Gowanus in Brooklyn, NY – that the location of a Whole Foods store in a 'soon-to-be gentrifying' or already gentrifying neighbourhood galvanizes interest by real estate agents, property developers and property buyers in these neighbourhoods. The stores have become bellwether sites, or 'anchor businesses' in the language of property developers (Miller, 2014), that indicate when an urban area is transforming into a 'desirable' location for property investment (Bendix, 2016). For example, an article about Whole Foods in the American arts and culture magazine, *Salon*, exclaims, 'Whole Foods is coming? Time to buy' – referring to a rush to purchase housing in urban neighbourhoods with a planned Whole Foods site (Doig, 2012). In addition to private sector interest in neighbourhoods with Whole Foods stores, Bendix (2016) notes that local governments in American cities are offering financial incentives to entice Whole Foods to locate and develop in a particular urban area. She writes that '(S)tores like Whole Foods are notorious for targeting pre-gentrifying or "up-and-coming" areas, where overhead costs are low and city governments are willing to offer generous subsidies to coax the chain to the neighborhood' (Ibid., 2016). Doig (2012) notes that Detroit's municipal government provided a substantial tax incentive to Whole Foods to attract the development of a store in the city's gentrifying Midtown district, with the broader intention of stimulating private sector-led residential and commercial development in the area. In keeping with government and private sector discourses of urban intensification, the siting of a Whole Foods store is considered by both government and private sector actors to connect with and generate interest in higher density residential and commercial development as a sustainability feature of compact city planning (Johnson Gardner, 2007).

In addition to being a harbinger in the production of gentrifying neighbour-hoods in certain North American and British cities, Whole Foods attempts to cultivate a sense of authenticity through place-based insertions where stores are located, as a way to meet the consumer interests of neighbourhood gentrifiers and claim a stake in the dynamics of local communities. Whole Foods has an explicit corporate mission to 'give back' to the neighbourhoods in which they locate; a form of commodified altruism that maintains complicity with neighbourhood gentrification while at the same time contributing to progressive social and environmental community work. For example, staff of the Whole Foods store in Stoke Newington, London, UK, a neighbourhood considered to be one of the more rapidly gentrifying neighbourhoods of east London and an area that is well known for 'hipster' gentrifiers (P. Brown, 2016; The Economist, 2013), enact local social and environmental outreach initiatives with the participation of customers. These include hosting 'green education' workshops for local residents about topics such as waste reduction through recycling and composting practices, the donation of surplus food to local food banks such as those operated by the Hackney Migrant Centre and North London Action for Homeless (an organization that also raises awareness about affordable housing shortages caused by gentrification in east London) (Spinks, 2015), and a '5 per cent day charity' program that channels 5 per cent of daily store revenue into non-profit organizations and programs in the neighbourhood (Whole Foods Market, 2016). These activities not only point towards the engagement of gentrifiers with a store that focuses on environmentally sustainable merchandise but also to a celebratory role of social and environmental corporate citizenship intended to provide a softer and kinder angle to gentrification. This image also strategically mitigates resistance by community activists to the siting of Whole Foods stores in certain neighbourhoods. Anguelovski's (2015) study of community resistance to the site planning and development of a Whole Foods store in the Jamaica Plain neighbourhood of Boston, historically a Hispanic and working class area, underlines community concerns over the negative impacts of gentrification; in this context, over concerns about the high purchase cost of Whole Foods products and that the store would cater to white, middle class gentrifiers instead of the needs of Hispanic residents. A campaign to protest the development of a Whole Foods store in Jamaica Plain was started in 2011 by a community organization concerned about gentrification, however municipal government support for the store allowed the development to proceed (Anguelovski, 2015; Greenspan, 2013). Anguelovski notes that Whole Foods declined to sign a formal 'Community Benefits Agreement' that would have provided financial benefits to community residents based upon their needs and ignored a community request to establish a fund to assist residents facing housing eviction (Anguelovski, 2015). Instead, Whole Foods attempted to mitigate community resistance and connect with Hispanic residents through the provision of Latin American products in the store and donation of surplus food to neighbourhood schools with Hispanic student populations (Greenspan, 2013).

These situations demonstrate the existence of community-based conflict over the location of Whole Foods stores in gentrifying urban neighbourhoods, which suggests that Whole Foods has not only become a new hallmark of gentrification but now also has symbolic meaning for anti-gentrification activism. The role of Whole Foods in creating a nuanced community-oriented philanthropic image that sits well with the social and environmental interests and concerns of new types of gentrifiers is also underlined. In the example of Whole Foods store in Stoke Newington, London, this philanthropy is even directed towards organizations that work to mitigate and resist social pressures caused by gentrification while at the same time the store is complicit with gentrification. Although Whole Foods can be considered as a symbol of environmental gentrification and 'gentrification to come' within neighbourhoods of certain North American and British cities, it also signifies a shift towards more specialized commercial spaces that cater to gentrifiers interested in environmentally friendly activities and products. Whole Foods is, however, a more mainstream and corporate example of commercial connections between sustainability and gentrification by comparison with more independently owned and operated commercial spaces oriented towards sustainability practices that are addressed in the following section.

New urban pioneers of gentrification: cultivating nostalgia in local sustainability practices

Gentrifiers who seek out alternative experiences in cities and purposely search for edgy and distinctive places with 'creative' social and environmental amenities are also creating embodied sustainability practices that promote independent, 'do-it-yourself' (DIY) approaches that generate feelings of authenticity and uniqueness. At the same time that particular urban neighbourhoods are identified by gentrifiers for their cultural diversity, lower cost housing and grittier character, there is also a related movement towards living in simpler ways and engaging in locally oriented sustainable initiatives and projects. Urban 'hipsters', who may or may not directly participate in creative professions, have played a central part in cultivating romanticized notions of 'simple living' through efforts to revive and create trends out of low carbon, traditional cottage industry activities and micro-enterprises in cities, such as craft beer and liquor making, sewing and knitting (Figure 3.1), bicycle sharing, clothing and household ware swaps, permaculture and foraging practices, apiculture and small livestock raising. There is a simultaneous adoption of components of modern, technological consumerist urban lifestyles – the use of smart phones, software applications and social media, for example – with a pastoralism that both romanticizes and simulates a 'by-gone era' through attachment to hands-on labour and small-scale crafting and agricultural practices more commonly associated with rural areas. These types of activities are similar to those of the urban homesteading movement[1] in the United States and practices found in urban eco-villages, both of which stress 'back to the land' self-sufficiency through small scale ecological initiatives in city locations (as discussed in Chapter 5). However, these types of activities by gentrifiers and within gentrifying neighbourhoods indicate a complicity with and an uncritical engagement with the processes and negative outcomes of gentrification. In these contexts, small scale, local and pastoral activities are nostalgic practices that are components in the production of place-based authenticity and uniqueness, and which dovetail with the ambitions of property agents and developers in the marketing of urban neighbourhoods.

Figure 3.1 Photo of Yarn Shop, Kensington Market, Toronto

While ostensibly contributing to alternative, more environmentally sustainable ways of living in cities, these practices have also become highly stylized
activities that are part of urban middle class consumer culture. Such activities
have been particularly significant in the case of traditionally working class
neighbourhoods undergoing gentrification in North American and European
cities. Harris (2011), for example, observes how gentrifiers in the Hoxton
area of Hackney, London, have romanticized the working class characteristics and industrial history of the neighbourhood through artistic 'odes' to
Cockney slang and cultivated notions of the urban pastoral through activities
such as hosting garden-style fetes – usually found in the English countryside
– on local streets, which have formed 'new cultural landscapes of gentrification' (Harris, 2011, p. 227). In addition to independent stores, workshops, and other spaces for small-scale, DIY initiatives that constitute new
neighbourhood-oriented landscapes of gentrification, a performative, embodied
aesthetic characterization of a pastoral, locally-focused lifestyle is also
produced through the type of dress styles that gentrifiers choose. This is
demonstrated in the use of a neo-victorian and pioneer 'pastiche' of clothing
items such as plaid jackets traditionally worn by North American lumber-jacks,
suspenders worn with high-waisted 'farmer' pants, the use of old-fashioned
monocles and spectacles, floral pioneer-style dresses and other thrift shop finds

(Ferrier, 2014; O'Neil, 2014). As a stylistic embodiment of Neil Smith's (1996) original notion of gentrifiers as urban pioneers in search of new urban frontiers, gentrifiers now take on the perceived aesthetic characteristics of pioneers in a form of tribute to the past. The archetype of the 'lumbersexual', an individual who embodies a rugged rural or wilderness-oriented masculine aesthetic sensibility while at the same time being comfortable with gender fluidity and more at home in urban locations, has become a popular cultural and media symbol for both critiques and celebrations of 'hipster' gentrifiers. These paradoxical characteristics are encapsulated in the following description:

> He is bar-hopping, but he looks like he could fell a Norway Pine. He looks like a man of the woods, but works at The Nerdery, programming for a healthy salary and benefits. His backpack carries a MacBook Air, but looks like it should carry a lumberjack's axe.
>
> (GearJunkie in O'Neil, 2014)

This characterization is also found in the popular television series and book, *Portlandia* (Armisen and Brownstein, 2012), which simultaneously celebrates and pokes fun at a 'hipster environmentalist' aesthetic among urban professionals in Portland, Oregon, a city known for the dedication of its residents to socially alternative and local scale environmental practices. Ferrier (2014) points out, however, that the more popular the archetype of the hipster 'lumbersexual' becomes in popular culture, the more individuals will begin distance themselves from and reinvent the 'hipster' label as it becomes more mainstream and ubiquitous; pointing towards an endless cultivation of new trends in order to be on the vanguard of authenticity and uniqueness in cities and urban popular culture.

The proliferation of independent, craft-oriented shops, bicycle repair stores and allotment garden spaces, and gentrifiers dressing like pioneers in 'edgier' gentrifying neighbourhoods cultivates an urban pastoralism that reinvents a notion of rusticity as well as a desire for authenticity. Machor (1987), in writing about the nature of urban pastoralism in the United States, suggests that there is a long-standing historical ambivalence about urban living that is reflected in a cultural fascination with the natural environment, rurality, a view of nature 'through a pastoral filter' of back-to-the-land practices and rustic settings (p. 4). In the context of urban gentrification, this is coupled with a complex post-industrial nostalgia for the urban industrial past (Kohn, 2010) that romanticizes historical forms of industrial labour while at the same time emphasizing more rustic notions of small-scale, cottage industry. For example, Mathews and Picton's (2014) analysis of the increasing production and consumption of independently and locally produced 'artisanal' craft beer in gentrifying urban districts demonstrates how a post-industrial commodification of heritage selectively glamourizes certain aspects of a city's industrial past.

Property sales firms have also started to profit from interests in rustic and sustainable practices. For example, in Toronto's rapidly gentrifying Bloorcourt (Bloor and Dovercourt) neighbourhood, Royal LePage, a Canadian real estate company, now holds a regular yard sale (rummage sale) on a residential street corner that connects with resident interest in recycling, reuse and 'street finds' – free furniture and household items that are commonly left in front of houses for others to use – while at the same time providing information about local properties for sale. In this way, the free sharing and reuse of old items is considered to associate with sustainability and a rustic feeling of village-like 'community' while contributing to the property sales objectives of the real estate company.

The cultivation of nostalgia for rusticity also hides the socially problematic aspects of the past and ignores issues such as environmental pollution, labour inequities, gender discrimination, and racism. In a discussion of the nuanced meanings of place-based nostalgia in the context of gentrified urban redevelopment sites, Kohn (2010) notes that nostalgia for activities of the past can offer progressive ideas of alternative ideas and practices that might be maintained or reintroduced. Yet, place-based nostalgia can also work to uncritically bypass or even evoke a sense of loss for a past of 'patriarchy and unquestioned white privilege' (Kohn, 2010, p. 365). These are interesting observations for sifting through complexities in the cultivation of nostalgia and the rustic pastoral in the practices of 'hipster' gentrifiers, the characteristics of which have been critiqued for promoting a 'color-blind experience of whiteness' (Marchiony, 2014). The activities that are considered on one hand to be environmentally sustainable – crafting, sewing, growing food, bicycling, item sharing and swapping – can also be viewed as a way to reproduce whiteness, inequitable gendered divisions of labour (the gendered labour of foraging, cooking from scratch, crafting and knitting, for example), and a retrenchment of class-oriented definitions of culture and labour when placed within a context of nostalgia for the past and a romanticization of subsistence-oriented 'pioneer-style' living in gentrifying areas. The emergence of small scale and local activities that evoke the past overlap with neighbourhood-based urban sustainability practices that frequently link with official policy and planning initiatives. Safransky (2014, p. 241), for example details how the abundance of vacant land lots in Detroit is attracting new 'pioneers' to the city interested in 'working the land' through participation in urban agricultural initiatives, which are supported by a broader urban policy and planning agenda of urban greening as a way to repurpose land. An emergent urban pastoralism and the identification of an evolving shape of 'urban pioneer' offers a window into analyses of the creation and use of environmental spaces at the neighbourhood level in cities and community-based initiatives that are, perhaps unknowingly at times, complicit with gentrification processes, as well as those which reproduce a largely middle class and professionalized notion of environmentalism.

Gentrification and local environmental practices: community gardening and local food production

Notable linkages have been made between environmental practices at the neigh-bourhood level and the reproduction of embodied and discursive forms of whiteness and middle-class sensibilities and attitudes towards environmental protection (cf. Aptekar, 2015; Kato, 2013; Slocum, 2007). Much of the discussion around race, racialization and the environment and the insertion of middle-class values into environmental organizations and movements has grown from academic and civil society research and activism on issues of environmental racism and environmental injustice. Work on environmental (in)justice has premised that racialized and low-income communities suffer disproportionately more from the location of unwanted land uses such as industrial factories and waste disposal sites near to their residential communi-ties, which is related to one or a combination of unjust zoning regulations, lower land and property values and lessened political ability to advocate against the proximity of environmental pollutants and poor environmental quality within communities (Agyeman, Bullard, and Evans, 2003; Agyeman, Scholsberg, Craven, and Matthews, 2016; Bullard, 1990, 1999; Pulido, 2000; Shiva, 2005). Concurrently, analyses of the lack of social justice and equity concerns in environmental sustainability discourse has underlined how necessary these concerns are for establishing, as Agyeman (2008) states, a more justice-oriented sustainability dynamic where sustainability takes on a more socially transformative 'redistributive function' rather than serving to gently reform existing policies and plans (2008, p. 752). Environmental justice work has shown that discourses of environmentalism and the environmental movement have been constructed through the aspirations of largely white, formally educated and middle class actors focused on mitigating environmental problems while often ignoring issues of racialization and poverty, particularly in urban locations (Agyeman, 2008). It has also deconstructed the role of white privilege in environmental practices and the environmental movement more broadly, underlined as assumptive behaviours and attitudes that are enacted in formal and informal ways and discussed as an 'unmarked category against which difference is constructed, whiteness never has to speak its name, never has to acknowledge its role as an organizing principle in social and cultural relations' (Lipsitz in Pulido, 2000, p. 13). Reflections on the environmental movement in Canada, for example have focused on how it has been constituted by and become representative of white, liberal and middle class values and reproduced white privilege while at the same time implicitly excluding those who do not have the same privileges largely as a result of being racialized (Gosine and Teelucksingh, 2008). Moving specifically into the realm of community-based environmental practices, sustainability practices, either shaped by the work of non-profit, non-governmental community organizations or by government policy and planning interventions, can reproduce environmental approaches that assume and re-perform societal privileges and give less priority to social equity and justice issues. These situations are reflected in connections between local environmental practices and gentrification, as well as in socio-spatial tensions between gentrifiers and lower income and often racialized residents, in sustainability initiatives such as community gardening and local food production; practices that often work through the directives of local government sustainability policies and plans.

The participation of gentrifiers in everyday environmental activities suggests that these initiatives are now components of broader spatial processes of gentrification in certain urban locations. This is demonstrated in emergent landscapes of 'foodie gentrification' (Miewald and McCann, 2014), that celebrate the consumption of locally sourced and wholesome food in cafes and restaurants in these neighbourhoods. Miewald and McCann (2014) outline contradictions between local government policies in Vancouver that forward sustainable local food production through community gardening and fruit tree harvesting, government strategies to encourage private sector-led residential development in certain historically marginalized downtown areas such as the Downtown Eastside, and emerging gentrification in these areas led through the 'promotion of a high-end "foodie culture", evident in the growing number of upscale cafes, bars, bistros, and restaurants' (p. 548). They note that these processes are juxtaposed against problems faced by low-income residents in accessing basic food necessities and precarious government funding for community-based programs that mitigate issues of food insecurity for marginalized residents in the same downtown neighbourhoods, pointing to emergent socio-environmental inequities in local food production and consumption within gentrifying areas.

Community gardening is often viewed in light of its value as an environmental initiative that expands the capacity of local residents to grow and share edible produce and as sites for low-income communities to offset the problems of food insecurity while, at the same time, build social connections between participants (Schmelzkopf, 2002; Wakefield, Yeudall, Taron, Reynolds, and Skinner, 2007). The production of local food to mitigate food insecurity is particularly important in urban neighbourhoods known to be 'food deserts' or 'food mirages' based upon the limited availability of affordable grocery shops and/or presence of very expensive grocery shops within a certain geographic area (Anguelovski, 2015; Breyer and Voss-Andreae, 2013). As Schmelzkopf (2002) and Martinez (2010) note in relation to community gardens in New York City, and Rosol (2012) suggests in reference to community gardening in Berlin, community gardens can be progressive spaces for community-based self-determination. They can also be progressive components of plans to reclaim urban land for ownership by communities, as discussed in Chapter 5. Conflicts over gentrification in local sustainability practices however, are also evident in the daily relational associations of community gardeners in subsistence-oriented food production, along with their relations with non-gardeners. These are demonstrated in problems over the location of community gardens and associated uses within public park spaces; for example, where gardens are sited near areas which are considered to be more 'undesirable'. For instance, in Toronto's Christie Pits park, located within a rapidly gentrifying neighbourhood, the organic community garden space and bake oven are located directly beside the basketball courts; a site for diverse youth to exercise and socialize, where recreational drug use often takes place, and an area targeted for surveillance by local government park staff and city police (Ruocco, 2010). The community bake oven is operated by park volunteers with regulatory permission from municipal government and is primarily utilized by higher income professional residents and their families. The oven and community meal nights are sponsored by Freeman Real Estate Ltd., a Toronto-based luxury residential sales agency, with proceeds from the evenings donated to local environmental projects (Public Bakeovens, 2016). In addition to this rather complex assemblage of participants – some with explicit investment in the gentrification of the surrounding neighbourhood – the close proximity of these initiatives can appear as a spatial attempt by government staff to support the coexistence of park uses through a recent municipal plan for the renewal of Christie Pits park (Brissenden and Burchell, 2015). However, it may also act as a form of social control and source of conflict where the tranquil actions of gardening and family-oriented community meals supersede the interests of those engaged with the basketball courts (Figure 3.2). This raises questions of which park uses and interests of park users are prioritized and privileged over others, and how

Figure 3.2 Photo of community garden next to basketball court, Christie Pits Park, Toronto

these different interests are negotiated within the context of environmental initiatives and park uses in neighbourhoods undergoing gentrification. Aptekar (2015) makes a similar point in connection to relational associations within community garden spaces by suggesting that,

> a community garden in a gentrifying neighbourhood is especially likely to experience conflicts over what it should look like and how people should behave in it, in addition to disagreements over access, relations with the community, and organizational structure and resources.
>
> (2015, p. 212)

Here, differing social relations of participants within community garden spaces are indicative of the larger tensions over gentrification and are demonstrated through the practices of individuals who, perhaps unknowingly, celebrate the 'benefits' of gentrification by comparison with those who assume its negative consequences.

Several recent studies on community gardens and gardening practices in the context of gentrifying urban areas have also teased out some of the problems with community gardens as micro-spaces that reflect the values of gentrifiers and are representative of environmental gentrification more broadly. These issues lie in addition to the growing incorporation of community gardens by private developers into new-build housing as attractive environmental amenities (Quastel, 2009) and the adoption of environmental design standards in urban government policies and new private sector development that promote garden spaces, as mentioned in previous chapters. Aptekar's (2015) ethnographic study of a community garden within a gentrifying district of Queens, New York City, notes contrasts in enactments of power between gardeners based on income and ethno-cultural differences. She states that,

> some immigrant and minority gardeners, including those on the steering committee, felt that it was really the handful of white professionals – branded 'the lawyers' by some – who were making the important decisions

and that,

> (T)hese leaders also ran the garden meetings, using a style of facilitation that was ostensibly participatory but resulted in exclusion of those gardeners who had difficulties with English, or did not embrace middle-class cultural norms of community building.
>
> (Aptekar, 2015, p. 215)

Aptekar continues by linking the engagement practices of white, middle-class professionals, and their access to social networks and formalized education, to the production of a broader 'green space vision' that understood the community garden to serve as a beneficial and visually attractive environmental amenity within the neighbourhood area, which was, at the same time, receiving an influx of new affluent residents (Ibid., 2015, p. 217). These situations are important for thinking about different contexts in which the involvement and needs of lower-income and/or racialized communities in community gardening are co-opted through the engagement of middle class, professionalized gentrifiers who, perhaps with socially and environmentally progressive intentions, begin to dominate these spaces through practices of privilege in decision making, network building and abilities to identify and vocalize their needs and concerns.

Differences in decision making efforts over community garden spaces are also underlined in a study of the Recovery Park plan in Detroit, a non-profit neighbourhood revitalization initiative aimed at including marginalized and low-income residents through participation in urban agriculture and formulated for a depopulated and underinvested area of the city (Draus, Roddy, and McDuffe, 2014). Draus *et al.* describe the program as one that incorporates urban farming, the creation of local employment opportunities and substance abuse rehabilitation practices as methods of community and physical infrastructure revitalization within a 200-acre district (Draus *et al.*, 2014, p. 2524). They note that while the project raises multiple benefits in relation to social inclusivity, community economic development and local food production, the initiative has also produced concerns by African-American residents about being 'weeded out' [displaced] (Draus *et al.*, 2014, p. 2536) by the presence of new urban agricultural initiatives. Drawing from ethnographic interviews, Draus *et al.* suggest that while some residents welcomed the provision of agricultural spaces, others viewed it as a problematic change that could redevelop the area while displacing the social needs and spatial presence of existing residents. In the context of Draus *et al.*'s study this occurs within a new roll out of municipal urban redevelopment policy and planning in Detroit that emphasizes greening initiatives for the rejuvenation of city areas with multiple vacant land lots as one method for priming land and attracting global investment (Clement and Kanai, 2015; Safransky, 2014). Such tensions point to emerging concerns about racialized and income-based displacement through the production of community gardening and local food cultivation, particularly in light of broader policy and planning agendas that regulate and support comprehensive urban agriculture initiatives. There are evident disjunctures between formalized policy and planning support for these initiatives and the varied and inequitable experiences of on-the-ground engagement based upon income differences, practices of racialization, and differing levels of formal education and access to social networks and resources. In this sense, community gardens, located within areas of cities that are vulnerable to gentrification or that are already gentrifying, have become interesting socio-ecological spaces for observing and contesting the enactments of gentrifiers, on-the-ground issues and concerns about physical displacement and dynamics of social inclusion and exclusion.

Conclusion

Exploring the role of gentrifiers in the production of sustainability policy and planning and in everyday and informal environmental practices provides insight into the connections between sustainability and gentrification in cities more broadly. This chapter has suggested a re-framing of who gentrifiers are in light of the adoption of environmental practices into gentrification; moving from traditional middle class 'young urban professionals' who aspire to reside in more opulent neighbourhoods and pursue more affluent lifestyle choices to middle-class professionals who incorporate environmentally friendly actions into their experiences and seek out more socially and environmentally progressive and authentic urban places, such as 'grittier' socio-economically and culturally diverse urban neighbourhoods often with a social activist history. This differs from more traditional 'artist-led gentrification' as new gentrifiers are individuals with higher incomes and professional occupations but are also interested in social and environmental issues and who can easily reconcile their engagement with certain consumerist practices (attainments of expensive technological devices, pursuits of good design, style and fashion, and 'foodie culture', and preferences for commercial spaces such as Whole Foods) with environmentally progressive actions. This is underlined through the role of urban 'bourgeois-bohemians (bo-bos)' or 'hipsters' and demonstrated through a pursuit of authenticity through social and environmental practices that cultivate nostalgic ideas of the past and romanticized, pastoral notions of urban living. While hipster or bo-bo gentrifiers do not exist in all cities and are not homogeneous, there are emergent practices and enactments that notify a shift towards their presence in sustainability initiatives within gentrifying urban areas. Leisure and commercial activities such as crafting, community gardening, bicycling and cycle repair, farmer's markets and thrifting have now become incorporated into the social relations and material landscapes of gentrification in cities.

The individual activities of gentrifiers shape urban policies and planning directives through engagement with governmental actors and participation in environmental planning initiatives such as local government planning meetings and design charrettes. Increases in creative city policies that promote sustainability initiatives, for example, aim to attract new types of middle class professionals to urban centres and attempt to reflect their values, but can also be implemented through their efforts and involvement in local planning and place-making projects. As noted in the practices of community gardening within gentrifying urban neighbourhoods, the participation of gentrifiers in sustainability activities evokes differences and tensions between the needs and visions of middle class gentrifiers for garden spaces and the engagement and needs of low-income residents and/or racialized communities, and which emerge in varied abilities to access resources, build networks of support, and participate in decision making. Existing and emerging environmental spaces in cities, such as community gardens, are increasingly important sites where the connections between sustainability policies, planning strategies and implementation and on-the-ground dynamics between residents are experienced and the politics and enactments of gentrification take place. These contexts also underline spaces of importance for environmental justice work in relation to the challenges of displacement and eviction caused by gentrification. As such, these same types of environmental spaces can be sites of local resistance to gentrification, where the power imbalances instigated by gentrifiers can also act as reflexive and transformative moments for communities that are threatened by exclusionary and direct forms of displacement. These situations will be discussed in Chapter 5 through an exploration of community-based sustainability initiatives that have formed in resistance to gentrification and emergent challenges of affordability in urban neighbourhoods, and the possibilities that these actions and spaces offer as an alternative.

References

Agyeman, J. (2008). 'Toward a "just" sustainability?' *Continuum – Journal of Media and Cultural Studies*, *22*(6), 751–757.
Agyeman, J., Bullard, R., and Evans, B. (eds) (2003). *Just Sustainabilities: Development in an Unequal World*. Cambridge, MA: MIT Press.
Agyeman, J., Schlosberg, D., Craven, L., and Matthews, C. (2016). Trends and Directions in Environmental Justice: From Inequity to Everyday Life, Community, and Just Sustainabilities. *Annual Review of Environment and Resources*, *41*, 321–340.
Anguelovski, I. (2015). Alternative food provision conflicts in cities: Contesting food privilege, injustice, and whiteness in Jamaica Plain, Boston. *Geoforum*, *58*, 184–194.
Aptekar, S. (2015). Visions of Public Space: Reproducing and Resisting Social Hierarchies in a Community Garden. *Sociological Forum*, *30*(1), 209–227. doi:10.1111/socf.12152
Armisen, F., and Brownstein, C. (2012). *Portlandia: A guide for visitors* (1st edn). New York: Grand Central Publishing.
Atkinson, R., and Bridge, G. (eds) (2005). *Gentrification in the Global Context: The new urban colonialism*. London and New York: Routledge.
Bendix, A. (2016). Are trader Joe's and whole foods gentrifying neighborhoods? Retrieved from www.citylab.com/housing/2016/01/whole-foods-grocery-store-gentrification/427020/
Bourdieu, P. (1977). *Outline of a theory of practice*. Cambridge, UK: Cambridge University Press.
Breyer, B., & and Voss-Andreae, A. (2013). Food mirages: Geographic and economic barriers to healthful food access in Portland, Oregon. *Health & Place*, *24*, 131–139.
Bridge, G. (2001). Bourdieu, rational action and the time-space strategy of gentrification. *Transactions of the Institute of British Geographers*, *26*(2), 205–216. https://doi.org/10.1111/1475–5661.00015

Bridge, G. (2006). Perspectives on cultural capital and the neighbourhood. *Urban Studies*, *43*(4), 719–730. https://doi.org/10.1080/00420980600597392

Brissenden, A., and Burchell, B. (2015). Christie pits renewal set to begin. *Gleaner Community Press*. Retrieved from http://gleanernews.ca/wp-content/uploads/2015/07/Page11Christie-Pts_Communit.jpg

Brooks, D. (2000). *Bobos in paradise: The new upper class and how they got there.* New York: Simon and Schuster.

Brown, J. (2015). Home from home? Locational choices of international 'creative class' workers. *European Planning Studies*, *23*(12), 2336–2355.

Brown, P. (2016, January 26). Is it a Tea House or Public House? *Morning Advertiser.co.uk*. Retrieved from www.morningadvertiser.co.uk/Drinks/Beer/Stoke-Newington-Tea-House-wins-over-hipster-worrying-locals

Budd, W., Lovrich, N., Pierce, J. C., and Chamberlain, B. (2008). Cultural sources of variations in US urban sustainability attributes. *Cities*, *25*(5), 257–267. https://doi.org/10.1016/j.cities.2008.05.001

Bullard, R. (1990). *Dumping in dixie: Race, class, and environmental quality.* New York: Westview Press.

Bullard, R. (ed.). (1999). *Confronting environmental racism: Voices from the grassroots.* New York: South End Press.

Butler, T., and Robson, G. (2001). Social capital, gentrification and neighbourhood change in London: A comparison of three south London neighbourhoods. *Urban Studies*, *38*(12), 2145–2162. https://doi.org/10.1080/00420980120087090

Catungal, J. P., Leslie, D., and Hii, Y. (2009). Geographies of displacement in the creative city: The case of liberty village, Toronto. *Urban Studies*, *46*(5–6), 1095–1114. https://doi.org/10.1177/0042098009103856

Choi, D. (2009, August 26). Are you a hipster, a bobo or a bananowe dziecko? Retrieved from www.cafebabel.co.uk/society/article/are-you-a-hipster-a-bobo-or-a-bananowe-dziecko.html

Clement, D., and Kanai, M. (2015). The detroit future city: How pervasive neoliberal urbanism exacerbates racialized spatial injustice. *American Behavioral Scientist*, *59*(3), 369–385.

Cohen, D. (2015). Grounding mobile policies: Ad hoc networks and the creative city in Bandung, Indonesia. *Singapore Journal of Tropical Geography*, *36*(1), 23–37. https://doi.org/10.1111/sjtg.12090

Cowen, D. (2006). *Hipster urbanism* (September/October). Retrieved from www.socialistproject.ca/relay/relay13_hipster.pdf

Cretella, A., and Buenger, M. S. (2016). Food as creative city politics in the city of Rotterdam. *Cities*, *51*, 1–10. https://doi.org/10.1016/j.cities.2015.12.001

Desfor, G., and Keil, R. (2004). *Nature and the city: Making environmental policy in Toronto and Los Angeles.* Tucson, AZ: University of Arizona Press.

Doig, W. (2012). Whole Foods is coming? Time to buy. Retrieved from www.salon.com/2012/05/05/whole_foods_is_coming_time_to_buy/

Ferrier, M. (2014, June 21). The end of the hipster: How flat caps and beards stopped being so cool. *Guardian*. Retrieved from https://www.theguardian.com/fashion/2014/jun/22/end-of-the-hipster-flat-caps-and-beards

Florida, R. (2002). *The rise of the creative class: And how it's transforming work, leisure, community and everyday life.* New York: Basic Books.

Florida, R. (2005). *Cities and the creative class.* Routledge.

Fowler, E. P., and Hartmann, F. (2002). City environmental policy: Connecting the dots. In E. P. Fowler and D. Siegel (eds), *Urban policy issues: Canadian perspectives*. Toronto: Oxford University Press.

Gordon, D. J. (2016). Lament for a network? Cities and networked climate governance in Canada. *Environment and Planning C: Government and Policy, 34*(3), 529–545. https://doi.org/10.1177/0263774X15614675

Greenspan, E. (2013, December 17). A whole foods grows in Brooklyn. *New Yorker*. Retrieved from www.newyorker.com/business/currency/a-whole-foods-grows-in-brooklyn

Harris, A. (2011). Art and gentrification: Pursuing the urban pastoral in Hoxton, London. *Transactions of the Institute of British Geographers, 37*, 226–241.

Hutton, T. A. (2009). *The new economy of the inner city: Restructuring, regeneration and dislocation in the 21st century metropolis*. Routledge.

Isin, E. F. (2002). *Being political: Genealogies of citizenship*. University of Minnesota Press.

Johnson Gardner. (2007). *An assessment of the marginal impact of urban amenities on residential pricing*. Portland, OR. Retrieved from www.reconnectingamerica. org/resource-center/browse-research/2007/an-assessment-of-the-marginal-impact-of-urban-amenities-on-residential-pricing/

Kato, Y. (2013). Not Just the Price of Food: Challenges of an Urban Agriculture Organization in Engaging Local Residents. *Sociological Inquiry, 83*(3): 369–391. doi:10.1111/soin.12008

Kern, L. (2012). Connecting embodiment, emotion and gentrification: An exploration through the practice of yoga in Toronto. *Emotion, Space and Society, 5*(1), 27–35. https://doi.org/10.1016/j.emospa.2011.01.003

Kern, L. (2015). From toxic wreck to crunchy chic: Environmental gentrification through the body. *Environment and Planning D: Society and Space, 33*(1), 67–83.

Kohn, M. (2010). Toronto's distillery district: Consumption and nostalgia in a post-industrial landscape. *Globalizations, 7*(3), 359–369.

Krueger, R., and Buckingham, S. (2009). Creative-city scripts, economic development, and sustainability. *Geographical Review, 99*(1), iii–xii.

Krueger, R., and Buckingham, S. (2012). Towards a 'Consensual' urban politics? Creative planning, urban sustainability and regional development. *International Journal of Urban and Regional Research, 36*(3), 486–503. https://doi.org/10.1111/ j.1468–2427.2011.01073.x

Landry, C. (2000). *The Creative City: A toolkit for urban innovators*. London: Earthscan Publications.

Lederman, J. (2015). Urban fads and consensual fictions: Creative, sustainable, and competitive city policies in Buenos Aires. *City & Community, 14*(1), 47–67. https://doi.org/10.1111/cico.12095

Ley, D. (1996). *The new middle class and the remaking of the central city*. Oxford: Oxford University Press. Retrieved from http://link.library.utoronto.ca/eir/EIRdetail. cfm?Resources__ID=1045679&T=F

Ley, D. (2003). Artists, aestheticisation and the field of gentrification. *Urban Studies, 40*(12), 2527–2544.

Long, J. (2016). Constructing the narrative of the sustainability fix: Sustainability, social justice and representation in Austin, TX. *Urban Studies, 53*(1), 149–172. https:// doi.org/10.1177/0042098014560501

Machor, J. L. (1987). *Pastoral cities: Urban ideals and the symbolic landscape of America*. Madison, WI: University of Wisconsin Press.

Marchiony, V. (2014). *The colorblind hipster: Deconstructing a cultural identity in crisis*. Journalism Honors Progam Thesis, Temple University. Retrieved from http://honors.temple.edu/about/students/profile/921

Martinez, M. (2010). *Power at the roots: Gentrification, community gardens, and the Puerto Ricans of the Lower East Side*. MD: Lexington Books.

Mathews, V., and Picton, R. M. (2014). Intoxifying gentrification: Brew pubs and the geography of post-industrial heritage. *Urban Geography*, *35*(3), 337–356. https://doi.org/10.1080/02723638.2014.887298

May, J., Wills, J., Datta, K., Evans, Y., Herbert, J., and McIlwaine, C. (2007). Keeping London working: Global cities, the British state and London's new migrant division of labour. *Transactions of the Institute of British Geographers*, *32*(2), 151–167. https://doi.org/10.1111/j.1475–5661.2007.00241.x

McLean, H. (2014). Digging into the creative city: A feminist critique. *Antipode*, *46*(3), 669–690.

McLean, H. (2016). Hos in the garden: Staging and resisting neoliberal creativity. *Environment and Planning D: Society and Space*, 263775816654915. https://doi.org/10.1177/0263775816654915

McLean, H., and Rahder, B. (2013). The exclusionary politics of creative communities: The case of Kensington Market pedestrian sundays. *Canadian Journal of Urban Research*, *22*(1), 90–110.

McLean, H., Rankin, K., and Kamizaki, K. (2015). Inner-suburban neighbourhoods, activist research, and the Social Space of the Commercial Street. *ACME: An International E-Journal for Critical Geographies*, *14*(4), 1283–1308.

Miewald, C., and McCann, E. (2014). Foodscapes and the Geographies of Poverty: Sustenance, Strategy, and Politics in an Urban Neighborhood. *Antipode*, *46*(2), 537–556.

Miller, B. (2014, November 3). The Whole Foods effect: What the specialty grocer means for development. Retrieved from https://urbanful.org/2014/11/03/whole-foods-effect/

O'Neil, L. (2014). 'Lumbersexual' trend thrusts rugged hipsters into men's fashion spotlight – Your Community. Retrieved from www.cbc.ca/newsblogs/your community/2014/11/lumbersexual-trend-thrusts-rugged-hipsters-into-mens-fashion-spotlight.html

Peck, J. (2005). Struggling with the creative class. *International Journal of Urban and Regional Research*, *29*(4), 740–770.

Peck, J. (2012). Recreative city: Amsterdam, vehicular ideas and the adaptive spaces of creativity policy. *International Journal of Urban and Regional Research*, *36*(3), 462–485.

Peck, J., and Tickell, A. (2002). Neoliberalizing Space. *Antipode*, *34*(3), 380–404. https://doi.org/10.1111/1467–8330.00247

Podmore, J. (1998). (Re) reading the 'loft living' habitus in Montreal's inner city. *International Journal of Urban and Regional Research*, *22*(2), 283–302.

Public Bakeovens. (2016). *Christie Pits Park Bake Oven* www.publicbakeovens. ca/wiki/wiki.php?n=ChristiePits.FrontPage

Pulido, L. (2000). Rethinking environmental racism: White privilege and urban development in southern California. *Annals of the Association of American Geographers*, *90*(1), 12–40.

Quastel, N. (2009). Political Ecologies of Gentrification. *Urban Geography, 30*(7), 694–725. https://doi.org/10.2747/0272–3638.30.7.694

Rankin, K. N., and McLean, H. (2015). Governing the commercial streets of the city: New terrains of disinvestment and gentrification in Toronto's inner suburbs. *Antipode, 47*(1), 216–239.

Recovery Park. (2014). www.recoverypark.org

Rose, D. (1999). Urban hierarchies and the changing characteristics of 'urban professionals' in Toronto and Montreal: Between convergence and divergence. *Canadian Journal of Regional Science, 22*(1), 2.

Rosol, M. (2012). Community volunteering as neoliberal strategy? *Green Space Production in Berlin Antipode, 44*(1), 239–257.

Ruocco, J. (2010). Police search for gunman in Bloor Street double shooting. *National Post* October 20, 2010. Retrieved from http://news.nationalpost.com/posted-toronto/police-search-for-gunman-in-bloor-street-double-shooting

Safransky, S. (2014). Greening the urban frontier: *Race, property and resettlement in Detroit Geoforum, 56*, 237–248.

Sassen, S. (2000). *Cities in a world economy.* Thousand Oaks, CA: Pine Forge Press.

Sassen, S. (2001). *The Global City: New York, London, Tokyo.* Princeton University Press.

Schmelzkopf, K. (2002). Incommensurability, land use, and the right to space: Community gardens in New York City. *Urban Geography, 23*(4), 323–343.

Shiva, V. (2005). *Earth Democracy: Justice, Sustainability, and Peace South End Press*, New York.

Slocum, R. (2007). Whiteness, space and alternative food practice. *Geoforum, 38*(3), 520–533.

Smith, L. C. (2012). The 'Whole Foods' paradox. Food sovereignty, eco-iconography, and urban indigenous discourse. *ELOHI. Peuples Indigènes et Environnement*, (2), 59–77.

Spinks, R. (2015, March 2). Long-time east Londoners on Hackney hipsters: 'They need a humour injection'. *Guardian.* Retrieved from www.theguardian.com/cities/2015/mar/02/east-london-hackney-hipsters-humour-locals

The Economist. (2013, August 9). Gentrification blues. *Economist.* Retrieved from www.economist.com/blogs/blighty/2013/08/londons-demography

Timm, J. (2014, March 22). *Millennials: We care more about the environment.* Retrieved from www.msnbc.com/morning-joe/millennials-environment-climate-change

Wakefield, S., Yeudall, F., Taron, C., Reynolds, J., and Skinner, A. (2007). Growing Urban Health: *Community gardening in South-East Toronto Health Promotion International, 22*(2), 92–101.

Wetherall, T. (2013, October 31). *London's hot clapton neighborhood under the radar.* Retrieved from www.10best.com/interests/travel-features/londons-hot-clapton-neighborhood-under-the-radar/

Whole Foods Market. (2016). *Community giving in east London.* Retrieved from www.wholefoodsmarket.com/service/community-giving-16

Zukin, S. (2008). Consuming authenticity: From outposts of difference to means of exclusion. *Cultural Studies, 22*(5), 724–748. https://doi.org/10.1080/09502380802245985

Zukin, S., Trujillo, V., Frase, P., Jackson, D., Recuber, T., and Walker, A. (2009). New retail capital and neighborhood change: Boutiques and gentrification in New York City. *City & Community*, *8*(1), 47–64.

5 Searching for equity and justice in sustainability in the gentrifying city

Introduction

Alternatives to the aforementioned connections between sustainability policies, planning initiatives and gentrification are emerging in response to concerns about the everyday impacts of gentrification. This chapter addresses community-level organizational practices that either implicitly or explicitly challenge these connections as a way to generate new understandings of social and environmental equity and justice. Discussions about alternative practices that counter gentrification have been notably absent from gentrification scholarship (Slater, 2009). Yet, as Slater underlines, researchers must reorient gentrification research towards social justice issues and a reframing of traditional understandings of property and its ownership and exchange (2009, p. 307). This suggestion widens a space for the consideration and integration of scholar-activist and community-based activist perspectives that challenges the threats and outcomes caused by gentrification in cities. Community-based organizations (CBOs) and resident activists are often on the front lines of addressing gentrification in cities and are left to enact the service and care work of tending to its outcomes and impacts on individuals and families, such as physical eviction from housing, to the search for free legal services, childcare and affordable housing alternatives. Such work has been well documented in research that identifies the important role of CBOs in providing care for communities that are facing complex problems caused by gentrification. Often, this literature has demonstrated how community-based strategies to resist gentrification pressures can include different practices that aim to defy displacement or which encourage the community control of land and housing stock as practices of de-commodification (Blomley, 2004; DeFillippis, 2004; Gibson-Graham, Cameron, and Healy, 2013; London Tenants Federation, Lees, Just Space, and Southwark Notes Archive Group, 2014; Medoff and Sklar, 1999; Rameau, 2008; Robinson, 1996).

Some urban CBOs have also created explicit mandates to resist gentrification through street-level direct action protests and programs to highlight the struggles of low-income and often racialized communities facing eviction and displacement in light of rising housing prices, land privatization, and increasing land values in their neighbourhoods and cities (cf. Alternatives for Community and Environment, 2015; Class War, 2015; Eviction Free San Francisco, 2016; Ontario Coalition Against Poverty, 2016; Rose, n.d.; Serve the People/Servir al Pueblo Los Angeles, 2016; Seminary of the Street, n.d.). In response to environmental and other forms of gentrification, some CBOs work outside the parameters of or seek to emancipate urban sustainability initiatives from the directives of government policy and planning in order to resist gentrification threats and displacement issues. Other CBOs collaborate with different levels of government and/or with the support of private philanthropic organizations to plan and implement local projects that challenge gentrification. Asking the question of how community-based urban sustainability initiatives can challenge gentrification creates room for insertions of social and environmental (socio-environmental) equity and justice approaches into projects that might otherwise be vulnerable to co-optation by gentrifiers, as observed in Chapter 4, or which serve to augment rather than resist gentrification. The following sections explore urban Community land trusts (CLTs), defined as land held in trust by a CBO for purposes of community management and stewardship, and eco-village organizations as social and environmental practices that incorporate equity and justice concerns and mitigate the trajectory of gentrification in several ways. While not all CLTs and eco-village organizations have equity and justice mandates, an explicit focus on the de-commodification of land and housing in the case of CLTs and engagement in small-scale, subsistence-based environmental practices by urban eco-villages provide alternatives for urban living within the context of the wider profit-oriented urban development and consumerist logic of gentrification. As intentional communities, these two approaches are aspirational initiatives for countering gentrification at the local level; CLTs and eco-villages are intended to be discursive, relational and material spaces where people are able to interact and share ideas about emergent community issues as well as solutions (Chitewere, 2010; Ergas, 2010; Litfin, 2014; Pickerill, 2016; Thompson, 2015).

A study of CLTs and eco-villages explores how these initiatives move beyond being societal responses to the outcomes of gentrification by acting as preemptive spaces before the start of or in the early stages of gentrification. This suggests a usefulness for their study in urban planning and possibilities for their implementation in cities across the globe that are experiencing different levels and forms of gentrification. CLTs have emerged over the past several decades in cities in the United States, and more recently in Canada, Australia and the United Kingdom, as well as in Kenya (Midheme and Mouleart, 2013). Eco-village communities have had a more extensive global reach through a formalized non-governmental organization, Global Ecovillage Network (GEN), that links together (as of 2014), approximately 400 eco-villages in urban and rural locations in Africa, North America, Latin America, Europe and Asia, and liaises with regional network organizations (GEN, 2014; Litfin, 2014). CLT and eco-village practices are not complete solutions to the threats and outcomes of gentrification and, like other locally oriented sustainability initiatives, they are vulnerable to becoming absorbed into neighbourhood-level gentrification processes through the participation of environmentally conscious gentrifiers or as positive externalities that may work to enhance property values and cultivate a socially and environmentally progressive image of a particular area. Through examples of urban CLTs and eco-villages that have formed with an aim to resist and lessen the impacts of gentrification and which implicitly resist gentrification in everyday activities that occur in these spaces, the following sections examine the possibilities for resistance to gentrification and for building social and environmental equity and justice through community-based land stewardship.

A central aspect of the role of CLT organizations in countering gentrification is the emphasis on the de-commodification of land through its removal from the speculative property market. CLT organizations hold title to a single land lot or parcels of land, acquired through donation by governments or private owners or purchased by the CLT organization for lower than market cost. Land can also be leased to a CLT organization on long-term (approximately 99 years) contracts, which is often the case for government-owned land. The objectives of the community-based ownership of land are to capture land value at the time the land is acquired in order to retain land affordability and to mitigate profit attainment from any future resale of the land (Aird, 2010; Davis, 2010; Crabtree, 2010, 2014; Sungu-Erylimaz and Greenstein, 2007). Some urban eco-villages, such as the Vauban eco-village in Frieburg, Germany and the Los Angeles eco-village that are discussed in this chapter, use a CLT model in order to attain and manage the community ownership of land. Both CLTs and eco-villages can be viewed as engagements with the commoning of urban land; as ways to create a different vision for urban space through a commoning of private property, defined by Gibson-Graham *et al.* as a method of allowing 'non-owners to have access to and use of privately owned property' and to share private property in ways that benefit a wider community (2013, p. 154). Additionally, the relational connections between community residents that are inscribed in the physical spaces of these initiatives suggest an attempt to build a sense of commons in terms of collectivized purpose and actions (cf. Caffentzis and Federici, 2014; Federici, 2010; Susser and Tonnelat, 2013). In these ways, they are counter-normative approaches to the planning and governance of the current and future use of urban land (Bunce, 2016; Thompson, 2015). Madden and Marcuse suggest that CLTs are 'the most prominent alternative tenures' in current use (Madden and Marcuse, 2016, p. 209). As noted in the context of the Dudley Street land trust in Boston, CLTs advance the ideas of community-based development that strengthen connections between residents and social and environmental activities within a neighbourhood area without producing gentrification and outcomes of displacement. Community ownership of land has helped to augment an objective of 'development without displacement' in the Dudley Street initiative

(Louie, 2016; Medoff and Sklar, 1994). The possibilities of CLT and eco-village organizations lies in their contributions to addressing social, environmental and spatial inequities and injustices at the neighbourhood level and the provision of sustainability activities, including sustainable land stewardship practices. The following examples of CLTs in Boston, London and Toronto focus on the ways in which these particular CLTs have formed with an objective of countering gentrification while at the same time producing new social and environmental spaces on community owned land. Through these examples, the challenges of acquiring community land in light of gentrification in these cities are also discussed. The Vauban eco-village in Germany and the Los Angeles eco-village, as intentional communities that have cultivated land ownership through a land trust model, demonstrate the connection between social and environmental practices in promoting visions of equity and justice. At the heart of these community-based solutions to gentrification is a notion of collective rights to the preservation of land and rights over equitable, sustainable land stewardship. This is particularly important in light of the challenges that gentrification causes for existing residents who struggle to afford living necessities, and the loss of the right to remain in urban areas that are no longer affordable. Alongside the production of equitable social practices in cities, these initiatives suggest important contexts for the future of sustainability initiatives in cities.

Urban community land trusts

CLTs are non-governmental, non-profit organizations that acquire donated or purchased land within a community area, the spatial boundaries of which are defined by the organization's members. The organization identifies uses for the land based upon collaborative discussions with organizational membership and local residents. The most prominent use of CLT land over the years has been for the provision of affordable housing, in relation to community needs and gentrification pressures, but more recent uses include the presence of social enterprises aimed at bolstering community economic development, and community gardens and urban farms for local food production (Yuen, 2014; Yuen and Rosenberg, 2013). CLTs hold land in trust for community stewardship – ideally with the goal of the land being perpetually in trust for a community – and place legal restrictions on the resale of the land and buildings.[1] The resale restrictions act to capture land value and prevent profit generation from future increased land valuations and building prices in the surrounding area (Davis, 2007). Building stock on the land can be owned by individuals that are connected to the CLT organization, however, the separation of land ownership from building stock on the land is embedded in a ground lease, created by the CLT, that delineates the organization as the land owner and prevents or mitigates future profit making upon the resale of housing by the owner. It also ensures the limitation or absence of rental increases for buildings owned by the CLT (Aird, 2010; Angotti, 2007; Bunce, Khimani, Sungu-Erylimaz, and Earle, 2013; Crabtree, 2010, 2014; Davis, 2007, 2010; Gray, 2008; Greenstein and Sungu-Eryilmaz, 2005; Meehan, 2014).

The modern origins of CLTs[2] are based in community organizing by African-American tenant farmers in the southern United States as part of the civil rights movement and the activism of civil rights advocates Slater King (a cousin of Martin Luther King, Jr.) and Bob Swann. Community ownership of land and holding land in trust were viewed to be acts of resistance against racism and the lack of available opportunities to access farming land by African-American tenant labourers (Curtin and Bocarsly, 2010; Davis, 2010). The first CLT, New Communities, Inc., was created in 1967 through the efforts of King and Swann in rural Georgia and operated as a way for African-American farmers to collectively own and steward approximately 5000 acres of agricultural land (Davis, 2010; White, 1992). After gaining importance in rural areas, the first urban CLT was created in Cincinnati in the early 1980s, in a low-income, primarily African-American, inner-city neighbourhood of Cincinnati, as a way to protect land for community purposes in light of public sector disinvestment (Ibid., 2010). More broadly, urban CLTs in the United States have most frequently organized as community-based development practices for local residents and for the biophysical revitalization of urban neighbourhoods (Angotti, 2007; DeFilippis, 2004; Thaden and Lowe, 2014). In American cities, CLT organizations have been established in low-income and racialized urban neighbourhoods with patterns of public sector disinvestment alongside the presence of neglectful and/or absentee private landowners. They have also formed as an anti-gentrification strategy in order to gain community control over land, provide affordable housing and other community-oriented services and programs on the land, and combat land inflation in areas on the cusp of gentrification (Davis, 2010; Medoff and Sklar, 1994). An increase of CLT organizations in cities in the United States since the 1980s underlines the popularity of their adoption likely in relation to the neoliberal retraction of government funding for social housing provision and the off-loading of responsibility for social and community-level program delivery to non-governmental CBOs over the past several decades. A survey of urban CLTs in the United States, conducted in 2007, noted the existence of approximately 250 CLT organizations in American cities (Sungu-Eryilmaz and Greenstein, 2007). Alongside this increase has been a growing capacity of regional and national level networks, such as the National CLT Network (2016), that have facilitated funding and educational support for CLT development and growth in both rural and urban locations across the United States. A similar emergence of CLTs in Britain is noted, with approximately 150 CLT organizations counted in England and Wales and found in cities such as Liverpool, Bristol, Leeds and London (Bunce, 2016; Moore and McKee, 2012; Thompson, 2015). There has been considerable policy mobility and idea transfer between CLT advocates, networks, and organizations in Britain and the United States, in particular, with more peripheral interest in the use of CLTs in Canada, Australia and Kenya. While not all CLTs espouse an activist mandate and simply act to provide community services based upon identified needs of local residents, other CLTs take a decidedly more activist-oriented approach to their development and operation with a focus on raising community and broader public awareness about problems of accessing affordable land and housing and emphasizing individual and community-based empowerment, in keeping with the civil rights and access to land origins of CLT use.

Dudley street neighborhood initiative, Boston

One of the more long-standing and significant urban CLTs in the United States is the Dudley Street organization founded in the 1980s in the Dudley Triangle area of the Roxbury neighbourhood in south Boston. The Dudley Street Neighborhood Initiative (DSNI) formed in 1984 as a community development organization with the purpose of addressing issues of private property neglect and abandonment, regular occurrences of arson fires and waste disposal on abandoned privately owned lots and a biophysical and social landscape of government neglect and redlining by financial institutions, in a largely African American, African (Cape Verdean), and Hispanic community (Holding Ground, 1996; Louie, 2016; Medoff and Sklar, 1994). DSNI formed Dudley Neighbors, Inc. (DNI) as a CLT organization in 1988 after several years of social and environmental justice activism and initiating community development projects. Louie (2016) notes that DNI was formed in response to the challenges of pursuing community development work in light of the levels of privately owned abandoned and vacant land and lack of community resident land ownership. She observes that the CLT model was chosen to foster resident land ownership and to promote a 'development without displacement' approach so as to 'prevent families from being priced out as they organized to improve their neighborhood' (2016, p. 2). She writes that, '[in] the Dudley Triangle, almost half of the land area – 30 acres – lay vacant and filled with garbage. . . . (M)ore than 60 per cent of the owners lived outside the neighborhood' (Louie, 2016, p. 8). Following the completion of a DSNI and resident-led neighbourhood planning process for the Dudley area that resulted in a planning document, *The Dudley Street Neighborhood Initiative Revitalization Plan: A Comprehensive Community Controlled Strategy*, the formation of DNI as a separate urban redevelopment corporation allowed for an ability on the part of DSNI to lobby the City of Boston and the Boston Redevelopment Authority to obtain the use of eminent domain legislation (otherwise known as expropriation or compulsory purchase) to take over title to abandoned privately owned land lots and amass a land inventory. This was done through an activist campaign entitled 'Take a Stand, Own the Land', which, as Louie (2016) and Medoff and Sklar (1994) note, also had the endorsement of the mayor of

Boston who wanted to secure the on-going political support of African-American residents. In August 1988, DNI formally incorporated and was granted the right to use the mechanism of eminent domain to legally expropriate and acquire title to land in the Dudley Triangle. In doing so, DNI became the first non-governmental, non-profit community organization in the United States to be granted permission to use eminent domain and remains the only CBO to have received this authority (Louie, 2016; Taylor, 1995).

The eminent domain authority allowed for DNI to embark on land accruement within a 60-acre neighborhood radius (Loh, 2015) to be held in trust by the CLT organization. Louie (2016) notes that the use of eminent domain occurred through the formation of a committee consisting of municipal government representatives and DSNI members to identify which public land in the area would be transferred to DNI sold to DNI at $1 per public land parcel, and which privately owned lots would be expropriated. Second, the securement of a $2 million loan from a private philanthropic organization, the Ford Foundation, was used to financially compensate landowners following the expropriation of private land and was repaid by DNI in the early 1990s. Since the late 1980s, DNI has accrued 32 acres of land under CLT ownership and has collaborated with affordable housing developers to produce, as of 2016, 225 affordable home ownership, co-operative and rental housing units on much of this land, with assistance from government agencies and departments, municipal planners and affordable housing developers (DNI, 2016; Louie, 2016). The sustainability of affordable housing built on land owned by DNI has been noted to be a reason why municipal government officials, as well as federal government organizations such as the Fannie Mae Foundation, have suggested that the Dudley neigbourhood has been able to successfully balance gentrification threats with a large presence of homeownership by low and moderate income residents, secured through ground lease contracts with DNI that maintain housing affordability (Louie, 2016; Wyly, Cooke, Hammel, Holloway, and Hudson, 2000). The ownership of land by DNI captures its value and de-commodifies it by maintaining it in long-term trust for the community, despite rescent rising land values in the Roxbury neighbourhood (Louie, 2016) and broader pressures of gentrification in traditionally low-income, culturally diverse Boston neighbourhoods, such as Jamaica Plain.

As part of the community organizing work of DSNI – before the formation of the land trust and during the accruement of vacant lots through land expropriation – the remediation of vacant lots occurred through the organization's environmental justice campaign, 'Don't Dump on Us'. The campaign focused on engaging residents in clearing refuse from vacant lots and roadways, lobbying the City of Boston to eradicate non-municipal, non-licensed waste transfer stations from the neighborhood and improve municipal waste collection services for residents (Medoff and Sklar, 1994). Medoff and Sklar note that these efforts were also considered by DSNI as a method of community empowerment for residents who, in community meetings with municipal government representatives, identified how they felt that the neighborhood had been unfairly targeted and that local government had '[given] poor neighborhoods like Dudley poor service' (1994, p. 70). The campaign was successful in gaining an active response by government officials through more strenuous provision of municipal disposal and collection service and cultivating more long-term relationships with local government public facilities workers and planners, among other government officials, in the development of the community-directed neighborhood plan and following the formation of the CLT. Initiatives to enhance the neighborhood's environmental landscape have focused on cleaning up and redesigning the neighborhood park as a community-oriented space through a project that was launched in 1991, and more recently, the creation of community gardens and children's playgrounds on land owned by DNI (DNI., 2016). Louie (2016) notes the importance of the relationship between DNI's operation of the CLT and DSNI's broader community-based development and planning initiatives, and suggests that this has been very apparent in the creation of resident-led urban agriculture projects for local food production. Writing about one of these initiatives, she notes that,

In order to contribute to economic activity and access to affordable healthy food, DSNI built a 10,000-square-foot community greenhouse by reclaiming a contaminated garage site that had been abandoned. Its partner, The Food Project, a land-and food-based youth development nonprofit, manages the greenhouse and farms 1.5 acres on the land trust.

(Louie, 2016, p. 16)

Two more recent CLT projects have emerged in Toronto and London that reflect the more activist origins and leanings of the Dudley Street CLT initiative. Both CLTs are notable for their shared characteristics of being social justice-oriented organizations with a focus on acquiring land and community benefits for low-income residents in light of quite intensive gentrification pressures in Toronto and London. The Parkdale Neighbourhood Land Trust (PNLT) and the East London Community Land Trust (ELCLT) each emphasize participatory governance through a broad membership base of individuals from the local area and facilitate community engagement processes in order to identify community needs for land, in keeping with the common method of organizational governance for CLTs in the American context (Davis, 2010; Sungu-Erylimaz and Greenstein, 2007). Like Dudley Street, both CLT organizations emphasize a linking together of social and environmental practices, primarily through the creation of new productive green spaces and attention to sustainable design, in their approach to land stewardship and share common concern about increasing social equity and justice in the production of urban space.

Parkdale neighbourhood land trust, Toronto

Parkdale, located in the western central area of Toronto and one of Toronto's older neighbourhoods, has transitioned over the past two decades from being a community consisting largely of low-income residents and new refugees and immigrants, into an area that has attracted urban professionals and, more recently, 'hipster' gentrifiers searching for 'authentic' neighbourhood experiences. Slater (2004), in a detailed study of gentrification in Parkdale, noted that gentrification in the area emerged in the mid-1980s as property values rose in other central Toronto neighbourhoods and middle class professionals began to move into Parkdale with a focus on converting inexpensive Victorian-era duplexes or triplexes, frequently used for single-room tenancies, into single family homes. The low property costs suggested that new gentrifiers bought housing with the idea 'that property values [in Parkdale] would eventually rise as the neighbourhood's profile rose' (Slater, 2004, p. 312). The socially diverse aspects of Parkdale, as a residential area for new immigrants and refugees, a neighbourhood for artists in need of inexpensive housing and studio spaces and political activists, as well as an affordable area for out-patients from a nearby mental health and addiction treatment hospital, has given the neighbourhood an eclectic character that became an attractive feature for gentrification by artists and more progressively minded middle class residents (Slater, 2004). Additionally, Toronto's municipal government has implemented regulatory enactments to mitigate multi-unit and single-room occupancy rental housing as forms of inexpensive accommodation, which has limited the availability of affordable housing (Hennebury, 2016; Mazer and Rankin, 2011; Slater, 2004; Whitzman and Slater, 2006; Whitzman, 2009). Parkdale's gentrification has largely been impacted by the presence of what Zukin (1989) has more broadly called 'creeping gentrification', which has been caused by new-build, market-oriented and mixed-use residential and commercial districts such as the nearby Liberty Village (Catungal, Leslie, and Hii, 2009) and the presence of older gentrified neighbourhoods in close proximity.

Gentrification within Parkdale has largely occurred in the residential streets in the north end of the neighbourhood, with this area now inhabited by professionalized, middle-to-high income families. This transformation has increasingly encroached upon the southern area of the neighbourhood, known as South Parkdale, where the majority of multi-story apartment towers with rental accommodation and remaining duplex and triplex housing arrangements geared toward lower-income residents are located. Recently, gentrification has also emerged in the form of 'hipster' gentrification, with affluent but edgy gentrifiers moving into Parkdale in order to seek out proximity to the grittier elements of neighbourhood and local, independent, DIY culture. There has been notable increase in independent coffee shops, trendy and expensive restaurants with locally sourced food, craft workshops and bicycle sales and repair shops, among other types of independent commercial activities, that have transformed neighbourhood thoroughfares. In contrast to gentrification in Parkdale, however, the area is considered to be one of the few remaining places in downtown Toronto where new immigrants and refugees can access affordable housing and other settlement services (Logan and Murdie, 2016). Logan and Murdie's recent study of newcomer settlement in Parkdale demonstrates that 52 per cent of Parkdale residents were born outside of Canada and 71 per cent of the neighbourhood's recent newcomers are from South Asian countries (Logan and Murdie, 2016, p. 100). Recently, a large community of Tibetan refugees has settled in South Parkdale with a need for refugee settlement services and programs (Ibid., 2016).

Within this context, the PLNT formed through the 'Parkdale People's Economy' project, a research initiative that started in 2010 and was based at the Parkdale Activity Recreation Centre (PARC), a community activity and social program centre located in South Parkdale. The project first developed as a collaborative research study between students in a University of Toronto urban planning course and PARC staff that examined the impacts of gentrification on local food security (Richer *et al.*, 2010). The study recommended, among other ideas, the establishment of a CLT as a way to 'hold land in trust for the community of Parkdale, and rent it to community agencies, local businesses and residents for a variety of uses that meet the community's needs' (Ibid., 2010, p. ii). The report identified five suggestions for the creation of a CLT that would focus more on commercial and other alternate uses instead of affordable housing: (i) fostering a dialogue with a 'wide range of community members about the idea of using a CLT for protecting small businesses from gentrification, for leasing spaces to food-related program/projects' such as the West End Food Co-op; (ii) establishing an inventory of vacant land and government owned land and identification of 'sympathetic allies' who would consider donating or selling their land at a below-market rate to a CLT organization; (iii) creating a CLT non-profit organization with registered charitable status; (iv) establishing a financial plan and seeking governmental and philanthropic funding; (v) finding non-profit developers to construct or renovate buildings on CLT land (Ibid., 2010, pp. 30–31). The study was adopted by PARC in order to assess the feasibility of the recommendations and to further develop the CLT proposal.

The proposal developed into the creation of the PNLT following research on the CLT model and organizational governance structures and methods of land use by CLTs. The PNLT organization was incorporated as a non-profit NGO in 2014 and received funding from the Ontario Trillium Foundation, a granting foundation of the Ontario provincial government that funds non-profit and charitable projects, in order to develop a more comprehensive organizational governance structure with representation from local residents, community businesses and NGOs. The current mission of PNLT is as follows,

> through the community land trust model, PNLT will acquire land and use it to meet the needs of Parkdale by leasing it to non-profit partners who

can provide affordable housing, furnish spaces for social enterprises and non-profit organizations, and offer urban agriculture and open space.

(The Parkdale People's Economy Project, 2015)

While the initial report that informed the creation of PNLT explicitly acknowledged the negative impacts of gentrification in Parkdale and offered the CLT as a mitigating solution, recent communications of the PNLT have somewhat tempered that approach. Although PNLT emphasizes social and environmental justice as pursuits of CLT development, the organization has stated that,

Parkdale is changing rapidly. This change is not inherently good or bad, but it raises important questions about affordability, diversity, and community assets in Parkdale. How can we ensure that everyone, particularly those with fewer resources and lower income, benefit from these changes?

(The Parkdale People's Economy Project, 2015)

This inclusion of a 'value free' interpretation of neighbourhood change suggests that PNLT is hoping to broaden and attract more diverse participants in CLT activities. However, this interpretation does open possible space for the co-optation of CLT activities through a possible growth in participation by gentrifier residents who might consider themselves to be socially and/or environmentally progressive and have influential networks due to their social roles and professional occupations, yet who do not genuinely share the same social equity and justice concerns and needs as low-income residents. This points to a problem in how CLT organizations might position themselves in relation to being open and willing to accept donations, organizational network support and other resources that are necessary to pursue CLT initiatives that meet the needs of less affluent residents. Nonetheless, the official organizational values that the PNLT articulate and the initiatives that they pursue, such as a community garden, the hosting of community meetings on the negative impacts of gentrification in Parkdale and working on a collaborative community-based plan for Parkdale (*The Parkdale Neighbourhood Plan*), focus on equitable development for low-income and marginalized people, collective action and engagement and 'land as commons', among others (PNLT, 2016; PNLT Purpose Vision Values, 2015a).

The PNLT is currently in the stage of purchasing its first land parcel, of approximately 5500 square feet, following an offer of a 'lower-than-market' price for a lot in south Parkdale owned by a local family (Hennebury, 2016; Porter, 2016). Prior to the sale, the landowners had leased the land to an 'English as a Second Language' learning program for new immigrants and refugees in the community, operated by the publicly funded Toronto District School Board and provided for through the Parkdale branch of Toronto's public library system. The language program leased the space for use as a community garden – called the 'Milky Way Garden' in keeping the name of the laneway (Figure 4.1). The program largely engages with Tibetan refugees who develop English language skills and build social connections with other residents through interactions in the garden while at the same time growing and harvesting produce for their personal use and to share with other residents (Ibid., 2016). Through a collaboration with the language program and fund-raising through individual donations, PNLT are finalizing the purchase of the lot and will be embarking on a community planning process to identify uses for the site in addition to the community garden. Possible uses that have been identified by local residents are a small block of affordable rental housing units, a greenhouse and a community kitchen to prepare produce from the garden.

Although the land being acquired by the PNLT is relatively small, the process of securing the land under land trust ownership has created a sense of achievement and collaboration among and between PNLT advocates, local residents, the language students who use the garden and other Parkdale-based community organizations, in relation to PNLT's goal of common land ownership. In this way, the relevance of PNLT is not in relation to the quantity of land that is being acquired but, instead, the significance of what uses the land will have that meets community needs and the relational connections that are developed between residents in decisions over the common ownership of land. While not acting as a solution that will halt or mitigate neighbourhood or city-wide gentrification processes, it offers a new space in Parkdale – and in Toronto more broadly – for community-focused discussions about gentrifi-cation and the creation of more equitable and just social and environmental futures for the Parkdale neighbourhood while at the same time meeting the needs of low-income and marginalized residents. The PNLT has also fostered public discourse about the role of CLTs in Toronto and aided in the development of a new CLT organization in the Kensington Market area of the central city, a neighbourhood that shares similar gentrification processes (Hennebury, 2016).

East London Community Land Trust, London

The ELCLT was formed in 2007 as a charitable organization of London Citizens, a social justice NGO and a member of the larger UK-wide Citizens UK activist network. The ELCLT was organized as a way to address gentrifi-cation impacts in the eastern boroughs of London as well as concurrent affordable housing shortages and overcrowding in existing affordable housing units (ELCLT, 2010). As noted in Chapter 3, gentrification has become increasingly prevalent in eastern London boroughs such as Hackney over the past decade with evidence of growing social polarization based upon rising income disparities and an increased demand for and short supply of afford-able housing (Butler *et al.*, 2011; Butler, Hamnett, and Ramsden, 2013; New

Figure 4.1 Photo of Milky Way Community Garden (Parkdale Neighbourhood
Land Trust), Parkdale, Toronto (Photo credit: Tish Carnat/Permission
granted by Tish Carnat)

Policy Institute, 2015). In 2008, through extensive community engagement with different organizations and residents' groups in east London, the ELCLT selected a former National Health Service (NHS) location, St. Clement's hospital in the Mile End neighbourhood of the borough of Tower Hamlets, as a potential land acquisition. The site had initially been identified through research conducted by students at Queen Mary University, in collaboration with local institutions such as the East London Mosque and the Central Foundation School for Girls. The land and buildings – consisting of 4.6 acres of land and approximately 11,000 m² of existing building space – had been sold by the NHS to the Homes and Communities Agency (HCA) in 2005 (London Citizens, 2010). With emphasis on potential ownership of the property, the ELCLT facilitated discussions between 2008 and 2010 about possible community uses for the site, through community meetings for area residents and discussions with local NGOs and educational and faith-based institutions. The location in Mile End was particularly important in relation to the neighbourhood's proximity to intensive gentrification in south Hackney near Victoria Park (Butler *et al.*, 2011), commercial gentrification along the Regent's Canal as well as the existence of uneven, 'patchy gentrification' occurring in certain areas across the borough of Tower Hamlets (De Verteuil, 2015, p. 65). The ELCLT's process for securing community land has focused more on the ownership and stewardship of land for the provision of affordable housing rather than environmental practices; however, the communities that have engaged in the CLT organizing process have identified sustainable building design and community garden spaces as important components alongside the development of affordable housing.

In 2010, the HCA embarked on an open bid tendering process to request development proposals from NGOs and for profit developers. The ELCLT collaborated with Igloo Regeneration, a Manchester-based private development firm specializing in sustainable planning and design, and Poplar Harca, a local housing association, to submit a proposal for a CLT on the site. Following the devolution of the HCA's responsibilities to the Greater London Authority (GLA), the ELCLT was requested to submit a second proposal after having the organization's initial development proposal accepted. The ELCLT's second bid emphasized further development partnerships that included a mixture of for-profit housing, affordable rental and homeownership units provided by a housing association, ELCLT ownership of housing units and land and sustainable design components. The ELCLT was also emboldened by broader political support from politicians regarding a 'community trust arrangement' to be achieved on the land through the tendering process. This support also included London's mayor at the time, Boris Johnson, who had developed an electoral policy statement on affordable housing that discussed CLTs as a viable way to create affordable housing in London (Johnson, 2008). Ultimately, the GLA's final decision did not accept ELCLT's bid but instead selected a proposal by Galliford Try, a London-area for-profit residential developer that supported establishing a form of a 'community trust' on the site. The GLA suggested that Galliford Try collaborate with ELCLT organizers to initiate a CLT in the eventual development (Kelly, 2012). Following these deliberations, an agreement was negotiated between the GLA and Galliford Try that required the freehold of the St. Clement's site to be transferred to a yet unnamed community foundation upon completion of the development with a caveat that Galliford Try develop 223 housing units with 35 per cent of the units geared towards affordable rental or affordable homeownership (GLA, 2012). The final agreement underlined that the ELCLT will own and arrange the sale of approximately 21 affordable homeownership units while Peabody Trust, a London-based housing association, will eventually manage the affordable rental units (Ibid., 2012). While this was not the outcome that the ELCLT had anticipated, the inclusion of an eventual land trust arrangement for site reflected their advocacy work regarding the role of community land trusts that the organization had engaged in with diverse communities within the Mile End neighbourhood over multiple years.

In keeping with the ELCLT's dedication to securing affordable housing for local residents, the ELCLT's affordable homes – the number of which are now increased to 23 units – are being made available to Tower Hamlets residents who are unable to afford market rate housing and who are members of the ELCLT organization (London Community Land Trust, 2016). The units will cost approximately half of the average market rate for housing in Mile End (Right Move, 2016) and are priced at approximately £130,000 for a one-bedroom unit and £235,000 for a three-bedroom unit (London Community Land Trust, 2016). Eligibility for affordable housing will be measured against the average annual income of Tower Hamlets residents and, in keeping with the approach of CLTs, each new owner will enter into a legal contract with the ELCLT that will significantly reduce the capacity to gain a profit from the future resale of the housing unit in order to retain its affordability (National CLT Network, East London Community Land Trust, and Citizens UK, 2014; Smith, 2014).

The final decision over the development of the site has resulted in a lessened number of affordable housing units than was initially proposed in the ELCLT's first development proposal. Despite this situation, however, the ELCLT views the inclusion of a community trust arrangement and the ownership of affordable housing as a victory for raising public awareness about the current problems of property ownership and gentrification in east London and emphasizing the de-commodification of land and housing, and community needs for land, as responses (Smith, 2014). While focusing more on the acquisition of community-owned land for affordable housing provision, the ELCLT has engaged with sustainable planning and design ideas over the duration of the community-based planning meetings and workshops that will be inte-grated into the St. Clement's site. Additionally, public attention regarding the St. Clement's CLT and the role of CLTs in facilitating community land

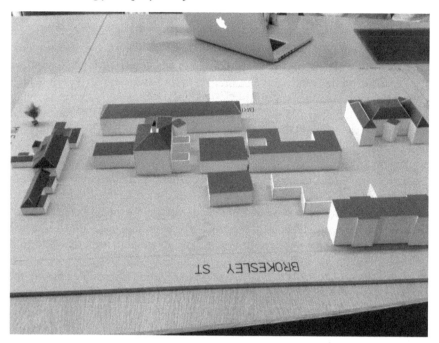

Figure 4.2 Photo of community design meeting – East London Community Land
        Trust, London, UK

stewardship and affordable housing provision has recently sparked CLT
initiatives in other boroughs of London, such as Camden and Lewisham. The
ELCLT has also initiated a name change to the London CLT in order to
better advocate for CLT development across the city (London CLT, 2016;
National CLT Network, East London Community Land Trust, and Citizens
UK, 2014). Like the PNLT, the broader relevance of the ELCLT and its role
in community-based development and challenging gentrification at the
neighbourhood level lies in the organization's ability to raise awareness about
the problems of commodified land and housing and the pressures caused
by gentrification.

Urban eco-villages

In a similar way to CLTs, eco-villages or ecocommunities support collective
decision making about land use and community assets. Eco-villaging, however,
places an emphasis on shared concerns about the biophysical environment and
environmental sustainability with the idea that eco-village spaces provide
respite from environmental problems and a forum for alternative lifestyles that
resist and challenge consumerist practices (Boyer, 2015; Ergas, 2010; Litfin,
2014). Pickerill (2016) writes that,

living in eco-communities is about acknowledging the interdependency of humans with each other and nature, and practicing mutual care . . . In this context, eco-communities are understood to be part of a wider movement advocating communing; to produce, live off and through the commons.

(p. 221)

Eco-villages were first examined by Robert Gilman in a 1991 report on intentional sustainable communities written for the environmental charity, Gaia Trust (Ergas, 2010). Ergas (2010) suggests that the use of the term 'eco-village' was a way to define emerging, self-determined, environmental communities that specifically focused on ecological planning and design and to differentiate these communities from other intentional settlements such as faith-based communities (Ibid., 2010). Increasingly, eco-village spaces and eco-villaging practices have become relevant in cities as a way for individuals to develop a collective, ideological, and spatial identity that opposes contemporary urban production and consumption practices. Urban eco-villages facilitate the pursuit of experimental eco-friendly lifestyles and community building within cities rather than in locations more commonly associated with the natural environment such as rural or wilderness locations (Boyer, 2015; Chitewere, 2010). As opposed to cities, rural and wilderness locations are often construed as more appealing spaces for eco-villages because of a better ability to disengage from society, go 'off-grid' in terms of disconnecting from physical infrastructure such as electrical and sewage systems, and pursue eco-village practices such as subsistence-oriented farming.

An increase in eco-villages across the globe has led to inter-organizational connectivity through the formation of international on-line and place-specific educational networks. The GEN is a United Nations Economic and Social Council affiliated NGO that connects over 400 eco-villages in Africa, North America, Latin America, Europe and Asia, with additional regional network organizations (GEN, 2014; Litfin, 2014). GEN Africa, for example, connects over 200 eco-villages across the continent and shares technical and educational resources (GEN Africa, 2014). The Eco-Yoff community in Dakar, Senegal is considered to be a global model for urban eco-villaging and hosts international conferences and workshops on urban eco-villaging practices (Birkeland, 2008; Gaia Education, 2016; GEN, 2014). Located in the northern section of the city and in close proximity to Senegal's international airport, the community emphasizes poverty alleviation through the formation of social and environmental micro-enterprises. Eco-Yoff prohibits automobile use in the community, operates an environmental education centre for local and inter-national visitors and engages in waste water recycling, solar electricity projects and additional planting of vegetation as a measure against climate change effects such as flooding that often occurs in Dakar during the summer months (Birkeland, 2008; Gaia Education, 2016; GEN Senegal, n.d.). Eco-Yoff organizers also identify land speculation in the coastal neighbourhoods surrounding Yoff as an emergent challenge to affordability and poverty alleviation (GENSenegal, n.d.). This relates to a recent occurrence of rising property values due to middle class residential and commercial gentrification and growing foreign investment in luxury vacation property development along Dakar's coastline; demonstrated in a stark increase (256 per cent) in the city's property prices between 1994 and 2010 (Global Property Guide, 2014). Eco-Yoff demonstrates how eco-village practices in cities in the global south are mobilized as community-oriented solutions to poverty, environmental problems, land speculation and property development. This is particularly important given an increasing occurrence of gentrification in major African cities and the proliferation of gentrification in cities in the global south (Lees, Shin, and Lopez-Morales, 2015, 2016; Simone, 2010; Simone and Abouhani, 2005).

The role of urban eco-village organizations in addressing the impacts of gentrification is less explicit than with CLTs but their significance rests in providing an alternative and environmental method of urban living that inherently opposes the production and consumerist practices of gentrification. Urban eco-villages must cope with the pressures and challenges of carving out an alternative space within broader political-economic contexts of urban development and growth, often in close spatial proximity to areas with rising property values. Eco-villages also have to address the everyday challenges of choosing subsistence living as a practice of resistance and sustainability within the context of a larger consumerist society. In writing about the alternative characteristics of eco-villages, Ergas (2010) suggests that they 'confront ideological differences from a dominant culture that designates status in terms of material possessions that require the perpetual extraction of precious resources' (p. 35). In her ethnographic study of eco-villagers and their personal motivations for living in alternative intentional communities, she notes that, 'ecovillagers believe they live a critique. Their everyday actions deny consumerist ideologies and are political in a dominant culture that sets the consumerist context' (Ergas, 2010, pp. 35–36). Certainly, common urban eco-villaging practices – such as permaculture and small livestock farming, clothes making and other cottage industries, the construction of housing using renewable materials and a reliance on reusable water and renewable energy sources – emphasize the internal use of material goods that are produced through the labour of eco-village residents and intended for community subsistence.

These practices certainly share commonalities with the emergence and romanticization of the 'urban pastoral' in the practices of new urban gentrifiers through increased demonstrations of fondness for pioneer-style aesthetics and DIY activities such as crafting and gardening, as discussed in Chapter 4. Yet, the more radical ethos of eco-villaging appears to challenge the consumerist pursuits of gentrifiers who are attracted to these activities because eco-village residents engage with an eco-community lifestyle that governs social and environmental practices through formal and informal processes rather than selectively participating in certain activities because of aesthetic appeal. Often this is done through a governance structure that dictates the need for income and tenure diversity in the membership and retention of eco-village residents. Chitewere (2010) notes the importance of social inclusion in eco-village development. While commenting on the similarities between environmental justice and eco-villaging in the pursuit of sustainable communities, she suggests that long-term sustainability of eco-villages 'requires the inclusion of all races, classes, and genders' (2010, p. 317). Chitewere argues that without social inclusion, eco-villages will develop as enclosed and exclusive spaces; as 'green gated communities and green segregated spaces' (2010, p. 317) that represent the values of white, middle-class environmentalism. The following examples of urban eco-villages demonstrate an organizational mandate for supporting income and tenure diversity, and in the case of the Los Angeles Ecovillage, support for poverty alleviation and cultural diversity.

Vauban eco-community, Freiburg, Germany

The Vauban neighbourhood was first envisioned as an intentional eco-community by the City of Freiburg government and a collective of different socially and environmentally progressive area residents interested in affordable housing and environmental issues between 1993 and 1994. The vision for the project focused on the design of a neighbourhood for 5000 residents with a focus on green space production and sustainable design, community building through resident participation and affordable housing provision through a diversity of tenure arrangements (City of Freiburg/Vauban District Association, 2009; Inclusive Cities Observatory, 2010). The planning process for the community, located in the south of Freiburg and the site for French military barracks until it was decommissioned by the French army in 1992, directly followed the purchase of the land area (approximately 38 hectares) by the City of Freiburg (Schroepfer and Hee, 2008). Vauban is an interesting example of an intentional eco-village where the local government has played a central role in the formation of the community alongside a representative non-governmental organization constituted by new residents. In this case, local government officials have facilitated the resident-focused orientation of the community and have sold parcels of land to co-operative groups of new residents over the course of the government's land ownership (City of Freiburg/Vauban District Association, 2009). Scheurer and Newman (2009) suggest that the City of Freiburg's impetus for facilitating the development of Vauban stemmed from the city having an established network of grass-roots activists, being on the vanguard of emergent sustainability discourse and environmental technology, and its role as an international centre for environmental institutions such as ICLEI and the Oko-Institut, a non-profit environmental research institute. The extension of these activities into the creation of Vauban guided a more grassroots approach to the planning of the district and an openness to collaborating with different resident interests in the community.

Following the withdrawal of French troops from the site in 1992, several of the barracks were squatted by a radical activist collective, the Self-Organized Independent Neighbourhood Initiative (SUSI), along with student union members. In purchasing the land in 1993, the City of Freiburg worked with SUSI to retain their use of the site for caravan space and to keep the use of four barracks as permanent, affordable housing (Inclusive Cities Observatory, 2010), as well as to follow upon the collective's environmental vision for the land. Local government planners facilitated a design competition for the neighbourhood and facilitated workshops to include different visions of residents interested in the community. This expansion of resident engagement occurred in 1994 through the formation of Forum Vauban, a representative community organization, and with the local government assigning responsibility to the organization for decision-making over issues such as traffic mitigation, energy conservation, residential collectives and gender issues (City of Freiburg/Vauban District Association, 2009). The City of Freiburg, as land owners, have facilitated a complex arrangement of different land ownership and land trust contexts within Vauban. The negotiations with the SUSI squatters led to the creation of a land trust arrangement where SUSI members own housing but have a long-term land lease with the City of Freiburg. In a different approach to the sale of publicly owned land, blocks of land have been sold to resident 'self-build' collectives (Baugruppen) (Hamiduddin, 2015), based upon their vision for that specific land parcel. In this way the residential collectives plan, design, and sometimes construct their own residential units and adhere to the larger social and environmental vision for Vauban. The resident collectives own parcels of neighbourhood land where their buildings are situated for the purpose of creating affordable options for housing and tenure. This approach greatly differs from the sale of publicly owned land to for-profit private developers as discussed in Chapter 3 in relation to new-build gentrification.

The funds generated by the City of Freiburg from land sales are redistributed into the government's ownership and management of neighbourhood infra-structure; observable in the provision of a tram line through the neighbourhood, parks and green landscaping such as grass trenches alongside paved roads to absorb stormwater, waste diversion through compost and recycling and the enforcement of the City's energy efficiency code for buildings (Ibid., 2009). The cooperative residential arrangements have produced an assortment of individual communities within the larger Vauban area, with each community being responsible for their own social and environmental practices (Scheuer and Newman, 2009) within the framework of publicly provided infrastructure. The Inclusive Cities Observatory, a research project through University College London, in a study of Vauban, has suggested that an exceptional feature of the district is the 'extremely diverse range of housing' (Inclusive Cities Observatory, 2010, p. 7) with an emphasis on a commitment by Forum Vauban to facilitating a long term and multigenerational residential commitment to 'aging in place' in the neighbourhood (City of Freiburg/Vauban District Association, 2009; Hamiduddin, 2015). Discourse about the neighbourhood is not framed in relation to combatting gentrification but in terms of facilitating social inclusivity in the occupation of housing. The Vauban District Association, the most recent residents' organization, posit that social inclusion in housing provision was emphasized from the start of the planning for Vauban in order to urge community control over housing access for residents with different income levels (City of Freiburg/Vauban District Association, 2009). The residential collectives have organized housing tenures such as home ownership cooperatives, publicly subsidized and private rental units and a self-governed rental housing cooperative (City of Freiburg/Vauban District Association, 2009; Scheurer and Newman, 2009). An emphasis on tenure diversity occurs alongside practices of spatial accessibility for age or disability-related mobility issues in residential design and neighbourhood spaces that represent the interests of different generations with a particular focus on the needs of children and seniors (City of Freiburg/Vauban District Association, 2009). Schroepfer and Hee's (2008) study of the sustainable design components of Vauban highlights the energy efficiency standards for buildings and notes that, on average, 65 per cent of energy for residential buildings in Vauban is derived from renewable sources such as solar paneling and heat retention through reinforced construction and a high density of buildings. They note that heating and electricity for housing in Vauban is generated through a district energy system that is fueled by the burning of wood chips (Schroepfer and Hee, 2008). The use of ground space in Vauban is constituted by street design intended to dissuade car use in residential areas, community gardens and poultry barns managed by the residential collectives, a community centre, parks and green playgrounds, sitting areas and bicycle storage and pathways, and services along the arterial road, which has produced a sense of Vauban as being a 'complete community'; a neighbourhood that meets the needs of residents in comprehensive ways (Figure 4.3). The broader impact of Vauban's contribution to ideas about sustainable community planning is indicated in the presence of international visitors to the neighbourhood as well as a United Nations Habitat award for best practices in 2002 (City of Freiburg/Vauban District Association, 2009).

Yet, while the emphasis on social inclusion has produced a sense of connectivity between generations and residents with different incomes and a less top-down implementation of a 'social mix' planning agenda in Vauban, it appears within a predominantly middle class and professionalized socio-cultural framework. Schroepfer and Hee (2008) note that while an attempt has

Figure 4.3 Photo of residential street, Vauban Eco-village, Freiburg, Germany

been made to form a heterogeneous community based on diversity in marital status, number of children, occupation and income, the efforts have resulted in a neighbourhood comprised of 'young married couples, middle-class white-collared workers, college students and those who share similar progressive mind sets' (Schroepfer and Hee, 2008, p. 70). The discourse around social equity and inclusivity in Vauban centres upon age demographics and countering imbalances in residential arrangements between the majority of adult-aged residents and a declining number of senior residents as well as imbalances between the larger number of families with children and families and individuals without dependents (Hamiduddin, 2015). There is a notable lack of attention towards the inclusion of cultural diversity in the neighbour-hood as well as in the social inclusion framework developed for Vauban by the City of Freiburg and Forum Vauban. The Vauban eco-community is a well-developed example of ecological sustainability, community land stewardship, social inclusion in residential provision and tenure, inclusivity based upon age, gender and ability, and comprehensive citizen engagement in community planning and design. The presence of a more fulsome discourse that explicitly addresses issues of cultural diversity, as noted in the next section in regard to the Los Angeles Ecovillage, would widen the approach taken by Vauban towards social inclusion.

Los Angeles Ecovillage

The Los Angeles Ecovillage (LAEV) is an income and culturally diverse eco-community situated in the downtown core of Los Angeles in the north end of the Koreatown/Wilshire neighbourhood. The eco-village was estab-lished with a focus on social, environmental and racial justice and identifies itself as a distinct community with spatial boundaries on two street blocks, but with porous associations with surrounding communities and neigh-bourhoods. Litfin (2014), in an ethnographic study of eco-villages, notes that the organizers of LAEV were explicitly influenced by a need for progressive, 'on the ground', community-based social and environmental justice responses following the Los Angeles riots in 1992 and a resultant awareness about the problems of racism and racialization in Los Angeles (2014, p. 30). As a quite informal and small eco-village, the community has also had to address pressures caused by gentrification and has mobilized to protect land and housing in the community from property speculation and development (Boyer, 2015). LAEV was initiated through the efforts of activists affiliated with a local non-profit NGO, the Cooperative Resources and Services Project, who envisioned an anti-consumerist 'neighbourhood of co-operatives' that would provide environmentally focused co-operative housing and programs in a community setting (Boyer, 2015; Litfin, 2014). Between 1986 and 1991, organizers of LAEV raised funds in an informal way to purchase inexpensive land and building stock while at the same time identifying uses and programs for the land. Following land purchase, members of LAEV have developed eco-village practices that focus on communal arrangements for residency, community gardening activities, cooking, eating and the sharing of other resources, and shared activities such as childcare. LAEV residents are also members of the Arroyo Seco Network of Time Banks, a time banking network based in Los Angeles where residents exchange their skills and labour for time credits that are exchanged for needed items or skills without monetary exchange (Los Angeles Ecovillage, 2017). Additional resident-led initiatives in the eco-village have focused on the creation of permeable walkways, a bicycle repair shop for eco-village residents and the surrounding neighbourhoods, a bulk food cooperative that sells organic food from local farms, and artistic events such as Eco-Maya, an annual festival that celebrates Mayan cultural history and the Hispanic culture of eco-village residents and surrounding communities (Boyer, 2015; Litfin, 2014; Los Angeles Ecovillage, 2016).

In response to increased property development in downtown Los Angeles in the 2000s and concerns about gentrification, LAEV residents formed the Beverly-Vermont Community Land Trust organization in 2007 (Beverly-Vermont Community Land Trust, 2016). This initiative transferred land ownership from the collection of residents who had originally purchased the land to the CLT organization and arranged a 99-year lease between the CLT organization as land owners and the eco-village's co-operative housing group. The integration and use of a CLT structure was a way to retain and protect long-term ownership and affordability of the land in light of increasing property development pressures, to place collective restrictions on land use, and prevent the possible resale of eco-village land and building infrastructure for profit (Beverly-Vermont Community Land Trust, 2016). In 2010, LAEV formed the Urban Soil/Tierra Urbana (USTU) housing co-operative that formalized the existing residential arrangements into a non-profit limited equity co-operative in two building complexes on eco-village land. The organizational mission of USTU is to 'provide permanently affordable housing to very low to moderate income households that sustains a diverse community whose members join together to publicly demonstrate higher quality living patterns while minimizing negative environmental and social impacts' (Los Angeles Ecovillage, 2017). The housing cooperative currently consists of 40 members that either rent or own residential units in the buildings and who engage in the governance and care of the community through labour on different work groups related to eco-village practices (Ibid., 2017). The formalization of organizational practices through the CLT and housing co-operative indicates a firm approach, through the presence of structure, toward maintaining the long-term sustainability of LAEV in light of external development pressures from the surrounding city.

The longevity of LAEV demonstrates a commitment to cultural diversity, to translating social and environmental justice ideas into practice through small-scale and collective land stewardship and building an intentional eco-community with strong organizational mechanisms such as the CLT to protect land ownership. While primarily self-sufficient and with a lessened reliance on relationship building with local government policy and planning, by comparison with the Vauban eco-village, LAEV still builds connections with surrounding neighbourhood and city initiatives. LAEV's self-organized yet fluid and less insular approach to eco-community building suggests a way forward in the progression of sustainable communities and acts as a small but meaningful local action against gentrification.

Conclusion

As alternative organizations and spaces, urban CLTs and eco-village organizations strive to resist and challenge both the spatial production and consumerist practices of gentrification. This chapter identifies some hopeful practices that may identify 'on the ground' ways to expand sustainable planning while at the same time resisting pressures of gentrification evident in rising property values, increasing enclosures on access to affordable housing and social and spatial dispossession and displacement. With varying degrees of governmental policy and planning involvement, all of the CLTs and eco-villages that are discussed in this chapter underline how local CBOs and residents can direct government policy and planning objectives to meet the needs of communities. Advocating for community needs relies upon community time and labour which can raise problems in light of the challenges faced by non-profit, non-governmental organizations, such as funding and capacity constraints. Yet, at the same time, local initiatives to own and steward land and affordable housing and care for the environment through sustainability activities can empower urban communities that directly experience gentrification.

In these ways, community organizations and residents act as policy-makers, through creating neighbourhood plans and as citizen planners in shaping social and ecological sustainability practices. Certainly, forms of citizen-led planning and the creation of intentional and self-directed communities raise their own challenges regarding equitable representation and voices in relation to community governance structures and decision-making, sometimes despite an explicit focus on the development of equitable processes. This is not to suggest that CLTs and eco-village organizations are comprehensive solutions or panaceas but, rather, initiatives that allow for individual and collective reflexivity about alternative social and environmental practices in cities. As noted in the examples discussed in this chapter, a strength of these initiatives lies in an ability to turn broader public attention towards issues of community rights over urban land in relation to threats posed by gentrification, raise discussions about collectively owned and stewarded urban land, and galvanize awareness about equitable and just social and environmental sustainability.

Although these organizations work at the local level, their collective efforts are now becoming increasingly relevant through the emergence of national and global networks. Although challenges exist for both approaches – particularly with regard to how easily land can be acquired in urban areas with high land values – CLTs and eco-villages offer emergent and important possibilities for countering more formal, top-down approaches to sustainability policy and planning along with the pressures caused by gentrification.

References

Aird, J. (2010). Reviving community ownership in England: CLTs are ready to take over the land. In Davis, J. (ed.), *The community land trust reader* (pp. 449–465). Cambridge, MA: Lincoln Institute of Land Policy.

Alternatives for Community and Environment. (2015). *Fighting gentrification and displacement.* Retrieved from www.ace-ej.org/node/11641.

Angotti, T. (2007). *Community Land Trusts and Low-Income Multifamily Rental Housing: The Case of Cooper Square, New York City.* Cambridge: Lincoln Institute of Land Policy.

Atkinson, R., and Bridge, G. (eds). (2005). *Gentrification in a global context.* Abingdon, UK: Routledge.

Beverly-Vermont Community Land Trust. (2016). *The Beverly-Vermont community land trust.* Retrieved from laecovillage.org/community-land-trust.

Birkeland, J. (2008). *Positive development: From vicious circles to virtuous cycles through built environmental design.* London: Earthscan.

Blomley, N. (2004). *Unsettling the city: Urban land and the politics of property.* Abingdon, UK: Routledge.

Boyer, R. (2015). Grassroots innovation for urban sustainability: Comparing the diffusion pathways of three ecovillage projects. *Environment and Planning A, 45,* 320–337.

Bunce, S. (2016). Pursuing urban commons: Politics and alliances in community land trust activism in east London. *Antipode, 48*(1), 134–150.

Bunce, S., Khimani, N., Sungu-Erylimaz, Y., and Earle, E. (2013). *Urban community land trusts: Experiences from Canada, the United States, and Britain.* Retrieved from www.academia.edu/2584425/Urban_Community_Land_Trust_Handbook_2013_

Butler, T., Hamnett, C., Miq, S., and Ramsden, M. (2011). *Ethnicity, class and aspiration: Understanding London's new east end.* Bristol: Policy Press.

Butler, T., Hamnett, C., and Ramsden, M. (2013). Gentrification, education and exclusionary displacement in east London. *International Journal of Urban and Regional Research, 37*(2), 556–575.

Caffentzis, G., and Federici, S. (2014). Commons against and beyond capitalism. *Community Development Journal, 49*(s.1), i92–i105.

Catungal, J., Leslie, D., and Hii, Y. (2009). Geographies of displacement in the creative city: The case of Liberty Village, Toronto. *Urban Studies, 46*(5/6), 1095–1114.

Chitewere, T. (2010). Equity in sustainable communities: Exploring tool from environmental justice and political ecology. *Natural Resources Journal, 50*(2), 315–339.

City of Freiburg/Vauban District Association (2009). *Quartier Vauban: A Guided Tour Freiburg: Stadtteilverein*, Vauban.

Class War. (2015). *Poor doors.* Retrieved from www.classwarparty.org.uk/category/poor-doors/.

Coulthard, G. (2014). Red skin, white masks: Rejecting the colonial politics of recognition. Minneapolis, MN: University of Minnesota Press.

Crabtree, L. (2010). Fertile ground for CLT development in Australia. In J.E. Davis (ed.). *The community land trust reader* (pp. 464–476). Cambridge, MA: Lincoln Institute for Land Policy.

Crabtree, L. (2014). Community Land Trusts and Indigenous Housing in Australia – Exploring Difference-Based Policy and Appropriate Housing. *Housing Studies, 29*(6), 743–759.

Curtin, J. and Bocarsly, L. (2010). CLTs: A growing trend in affordable home ownership. In J.E. Davis (ed.), *The community land trust reader* (pp. 289–314). Cambridge, MA: Lincoln Institute of Land Policy.

Davidson, M. (2011). Critical commentary: Gentrification in crisis–Towards consensus or disagreement? *Urban Studies, 48*(10), 1987–1996.

Davis, J.E. (2007). *Starting a community land trust: Organizational and operational choices* Burlington, VT: Burlington Associates.

Davis, J.E. (ed.). (2010). *The community land trust reader.* Cambridge, MA: Lincoln Institute of Land Policy.

DeFillippis, J. (2001). The myth of social capital in community development. *Housing Policy Debate, 12*(4), 781–806.

DeFillippis, J. (2004). *Unmaking goliath: Community control in the face of global capital.* Abingdon, UK: Routledge.

DeVerteuil, G. (2015). *Resilience in the post-welfare inner city: Voluntary sector geographies in London, Los Angeles, and Sydney.* Bristol, UK: Policy Press.

Dudley Neighbors, Inc. (DNI). (n.d.). *The community land trust: Land Trust 101.* Retrieved from www.dudleyneighbors.org/land-trust-101.html.

Ergas, C. (2010). A model of sustainable living: Collective identity in an urban ecovillage. *Organization & Environment, 23*(1), 32–54.

Eviction Free San Francisco. (2010). *Eviction free San Francisco: Taking direct action to save our homes and save our city.* Retrieved from Evictionfreesf.org.

Federici, S. (2010). Feminism and the politics of the commons. In C. Hughes, S. Peace, and T. Van Meter (eds). *Uses of a whirlwind: Movement, movements, and contemporary radical currents in the United States* (pp. 283–294). Oakland, CA: AK Press.

Gaia Education. (2016). *About gaia trust ecovillages.* Retrieved from www.gaia.org/gaia/education/living/.

GEN Africa. (2014). *Global ecovillage network Africa.* Retrieved from www.gen-africa.org/.

GEN Senegal. (n.d.). *GENSEN: Global ecovillage network senegal.* Retrieved from www.gensenegal.org/.

Gibson-Graham, J.K., Cameron, J., and Healy, S. (2013). *Take back the economy: An ethical guide for transforming our communities.* Minneapolis, MN: University of Minnesota Press.

Global Ecovillage Network (GEN). (2014). *Connecting communities for a sustainable world.* Retrieved from www.gen.ecovillage.org/.

Global Property Guide. (2014). *Senegal's property boom continues.* Retrieved from www.globalpropertyguide.com/Africa/Senegal.

Glynn, S. (2005). East End immigrants and the battle for housing: A comparative study of political mobilization in the Jewish and Bengali communities. *Journal of Historical Geography, 31,* 528–545.

Gray, K. (2008). Community land trusts in the United States. *Journal of Community Practice, 16*(1), 65–78.

Greater London Authority (GLA). (2012). *Request for mayoral decision – MD1028* July 16, 2012. London: Author.

Greenstein, R., and Sungu-Erylimaz, Y. (2005). Community Land Trusts: Leasing Land for Affordable Housing. *Land Lines Newsletter, 17*(2), April.

Gujit, I., and Shah, M. (eds). (1998). *The myth of community: Gender issues in participatory development.* London: Intermediate Technology Publications.

Hamiddudin, I. (2015). Social sustainability, residential design and demographic balance: Neighbourhood planning strategies in Freiburg, Germany. *Town Planning Review, 86*(1), 29–52.

Harvey, D. (2009). The 'New' imperialism: Accumulation by dispossession. In L. Panitch and C. Leys (eds), *Social register 2004: The new imperial challenge* (pp. 63–87). London: Merlin.

Harvey, D. (2012). *Rebel Cities: From the right to the city to the urban revolution.* London: Verso.

Hennebury, E. (2016). *Community land trusts as an anti-gentrification strategy: Case studies of Parkdale and Kensington Market, Toronto.* Master of Environmental Studies Major Paper, Faculty of Environmental Studies, York University, Toronto.

Hodkinson, S. (2012). The new urban enclosures. *City, 16*(5), 500–518.

Inclusive Cities Observatory. (2010). *Freiburg, Germany: Vauban sustainable urban district.* Committee on Social Inclusion, Participatory Democracy, and Human Rights, United Cities and Local Governments. Retrieved from www.uclg.org/cisdp/

Kelly, L. (2012). Community trust sparks move towards genuinely affordable housing in capital. *Guardian.* Monday, July 16, 2012.

Lees, L. (2012). The geography of gentrification: Thinking through comparative urbanism. *Progress in Human Geography, 36*(2), 155–171.

Lees, L., Slater, T., and Wyly, E. (2008). *Gentrification.* Abingdon, UK: Routledge.

Litfin, K. (2014). *Ecovillages: Lessons for sustainable community.* Cambridge, UK: Polity Press.

Logan, J., and Murdie, R. (2016). Home in Canada? The settlement experiences of Tibetans in Parkdale, Toronto. *International Migration and Integration, 17,* 95–113.

Loh, P. (2015). How one Boston neighborhood stopped gentrification in its Tracks. *Yes! Magazine.* January 28, 2015.

London Citizens (2010). www.citizensuk.org/

London Community Land Trust. (2016). *London Community Land Trust: Homes we can afford.* Retrieved from www.londonclt.org.

London Tenants Federation, Lees, L., Just Space, and Southwark Notes Archive Group. (2014). *Staying put: An anti-gentrification handbook for council estates in London.* London: Calverts Co-operative.

Los Angeles Ecovillage. (2016). *Reinventing how we live in the city.* Retrieved from http://laecovillage.org.

Los Angeles Ecovillage. (2017). *Urban soil/tierra urbana.* Retrieved from http://laecovillage.org.

Madden, D., and Marcuse, P. (2016). *In defense of housing: The politics of crisis.* London: Verso Books.

Mahan, L. (1996). *Holding Ground: The Rebirth of Dudley Street.* USA: New Day Films.

Mazer, K., and Rankin, K. (2011). The social space of gentrification: The politics of neighborhood accessibility in Toronto's Downtown West. *Environment and Planning D, 29*(5), 822–839.

Medoff, P., and Sklar, H. (1999). *Streets of hope: The fall and rise of an urban neighborhood.* Boston: South End Press.

Meehan, J. (2014). Reinventing real estate: The community land trust as a social invention in affordable housing. *Journal of Applied Social Science, 8*(2), 113–133.

Midheme, E., and Mouleart, F. (2013). Pushing back the frontiers of property: Community land trusts and low-income housing in urban Kenya. *Land Use Policy, 35,* 73–84.

Moore, T., and McKee, K. (2012). Empowering local communities? An international review of community land trusts. *Housing Studies, 27*(2), 280–290.

National CLT Network. (2016). *National community land trust network.* Retrieved from www.communitylandtrusts.org.uk/.

National CLT Network, East London Community Land Trust, and Citizens UK. (2014). *Evidence to the Review: Improving the secondary market for affordable homes.* London: Author.

New Policy Institute. (2015). Boroughs | poverty indicators | London's poverty report. Retrieved from www.londonspovertyprofile.org.uk/indicators/boroughs/

Ontario Coalition Against Poverty. (2016). Homelessness/housing. Retrieved from update.ocap.ca/housing.

Parkdale Neighbourhood Land Trust (PNLT). (2016). www.pnlt.ca

Parkdale People's Economy Project. (2015). Community land trust. Retrieved from www.pnlt.ca/about/

Pickerill, J. (2016). *Eco-homes: People, place, and politics.* London: Zed Books.

Porter, C. (2016). Activists' generosity blooms in Parkdale garden. *Toronto Star.* Friday, May 27, 2016.

Rameau, M. (2008). *Take back the land: Land, gentrification, and the Umoja Village Shantytown.* Oakland, CA: AK Press.

Richer, C., Htoo, S., Kamizaki, K., Mallin, M., Goodmurphy, B., Akande, A., and Molale, A. (2010). *Beyond bread and butter: Toward food security in a changing Parkdale.* Retrieved from www.pchc.on.ca/assets/files/beyond%20bread%20and%20butter.pdf.

Robinson, T. (1996). Inner-city innovator: The non-profit community development corporation. *Urban Studies, 33*(9), 1647–1670.

Rose, K. (n.d.). *Combating gentrification through equitable development.* Retrieved from www.reimaginerpe.org/node/919.

Scheurer, J., and Newman, P. (2009). *Vauban: A European model of bridging the green and brown agendas.* Case study prepared for Revisiting Urban Planning: Global Report on Human Settlements, United Nations Human Settlements Program.

Schroepfer, T., and Hee, L. (2008). Emerging forms of sustainable urbanism: Case studies of Vauban Freiburg and solar City Linz. *Journal of Green Building 3*(2), 65–76.

Serve the People Los Angeles. (2016). *Serve the People Los Angeles*. Retrieved from Servethepeoplela.org.

Seminary of the Street. (n.d.). *Meet as at the corner of love and justice!* Retrieved from www.seminaryofthestreet.org.

Simone, A. (2010). *City life from Jakarta to Dakar: Movements at the crossroads.* Abingdon, UK: Routledge.

Simone, A., and Abouhani, A. (2005). *Urban Africa: Changing contours of survival in the city*. London: Zed Books.

Slater, T. (2004). Municipally managed gentrification in South Parkdale, Toronto. *Canadian Geographer*, *48*(3), 303–325.

Slater, T. (2009). Missing Marcuse: On gentrification and displacement. *City*, *13*(2–3), 292–311.

Smith, D. (2002). Rural gatekeepers: Closing and opening up 'Access' to greentrified Pennine rurality. *Social and Cultural Geography*, *3*, 445–461.

Smith, D. (2007). The 'Buoyancy' of 'Other' geographies of gentrification: Going 'Back-to-the-Water' and the commodification of marginality. *Tijdschrift voor Economische en Sociale Geografie*, *98*(1), 53–67.

Smith, D. (2014). The half-price houses coming soon to east London. *Guardian.* Thursday, March 27, 2014.

Smith, N. (2002). New globalism, new urbanism: Gentrification as global urban strategy. *Antipode*, *34*(3), 427–450.

Sungu-Erylimaz, Y., and Greenstein, R. (2007). *A national study of community land trusts*. Cambridge, MA: Lincoln Institute of Land Policy.

Susser, I., and Tonnelat, S. (2013). Transformative cities: The three commons. *Focaal*, *66*, 105–121.

Taylor, E.A. (1995). The Dudley Street neighborhood initiative and the power of eminent domain. *Boston College Law Review*, *35*(5), 1061–1087.

Thaden, E., and Lowe, J.S. (2014). *Resident and community engagement in community land trusts*. Working Paper. Cambridge, MA: Lincoln Institute of Land Policy.

Thompson, M. (2015). Between boundaries: From commoning and guerilla gardening to community land trust development in Liverpool. *Antipode*, *47*(4), 1021–1042.

White, K. (1992). Bob Swann: An interview. In J.E. Davis (ed.) (2010), *The community land trust* reader (pp. 269–274). Cambridge, MA: Lincoln Institute of Land Policy.

Whitzman, C. (2010). *Suburb, Slum, Urban Village: Transformations in Toronto's Parkdale Neighbourhood, 1875–2002*. Vancouver: UBC Press.

Whitzman, C., and Slater, T. (2006). Village Ghetto Land: Myth, social conditions, and housing policy in Parkdale, Toronto, 1879–2000. *Urban Affairs Review*, *41*(5), 673–696.

Wyly, E. (2015). Gentrification on the Planetary Urban Frontier: The evolution of Turner's noosphere. *Urban Studies*, *52*(14), 2515–2550.

Wyly, E., Cooke, T., Hammel, D., Holloway, S., and Hudson, M. (2000). *Ten 'Just Right' urban markets for affordable homeownership*. Washington, DC: Fannie Mae Foundation.

Yuen, J. (2014). City farms on CLTs. *Land lines* (April Issue). Cambridge, MA: Lincoln Institute of Land Policy.

Yuen, J., and Rosenberg, G. (2013). Hanging on to the Land. *Shelterforce: The voice of community development* (February Issue).

Zukin, S. (1989). *Loft Living: Culture and capital in urban change.* New Brunswick, NJ: Rutgers University Press.

6   Conclusion

Future directions for
resisting gentrification

The previous chapters have explored the convergences between sustainability policy, planning and gentrification at multiple scales, with assemblages of public, private and civil society actors, and in different urban locations and environments. Identifying and untangling the connections between the production and implementation of urban sustainability policy and planning and gentrification processes in cities allows for more specific analyses regarding environmental gentrification and urban policy development and planning going forward. What is most striking about these connections are the para-doxical associations between the intended objectives of often progressive and environmentally focused sustainability policy and planning initiatives and the inequitable and unjust characteristics and practices of gentrification. Importantly, this is demonstrated in the ways by which assemblages of actors and interests engage with the creation of sustainability policy and planning initiatives that are complementary with and embedded within gentrification. As an emergent form of gentrification, environmental gentrification is defined as the convergence of environmental spaces and practices – environmental spaces such as parks, formalized policy and planning agendas and informal, everyday environmental activities – with the transformations created by rising residential property values, commercial services geared to higher income earners and other affluent amenity spaces in cities. These changes are evident in consumer demand for and policies and planning practices that produce and manage existing green residential neighbourhoods as well as market-geared newly built sustainable communities with ample parks and other environmental infrastructure and a growing interest of property developers in formal sustainable planning and design systems such as LEED and BREEAM. Environmental gentrification is also identified in the growing number of commercial spaces that cater to the tastes of higher income residents interested in environmental issues and environmentally responsible products, such as organic food stores and farmers' markets with locally sourced items, 'locavore' restaurants, and bicycle shops. It also includes the participation of gentrifiers in community-based sustainability activities such as crafting and community gardening as a way to seek out more 'authentic', grittier and alternative urban experiences and enact ostensibly progressive personal interests in and commitments to mitigating environmental problems. In these ways, we now observe an emergence of gentrified and environmentally friendly enclaves in cities that pose particular concerns for how gentrification will progress in cities. Critiquing gentrification becomes additionally complex and challenging when it includes environmental features and practices that are publicly considered to be progressive, well-meaning, and focused on conserving and protecting the natural environment. While this book demonstrates how urban gentrification processes are augmented by sustainability policy and planning ideas and projects, individual concerns about environmental issues that work to influence and co-create policy and planning initiatives, and public, private and civil society sector practices that combine to produce sustainable urban communities and spaces, it contributes, more broadly, to emergent discourse about environmental gentrification and associated forms of social and environmental inequity and injustice in cities. In light of global and localized governance concerns about the impacts of climate change in cities, multi-sectoral interest in building resilient and sustainable cities and public awareness about environmental issues, environmental forms of gentrification will continue to shape landscapes and social relations within cities as policies, planning directives and local initiatives further unfold in response to these issues.

Of particular concern are the implications of the entanglement of sustainability policy and planning directives and initiatives with gentrification for the continued production of uneven development in cities. Gentrification is implanted within the mechanics of profit accretion in cities and specifically through patterns of property investment and development and urban governance structures that support the endeavours of capital accumulation. As noted through the discussion of literature on policy-led and new-build gentrification in Chapter 2 and in examples presented through this book, gentrification has been increasingly guided by public–private sector alliances and arrangements. These arrangements are considerably identifiable in the urban policy and planning agenda of intensification where different governmental levels have envisioned the sustainability benefits of urban intensification yet largely relied on the involvement of private sector developers to implement this agenda through the redevelopment and production of new compact residential and commercial spaces. Across cities, gentrification produces uneven spaces and practices that support the aspirations of higher income earners and affluent persons while distinctly narrowing the availability of and equitable access to urban spaces and activities for lower income and marginalized residents. The integration of sustainability principles and initiatives into the logic of gentrification and the subsequent production of environmental spaces and practices that benefit the investment patterns, consumer demands and lifestyle pursuits of a higher income and professionalized demographic of urban resident produces myriad challenges for lower income residents regarding access to affordable housing and the right to reside within sustainable, green communities. Moreover, this situation raises the likelihood of more entrenched uneven environmental landscapes and relational associations in cities where affluent residents are able to engage in and benefit from the provisions of urban sustainability policies and sustainability planning endeavours while low-income and marginalized residents are further disconnected and excluded from these arrangements.

In analyzing the convergences between sustainability policies, sustainability planning directives and gentrification, the aim of this book was not to critique the necessary objectives of urban sustainability aspirations. Urban policy and planning directives that encourage sustainability are increasingly urgent for the mitigation of climate change effects, biodiversity loss, and the continuing presence of air, water and ground pollution. In keeping with Agyeman's notion of *just sustainability*, sustainability is a necessary concept but it must be reconceptualised to emphasize social equity and justice gains as core principles – a socio-ecological sustainability that prioritizes social and environmental justice. With this in mind, it then becomes important to critically assess how sustainability policy and planning initiatives are envisioned and implemented in 'on the ground' ways by different actors and interests, particularly by those with economic interests. This takes into consideration the post-political applications of sustainability management and arguments regarding the managerial and technocratic nature of institutionally created sustainability agendas and implementation practices, where actors focus more on short-term and stop-gap mitigation strategies than on longer term and more radical solutions to environmental problems (Swyngedouw, 2009, 2010). Literature that discusses the anthropocene as a way to define our current era of human-produced environmental crisis (cf. Castree, 2014a, 2014b; Chakrabarty, 2015), or the notion of the capitalocene as a delineation of how capitalism organizes nature (Moore, 2016, p. 6), demonstrates that the environmental crisis requires a deeper understanding of the impact of human and capitalist extractions from the natural environment. Further, as Castree (2014b) suggests, the age of the anthropocene as a period of environmental crisis compels humans to re-consider how they live in light of impending and increasingly serious environmental problems. In relating this back to the connections between sustainability policy, planning and gentrification, there is a complementarity with the ideas of alternative and community-based land ownership and the approaches of urban community land trusts and eco-villages, as discussed in Chapter 5. A concluding observation here is that in order to produce more equitable and just urban sustainability practices and mitigate the effects of gentrification a reframing of urban land ownership must occur. Such a reorientation would emphasize a collective and de-commodified understanding of how land might be shared and used and also allow for different forms of affordable housing and sustainable practices. These more hopeful ideas not only attempt to restructure the processes and outcomes of gentrification – by removing land from the speculative property market as in the case of community land trusts – but also shape an understanding about community-based urban land stewardship and everyday environmental practices as legitimate sustainability approaches. They may be more formalized through organizational policies and plans and in collaboration with local government, as demonstrated in the eco-village in Freiburg, Germany or more informal and ad hoc in their planning as per more non-governmental, resident-led approaches, but with the primary emphasis resting on urban sustainability as a political action that has benefits for lower income and other marginalized urban residents. Such an approach would be helpful in addressing problems of eviction and displacement caused by gentrification, in the sense that residents who are threatened by displacement would have the agency and ability to mobilize around ideas of collective land ownership as way to remain in place.

Certainly, any aspirational projects that aim to de-commodify urban land and housing must also include a decolonized understanding of land use and land rights in cities, particularly in those that have been built upon indigenous lands. In addition to the notion of gentrification as a neo-colonial practice that shares similar characteristics such as the taking over of urban land, dominant assumptions about the privileges of gentrifiers moving into particular sections of cities, and eviction and displacement, there is also an understanding of gentrification as a process that, quite literally, continues colonialist practices by displacing indigenous peoples. The Zibi development in Ottawa, Canada, discussed in Chapter 3, underlines this process in a situation where property developers proceeded with the planning of a new market-geared sustainable residential community despite local concern and tensions over indigenous land rights and with development occurring on unceded lands. In order to create more equitable and just urban sustainability policies and sustainable planning contexts and to foster collective land stewardship as a counteraction against gentrification a deeper commitment from governmental and non-governmental interests towards decolonized notions of urban land stewardship is required. In this way, land rights are instantly returned to indigenous persons who have had land taken away and traditional practices of land care and stewardship are affirmed. Discontinuing sustainability policies and planning agendas that perpetuate rather than dismantle historical settler–colonialist systems and that occur on land that has been taken from indigenous people through physical eviction or legal contracts over time is integral for a shift towards reframing sustainability as an equitable and just concept both in principle and in how it is implemented through the efforts of different actors. It also points to how gentrification analyses can continue to engage with indigenous scholarship in understanding the impacts of gentrification on indigenous persons and meanings of indigeneity in post-colonial cities and nations, as noted in Coulthard's analysis (2014) of gentrification as a neo-colonialist practice that imagines urban space as *urbs nullius* – terrain that is wrongly imagined as never being inhabited by indigenous persons and thus available for continued urbanization.

The roles and enactments of gentrifiers who assume environmental concerns and engage in socially and environmentally progressive initiatives, yet who are also complicit with the residential and commercial transformations activated by gentrification through their social positioning and property investments, are evident in gentrifying or already gentrified neighbourhoods and in newly built sustainable residential communities. The lifestyle choices of more 'bourgeois-bohemian' or 'hipster' gentrifiers have been reproduced through the expedient transmission of fashion and style trends to neighbourhoods in multiple cities. While the archetype of the 'hipster' gentrifier has localized characteristics dependent on place, a unifying feature is an emphasis on seeking out authentic experiences. This is represented in a form of gentrifier who is affluent in terms of income and professional positioning but who actively pursues grittier urban experiences and wishes to reside in traditionally working class and more culturally diverse urban areas, and who adopts lifestyle activities such as bicycle repair, urban farming, sewing and knitting and clothes swapping and thrifting that are either explicitly or inherently defined as sustainable actions and are evocative of a pastoralized notion of urban living. The trend of artisanal crafting evident in the production of local organic food and drink products such as craft beer, for example underlines this shift. The racialized characteristics of these types of practices, being activities that are engaged in by largely white, professionalized residents and which romanticize an unspecific and atemporal 'pioneer era', suggest a problematic connection between emerging localized enactments of sustainability, reproductions of white privilege and implied exclusions of racialized persons in urban spaces; associations that are discussed in environmental justice literature, but not to the same extent in gentrification scholarship. The participation of this shape of gentrifier as one actor in an assemblage of co-produced local governmental sustainability policies often occurs through social and professionalized connections where articulations and visioning of sustainable urban spaces are evoked and put forward. Engagement with governmental and non-governmental sustainable planning initiatives, such as community gardens as addressed in Chapter 4, indicates that spaces of sustainability are increasingly co-created through the efforts of gentrifiers. Yet, they are also places where the demands and lifestyle choices of gentrifiers are articulated and performed, often with a sense of moral philanthropy that espouses benefits for the environment and for the local area but without a critique of gentrification. Such experiences are likely to increase as environmental gentrification becomes more embedded in the everyday connections between sustainability policy and planning agendas and initiatives and urban spatial transformation, particularly in urban neighbourhoods. A concern here lies in the potential for the co-optation of sustainability initiatives created by and directed towards the needs of low-income and marginalized urban residents and how issues of co-optation can be avoided in emergent and future contexts.

As noted, a movement towards emulsifying sustainability policy directives and planning initiatives at localized scales, through governmental or non-governmental efforts and by meeting the needs of less affluent and socially marginalized urban residents, is a necessary response to the convergences of sustainability policy, planning and gentrification. While not wishing to romanticize urban communities and local spheres as the optimal places for these processes, the closer relational associations between assemblages of actors and interests at the local scale does suggest a more meaningful context for these discussions. This is identified in literature on localization, de-growth or 'no growth' (cf. De Young and Princen, 2012; Kallis, Demaria, and D'Alisa, 2015; Zovanyi, 2013) that delineates the importance of the de-commodification of land, a disengagement with consumerist practices and a re-orientation towards collectivity and cooperation as sustainable approaches at the community level. Kallis *et al.* (2015, p. 3), for example define de-growth as a critique of growth and underline that it argues for a 'decolonization of public debate from the idiom of economism and for the abolishment of economic growth as a social objective' and, in place, a move towards 'simplicity, conviviality, care, and the commons' as ways to re-think new and more sustainable ways by which to interact and live. Although this shares similar ideas with the aforementioned sustainability initiatives that are engaged with by gentrifiers, an emphasis is placed on de-commodification and a commitment to living in simpler and less consumerist ways through co-operative and subsistence-focused efforts. Applied to contexts of gentrification in cities, notions of de-growth might be useful in contemplating future environmental actions that do not connect with the expansionist growth and development imperatives of gentrification.

I have aimed to identify convergences of sustainability policy, planning and gentrification in cities, the assemblages of actors and interests involved in these processes, and the issues, contradictions, and tensions that emerge as a result of these connections. By ending with a hopeful tone, it is anticipated that some possible ideas, not prescriptions, for changes to these situations might be contemplated in future academic and practitioner discussions about urban sustainability agendas and projects. As an emergent form of gentrification in cities and as articulated through sustainability policies and planning agendas and initiatives, environmental gentrification is explored as a paradoxical and problematic process that is becoming increasingly embedded within the material spaces and social relations of cities.

References

Castree, N. (2014a). The anthropocene and geography I: The back story. *Geography Compass, 8*(7), 436–449.

Castree, N. (2014b). The anthropocene and geography III: Future directions. *Geography Compass, 8*(7), 464–476.

Chakrabarty, D. (2015). *The human condition in the anthropocene.* The Tanner Lectures in Human Values, Yale University, February 18–19, 2015.

Coulthard, G. S. (2014). *Red skin, white masks: Rejecting the colonial politics of recognition.* Minneapolis, MN: University of Minnesota Press.

De Young, R., and Princen, T. (eds). (2012). *The localization reader: Adapting to the coming.* Downshift Cambridge, MA: MIT Press.

Kallis, G., Demaria, F., and D'Alisa, G. (2015). Introduction: Degrowth. In G. D'Alisa, F. Demaria, and G. Kallis (eds), *De-growth: A vocabulary for a new era* (pp. 1–18). New York City: Routledge.

Moore, J. (2016). Introduction: Anthropocene or Capitalocene? Nature, History, and the Crisis of Capitalism. In J. Moore (ed.). *Anthropocene or capitalocene? Nature, History, and the Crisis of Capitalism* (pp. 1–13). Oakland, CA: PM Press.

Swyngedouw, E. (2009). The antinomies of the post-political city: In search of a democratic politics of environmental protection. *International Journal of Urban and Regional Research*, *33*(3), 601–620.

Swyngedouw, E. (2010). Apocalypse forever? Post-political populism and the spectre of climate change. *Theory, Culture & Society*, *27*(203), 212–232.

Zovanyi, G. (2013). The no-growth imperative: Creating sustainable communities under ecological limits to growth. London: Routledge.

Index

Numbers in *italics* refer to figures.